THE POINTS OF MY COMPASS

THE POINTS OF MY COMPASS

LETTERS FROM THE EAST, THE WEST,

THE NORTH, THE SOUTH

BY E. B. WHITE

HARPER & ROW, PUBLISHERS

NEW YORK, EVANSTON, AND LONDON

To WILLIAM SHAWN

CONTENTS

NOTE

The essay called "A Slight Sound at Evening" was published first in *The Yale Review,* under the title "Walden—1954." The other pieces in this book appeared first in *The New Yorker.* The postscripts are appearing here for the first time. Each piece carries the date on which it was written, not the date on which it was published. The arrangement is chronological except for the first two pieces, which are reversed.

FOREWORD

The visitor to the attic knows the risk he runs when he lifts the lid from a box of old letters. Words out of the past have the power to detain. Hours later he may find himself still crouched on the floor, savoring the pains and embarrassments of an early love, and with leg cramps to boot.

The letters that make up this book, when I dug them out and began rereading them, detained me in much the way I have described, and I have been in some pain. The world that I'm in love with has not resisted my advances with anything like the firmness it is capable of, and I love it as passionately as though I were young, and so it's no wonder I have been heavily involved, no wonder an occasional passage in the letters makes me wince.

These are period pieces. Some of them go back to remote times —to medieval days, when the world was in darkness, before Man had orbited, before Woman had twisted. In this century, things move with lamentable swiftness, events crowd in, and a writer must have a lot of cheek to exhume anything at all, lift any lid. All I can say in my own defense is that I have not cheated; the pieces have not been doctored in an attempt to remove traces of dust or fluff; I have not tried to give them an outward appearance of currency. Each letter carries its dateline, and the reader need never be in any doubt as to where he stands in time, although he may wonder where he stands in other respects, or where *I* stand. Most of the pieces appeared first under the title "Letter From

the East" (or some other point), and I have retained the original
titles while adding a somewhat more descriptive heading in each
case. For those who may be baffled by my private East, West,
North, and South, and find my geography capricious, I shall
start with an explanation, or key to the puzzle.

A few years ago, having forsworn weekly journalism but
wishing to continue writing, I invented a system of orientation
that would serve my convenience. In *The New Yorker*, "letters"
were appearing—"Letter from Paris," "Letter from London," letters from far distant or far-out places like Kenya or Washington.
I think I must have been envious of the persons who wrote these
letters, the foreign correspondents who enjoyed the aura of
romance that settles on that profession. At any rate, I decided
to become a letter writer. One obstacle stood in my way, and
it was a stubborn one: unlike other correspondents, I seldom
went anywhere or did anything. My activities smelled of the
hearth. Instead of being in London, I was home. Instead of being
in Karachi, I was in the barn, or in the bathtub. My life was
uneventful, my habits were fixed, and my thoughts to an alarm-
ing degree ranged back and forth over my small immediate affairs.
I regretted this but saw no likelihood that I would suddenly
change my ways or leave my haunts. Clearly, if I were to serve
as a foreign correspondent to a responsible publication I would
have to alter the world itself, and rearrange geography to give me
a wider range.

Not wanting to rule out any portion of the globe as my
territory, or any subject matter as my concern, I invented a
new compass and a more accommodating wind vane. Like many
useful inventions, mine was touched with simplicity (some will
call it simple-mindedness). I selected my office in midtown
Manhattan as a locus—a spot in air between Forty-third and
Forty-fourth streets, between Fifth and Sixth. In my new
design, anything east of this point was "the East," anything west
of it was "the West," and so on. Thus, by merely walking half

a block over to Sixth Avenue, I was in a position to write a
"Letter from the West." You can readily see what a convenience
this was to a foreign correspondent—no passport fuss, no plane
reservations, no packing of suitcases, no trouble with customs,
no dysentery from eating raw food. All I had to do was sit down
anywhere and I was somewhere.

It is conceivable that the editor of *The New Yorker*, when
I sprung this geographical distortion on him, regarded it as a
sly joke on the magazine. If he did, he never let on, and I did
not worry about it, as my motives were pure and my affection
for the magazine great. My letters were published, and not
many complaints came in about the compass. Geography today
is undergoing vast shifts anyway, with populations in turmoil
and the weathercock spinning wildly as the wind veers.

There is one other small matter that perhaps should be cleared
up. My home is in a town in Maine, and when I began writing
letters from there I needed a dateline, but did not want to use
the name of the town, as the whole scheme of my existence is
based on concealment. (If a man is foolish enough to reveal his
thoughts, the least he can do is conceal his whereabouts.) But in
writing of a place, it is easier if the place has a name, just as, if
you're calling a dog, it's a help if the dog has a name. For convenience, then, I gave my home a name—I called it Wormwood,
thinking this would sound enough like an English manor house so
that nobody would take it seriously. But some people did, and
even some of my friends began referring to my place as Wormwood, and this was too much even for me. In editing the pieces
for this book, I have dropped Wormwood and substituted Allen
Cove, a small arm of the sea that cradles my pasture.

To some of the letters I have added postscripts, and these, of
course, carry a more recent date. They contain afterthoughts
and later information.

Since most of my letters were from "the East," I had planned
to call this book "Letters from the East, and Other Points." But

when my wife got on to this, she said, "You can't do that, it would be misleading." And then, in one of those dazzling shifts of emphasis that are a true adornment of the sex, she added, "The book would be bought only by people interested in the Orient." In deference to her judgment I changed the title to *The Points of My Compass* and am prepared to have the book bought only by compass adjusters, of whom there must be quite a few scattered about. There used to be one in Rockland. His name was Crockett.

E. B. W.

July 30, 1962

THE POINTS OF MY COMPASS

THE EYE OF EDNA

Allen Cove, September 15, 1954

Two hurricanes have visited me recently, and except for a few rather hasty observations of my own (which somehow seem presumptuous), all I know about these storms is what I've heard on the radio. I live on the Maine coast, to the east of Penobscot Bay. Formerly, this coast was not in the path of hurricanes, or if it was we didn't seem to know it, but times change and we must change with them. My house is equipped with three small, old-fashioned radios, two of them battery sets, one a tiny plug-in bedside model on which my wife sometimes manages to get the Giants after I have turned in. We do not have TV, and because of this curious omission we are looked upon as eccentrics, possibly radicals.

Hurricanes, as all of us know to our sorrow, are given names nowadays—girls' names. And, as though to bring things full circle, newborn girl babies are being named for hurricanes. At the height of the last storm, one of the most dispiriting crumbs of news that came to me as the trees thrashed about and the house trembled with the force of the wind was that a baby girl had been born somewhere in the vicinity of Boston and had been named Edna. She is probably a nice little thing, but I took an instant dislike to her, and I would assume that thousands of other radio listeners did, too. Hurricanes are the latest discovery of

3

radio stations and they are being taken up in a big way. To me, Nature is continuously absorbing—that is, she is a twenty-four-hour proposition, fifty-two weeks of the year—but to radio people, Nature is an oddity tinged with malevolence and worthy of note only in her more violent moments. The radio either lets Nature alone or gives her the full treatment, as it did at the approach of the hurricane called Edna. The idea, of course, is that the radio shall perform a public service by warning people of a storm that might prove fatal; and this the radio certainly does. But another effect of the radio is to work people up to an incredible state of alarm many hours in advance of the blow, while they are still fanned by the mildest zephyrs. One of the victims of Hurricane Edna was a civil-defense worker whose heart failed him long before the wind threatened him in the least.

I heard about Edna during the morning of Friday, September 10th, some thirty-six hours before Edna arrived, and my reaction was normal. I simply buttoned up the joint and sat down to wait. The wait proved interminable. The buttoning-up was not difficult—merely a couple of hours of amusing work, none of it heavy. I first went to the shore, hauled my twelve-foot boat up above high-water mark, and tied it to a stump. I closed and barricaded the boathouse doors. Then I came back up through the meadow, tolled the sheep into the barn, hooked the big doors on the north side, and drove nails in next to the hooks, so they couldn't pull out when the doors got slatting around. I let the geese in and fed them some apples—windfalls left over from Hurricane Carol. There was no good reason to shut the geese in, as they had roamed all over the place during Carol, enjoying the rough weather to the hilt and paying frequent visits to the pond at the height of the storm, but I shut them in from tidiness, and because the radio was insisting that everyone stay indoors. I got a couple of two-by-fours and some pegs, and braced the cedar fence on the west side of the terrace. Anticipating power failure, I drew extra water for drinking and cooking, and also set a pail of water next to each toilet, for a spare flush. My wife, who enters quickly into the spirit of disaster, dug up a kerosene lamp, and there was a lot of commotion about cleaning the globe and the chimney—until it was discovered that there was no wick. The potted fuchsia was moved indoors, and also the porch rocker, lest these objects be carried aloft by the wind and dashed against windows. The croquet set was brought in. (I was extremely skeptical about the chance of croquet balls' coming in through the window, but it presented a vivid picture to the imagination and was worth thinking about.) The roof of the pullet house had blown off during Carol, and the pullets had developed a prejudice against hurricanes, so I shut them up early. I went to bed that night confident that all was in readiness.

Next morning, everything was in place, including the barometric pressure. The power was on, the telephone was working, the wind was moderate. Skies were gray and there was a slight rain. I found my wife curled up in bed at ten of seven with her plug-in going, tuned to disaster. In the barn, I received an ovation from the geese, and my failure to release them caused an immense amount of gossip. After breakfast, the whole household, with the exception of our dachshund, settled down to the radio, not in a solid family group but each to his own set and his own system of tuning. No matter where one wandered, upstairs or down, back or front, a radio voice was to be heard, bringing ominous news. As near as I could make out, the storm was still about a thousand miles away and moving north-northeast at about the speed of a medium-priced automobile. Deaths had been reported in New Jersey. A state of emergency had been declared in New London, Connecticut, and in Portland, Maine. Something had happened to the second shift at the Commercial Filters Corporation plant in Melrose, Massachusetts, but I never learned what. A man named Irving R. Levine wished me "good news." The temperature in Providence, Rhode Island, was sixty-eight degrees.

It became evident to me after a few fast rounds with the radio that the broadcasters had opened up on Edna awfully far in advance, before she had come out of her corner, and were spending themselves at a reckless rate. During the morning hours, they were having a tough time keeping Edna going at the velocity demanded of emergency broadcasting. I heard one fellow from, I think, Riverhead, Long Island, interviewing his out-of-doors man, who had been sent abroad in a car to look over conditions on the eastern end of the island.

"How would you say the roads were?" asked the tense voice.

"They were wet," replied the reporter, who seemed to be in a sulk.

"Would you say the spray from the puddles was dashing up around the mudguards?" inquired the desperate radioman.

"Yeah," replied the reporter.

It was one of those confused moments, emotionally, when the listener could not be quite sure what position radio was taking— *for* hurricanes or *against* them.

A few minutes later, I heard another baffling snatch of dialogue on the air, from another sector—I think it was Martha's Vineyard.

"Is it raining hard there?" asked an eager voice.

"Yes, it is."

"Fine!" exclaimed the first voice, well pleased at having got a correct response.

At twenty-one and a half seconds past eleven o'clock, a New England prophet named Weatherbee, the WBZ weatherman, reported that the storm was moving north-northeast at fifty miles an hour and said that New England as a whole would not get the sustained force of the wind. This prediction was followed by a burst of inspirational music, and I wandered away and into the kitchen, where I found Mrs. Freethy mixing up a spongecake. "Heard from Edna?" she asked with wry amusement as she guided the electric mixer on its powerful way through the batter. Mrs. Freethy takes her hurricanes where she finds them.

When I returned to the radio, a man was repeating the advice

I had heard many times. Fill the car with gas before the pumps lose their power. Get an old-fashioned clock that is independent of electricity. Set the refrigerator adjustment to a lower temperature. I weighed all these bits of advice carefully. The car had already been fuelled. The clocks in my house have never been contaminated by so much as a single jolt of electric current. And I decided against monkeying with the refrigerator, on the ground that the control knob was probably buried behind about eighteen small, hard-to-handle items of food left over from previous meals and saved against a rainy day like this one.

I switched to Rockland, 1450 on my dial. The town manager of Camden was speaking. He said preparations had been made for mass feeding, and that you could get fed at either the Grange Hall or the Congregational Parish House, and you were invited to bring your own food. A bulletin said the core of the storm would pass to the east of Rhode Island. From Bangor, the news was that the Gene Autry show would continue as planned. The Boston Fire Commissioner advised me to keep calm and follow instructions, and I thought again about my obstinacy in the matter of the refrigerator. In Nantucket, winds were seventy-seven miles per hour.

At noon, I took a short vacation from the radio and looked out at the familiar scene, which, because it bore so little relation to the radio scene, assumed a sort of unreality. It was thirty hours or more since I'd slipped into a hurricane mood, and I could feel the telling effects of such sustained emotional living. I went outdoors. A light breeze was blowing from the southeast. Rain fell in a drizzle. The pasture pond was unruffled but had the prickly surface caused by raindrops, and it seemed bereft without geese. The sky was a gloomy gray. Two rosebushes bowed courteously to each other on the terrace. I got a berry basket and walked out to the pullet yard, where I collected a few damp eggs. The pullets stood about in beachcombing attitudes, their feathers in disorder. As I walked back to the house, I measured with my eye the point on the roof where the biggest balm-of-Gilead tree would strike when it toppled over. I made a mental note to evacuate my people from front rooms if the wind should shift into the west, but was doubtful as to my chances of evacuating my wife from any room whatsoever, as she doesn't readily abandon well-loved posts, especially if they are furnished with traditional objects that she admires and approves of, and she is inclined to adopt a stiff-backed attitude about any change of location based on my calculations. Furthermore, she can present an overwhelming array of evidence in support of her position.

Back indoors, the storm, from which I had enjoyed momentary relief by taking a stroll in it, was on me again in full force—wild murmurings of advance information, almost impossible to make head or tail of. Edna's eye was at sea, and so was I. The eye was in New Jersey. No, it was in Long Island. No, it was not going to hit western Long Island or central Massachusetts. It was going to follow a path between Buzzards Bay and Nantucket. (This called for an atlas, which I produced.) All of New England will get the weaker part of the storm, but the Maine coast, "down Bar Harbor way," can be hit hard by Edna late this afternoon. I bridled at being described as "down Bar Harbor way."

Not only were the movements of the storm hard to follow but the voices were beginning to show the punchy condition of the poor, overworked fellows who had been blowing into their microphones at seventy miles per hour for so many hours. "Everything," cried one fellow, "is pretty well battered down in Westerly." I presumed he meant "battened down," but there was no real way of knowing. Another man, in an exhausted state, told how, in the previous hurricane, the streets of Providence had been "unindated." I started thinking in terms of unindated streets, of cities pretty well battered down. The wind now began to strengthen. The barometer on my dining-room wall was falling. From Rockland I got the "Top of the Farm News": 850,000 bales of cotton for August; a new variety of alfalfa that will stand up to stem nematode and bacterial wilt; a new tomato powder—

mix it with water and you get tomato juice, only it's not on the
market yet. Low tide will be at 4:23 this afternoon. The
barometer now reads 29.88 and falling. A chicken shoot is cancelled for tomorrow—the first chicken shoot I had ever heard of.
All Rockland stores will close at three o'clock, one of them
a store carrying suits with the new novelty weave and novel
button and pocket trim. If this thing gets worse, I thought, I'll
have to go outdoors again, even though they tell you not to.
I can't take it in here. At 1:55 P.M., I learned that visiting hours
at the Portsmouth Hospital, two hundred miles to the southwest
of me, had been cancelled, and, having no friend there, I did not
know whether to be glad about this or sorry.

The time is now two o'clock. Barometer 29.50, falling. Wind
ESE, rising. It seems like a sensible moment to do the afternoon
chores—get them over with while the going is good. So I leave
the radio for a spell and visit the barn, my peaceable kingdom,
where not a nematode stirs.

When I resumed my vigil, I discovered to my great surprise
that Rockland, which is quite nearby, had dropped Edna for the
time being and taken up American League baseball. A Red Sox–
Indians game was on, with the outfield (I never learned which
outfield) playing it straightaway. My wife, who despises the
American League, was listening on her set, and dialling erratically.
I heard a myna bird being introduced, but the bird failed to respond to the introduction. Then someone gave the rules of a
limerick contest. I was to supply the missing line for the following limerick:

> I knew a young lady named Joan
> Who wanted a car of her own.
> She was a sharp kid
> So here's what she did
> . . . .

The line came to me quickly enough: She ordered a Chevy by
phone. I was to send this to Box 401 on a postcard, but I didn't
know what city and I wasn't at all sure that it was a General

Motors program—could have been a competitor. The whole thing made no sense anyway, as cars were at that moment being ordered off the roads—even Joan's car.

At 2:30, it was announced that school buildings in the town of Newton were open for people who wanted to go to them "for greater personal security or comfort." Ted Williams, who had been in a slump, singled. WBZ said the Boston police had lost touch with Nantucket, electric power had failed in South Natick, Portland was going to be hit at five o'clock, Wells Beach had been evacuated, a Republican rally for tonight in Augusta had been cancelled, the eye of Edna was five miles north of Nantucket, a girl baby had been born, Katharine Cornell had been evacuated by police from her home on Martha's Vineyard, and all letter carriers had been called back to their stations in Boston on the old sleet-snow-wind theory of mail delivery. I made a trip to the barometer for a routine reading: 29.41, falling.

"The rain," said the Mayor of Boston in a hearty voice, "is coming down in sheets."

"That gigantic whirlpool of air known as Hurricane Edna," said Weatherbee, from his South Shore observation point, "is over the town hall of Chatham." Weatherbee also dropped the news that the eastern end of the Maine coast would probably get winds of hurricane velocity about six hours from now.

"Weatherbee," said a proud voice from the WBZ Communications Center, "is still batting a thousand." (At this juncture I would have settled for Ted Williams, who wasn't doing nearly so well.)

The rest of the afternoon, and the evening, was a strange nightmare of rising tempest and diminishing returns. The storm grew steadily in force, but in our neck of the woods a characteristic of hurricanes is that they arrive from the southwest, which is where most radio lives, and radio loses interest in Nature just as soon as Nature passes in front of the window and goes off toward the northeast. Weatherbee was right. The storm did strike here about six hours later, with winds up to ninety miles an hour, but when the barometer reached its lowest point and the wind shifted into the

NW and began to tear everything to pieces, what we got on the
radio was a man doing a whistling act and somebody playing
the glockenspiel. All the livelong day we had had our mild weather
to the sound of doom, and then at evening, when the power failed
and the telephone failed and the tide flooded and the gale exploded,
we heard the glockenspiel. Governor Cross, a Republican, who
also lives to the westward, had already announced that the worst
of the storm was over and that, except for a few benighted areas
along the coast, everything was hunky-dory. I notice he got voted
out of office a couple of days later, probably by an enormous out-
pouring of Republican turncoats from the coastal towns to the east
of him, whose trees were being uprooted at the time he was speaking.

My own evening was an odd one. As Edna moved toward me
across the Gulf of Maine, I watched the trees and the rain with
increasing interest, albeit with no radio support except from the
glockenspiel. At half past six, I evacuated my wife from a front
room, without police action, and mixed us both a drink in a back
room. At 6:55, she leaned forward in her chair and began neaten-
ing the books in a low bookshelf, pulling the volumes forward
one by one and lining them up with the leading edge of the shelf,
soldiers being dressed by their sergeant. By half past seven the wind
had slacked off to give Edna's eye a good peep at us, the glass was
steadying, and ten minutes later, watching the vane on the barn, I
saw the wind starting to back into the north, fitfully. The rain
eased up and we let the dachshund out, taking advantage of the
lull. (Unlike the geese, she had no use for rough weather, and she
had obeyed the radio faithfully all day—stayed put under the
stove.)

At 7:45, the Governor of New Hampshire thanked everyone for
his cooperation, and Logan International Airport announced the
resumption of flights. At eight o'clock, my barometer reached bottom—28.65. The Governor of Massachusetts came on to thank *his*
people, and somebody announced that the Supreme Market in
Dorchester would be open for business in the morning (Sunday).

Another voice promised that at eleven o'clock there would be a wrap-up on Hurricane Edna.

At this point, I decided to take a stroll. The night was agreeable —moon showing through gray clouds, light rain, hurricane still to come. My stroll turned out to be a strange one. I started for the shore, thinking I'd look over things down there, but when I got to the plank bridge over the brook I found the bridge under water. This caused me to wonder whether my spring, which supplies the house and which is located in the low-lying woods across the road, was being unindated. So, instead of proceeding to the shore, I crossed the road and entered the woods. I had rubber boots on and was carrying a flashlight. The path to the spring is pretty well grown over and I had difficulty finding it. In fact, I'm not sure that I ever did find it. I waded about in the swampy woods for ten or fifteen minutes, most of the time in water halfway up to my knees. It was pleasant in there, but I was annoyed that I was unable to find the spring. Failing in this, I returned to the house, kicked off my boots, and sank back into radioland. The Bangor station predicted ninety-mile winds within half an hour, and I discovered a scrap of paper on which my wife had scribbled "Bangor 9437, 7173, and 2313"—emergency numbers taken down just as though we were really in telephone communication with the outside world. (The phone had been gone for a long time.)

At 8:44, the power failed, the house went dark, and it was a whole lot easier to see Edna. In almost no time the storm grew to its greatest height: the wind (NW by this time) chased black clouds across the ailing moon. The woods to the south of us bent low, as though the trees prayed for salvation. Several went over. The house tuned up, roaring with the thunder of a westerly wind. For a little while, we were both battened down and battered down.

There are always two stages of any disturbance in the country —the stage when the lights and the phone are still going, the stage when these are lost. We were in the second stage. In front of the house, a large branch of the biggest balm-of-Gilead tree snapped and crashed down across the driveway, closing it off. On the north side, an apple tree split clean up the middle. And for half an hour or so Edna held us in her full embrace.

It did not seem long. Compared to the endless hours of the radio vigil, it seemed like nothing at all. By ten o'clock, the wind was moderating. We lighted the dog up to her bed by holding a flashlight along the stairs, so she could see where to leap. When we looked out of a north bedroom, there in the beautiful sky was a rainbow lit by the moon.

It was Taylor Grant, earlier in the evening, who pretty well summed things up for radio. "The weather bureau estimates that almost forty-six million persons along the east coast have felt some degree of concern over the movement of the storm," said Mr. Grant. "Never before has a hurricane had that large an audience." As one member of this vast audience, I myself felt a twinge of belated concern the next morning when I went over to the spring to fetch a pail of water. There in the woods, its great trunk square across the path, its roots in the air, lay a big hackmatack.

I never did get to hear the wrap-up.

P.S. (April 1962).   Since Edna's visit more than seven years ago, much has changed—in the home and on the air waves. Prehurricane suspense probably reached its peak in the storm described above; subsequent blows have been promptly forecast and fully reported, but without the wild note of enthusiastic hysteria that attended Edna.

A country dweller knows that he must be alert and ready for disaster at all times, not just in the hours before a hurricane. Nature has a bottomless bag of surprises, and most of them go unpredicted by broadcasters in studios. Our worst tree-fall did not occur during any of the great storms that have come our way; it took place on a bright, smiling Sunday morning in early summer last year, when, after thirty-six hours of heavy rain, the sun came out, the wind shifted into the northwest, and there was a brief squall. I happened to be looking out a front window and saw one of the big shade trees on the lawn buckle and go down, snapping off at a point about eight feet above the ground. I wasn't prepared for this, but nothing surprises me any more, and nobody got hit. The tree, a balm-of-Gilead, which had stood so valiantly through the great gales, must have been caught at a disadvantage by this small, brief, tricky wind. Its guard must have been down. When we examined it, in its fallen condition, it turned out to be as hollow as a pipe, and we sawed it up and hauled it to the dump, saving only an eight-inch section that I have since made into a memorial bird bath.

Weather, of course, is an obsession with the television people. Our home now boasts a TV set, and somebody is always telling me the temperature in Great Falls, Montana—which is like telling me that a man has just changed his shirt in Sicily. Moreover, the weather broadcasters have become emotionally involved with the natural scene, and feel personally responsible for inclemency. Odysseus in all his seafaring never had such a sense of the gods at work, helping and hindering. Two rainy weekends in succession put an almost unbearable strain on weather announcers, and they begin using queer meteorological terms like "gloomy," "dreary," and "miserable." Soon we will have weather tips sent to us by satellites on the prowl in space, and heaven knows what kind of view they will take of disturbances. There is much to be said for a pretty girl and her mass of cold air sweeping down from Canada.

I miss the geese around here, in all weather. (I have been compelled to trim my zoo and no longer entertain geese, or they me.) Any sort of disturbance, whether man-made or elemental, is of immense interest to a goose, and geese watch the world through eyes that often seem capable of seeing things not visible to men. I have always envied a goose its look of deep, superior wisdom. I miss the cordiality of geese, the midnight cordiality. And they are the world's best drinkers, forever at it.

A SLIGHT SOUND AT EVENING

Allen Cove, Summer, 1954

In his journal for July 10-12, 1841, Thoreau wrote: "A slight sound at evening lifts me up by the ears, and makes life seem inexpressibly serene and grand. It may be in Uranus, or it may be in the shutter." The book into which he later managed to pack both Uranus and the shutter was published in 1854, and now, a hundred years having gone by, *Walden*, its serenity and grandeur unimpaired, still lifts us up by the ears, still translates for us that language we are in danger of forgetting, "which all things and events speak without metaphor, which alone is copious and standard."

Walden is an oddity in American letters. It may very well be the oddest of our distinguished oddities. For many it is a great deal too odd, and for many it is a particular bore. I have not found it to be a well-liked book among my acquaintances, although usually spoken of with respect, and one literary critic for whom I have the highest regard can find no reason for anyone's giving *Walden* a second thought. To admire the book is, in fact, something of an embarrassment, for the mass of men have an indistinct notion that its author was a sort of Nature Boy.

I think it is of some advantage to encounter the book at a period in one's life when the normal anxieties and enthusiasms and rebellions of youth closely resemble those of Thoreau in that spring of 1845 when he borrowed an ax, went out to the woods, and began to whack down some trees for timber. Received at such a juncture, the book is like an invitation to life's dance, assuring the troubled recipient that no matter what befalls him in the way of success or failure he will always be welcome at the party—that the music is played for him, too, if he will but listen and move his feet. In effect, that is what the book is—an invitation, unengraved; and it stirs one as a young girl is stirred by her first big party bid. Many think it a sermon; many set it down as an attempt to rearrange society; some think it an exercise in nature-loving; some find it a rather irritating collection of inspirational puffballs by an eccentric show-off. I think it none of these. It still seems to me the best youth's companion yet written by an American, for it carries a solemn warning against the loss of one's valuables, it advances a good argument for travelling light and trying new adventures, it rings with the power of positive adoration, it contains religious feeling without religious images, and it steadfastly refuses to record bad news. Even its pantheistic note is so pure as to be noncorrupting—pure as the flute-note blown across the pond on those faraway summer nights. If our colleges and universities were alert, they would present a cheap pocket edition of the book to every senior upon graduating, along with his sheepskin, or instead of it. Even if some senior were to take it literally and start felling trees, there could be worse mishaps: the ax is older than the Dictaphone and it is just as well for a young man to see what kind of chips he leaves before listening to the sound of his own voice. And even if some were to get no farther than the table of contents, they would learn how to name eighteen chapters by the use of only thirty-nine words and would see how sweet are the uses of brevity.

If Thoreau had merely left us an account of a man's life in the woods or if he had simply retreated to the woods and there recorded his complaints about society, or even if he had contrived to include both records in one essay, *Walden* would probably not have lived a hundred years. As things turned out, Thoreau, very likely without knowing quite what he was up to, took man's relation to Nature and man's dilemma in society and man's capacity for elevating his spirit and he beat all these matters together, in a wild free interval of self-justification and delight, and produced an original omelette from which people can draw nourishment in a hungry day. *Walden* is one of the first of the vitamin-enriched American dishes. If it were a little less good than it is, or even a little less queer, it would be an abominable book. Even as it is, it will continue to baffle and annoy the literal mind and all those who are unable to stomach its caprices and imbibe its theme. Certainly the plodding economist will continue to have rough going if he hopes to emerge from the book with a clear system of economic thought. Thoreau's assault on the Concord society of the mid-nineteenth century has the quality of a modern Western: he rides into the subject at top speed, shooting in all directions. Many of his shots ricochet and nick him on the rebound, and throughout the melee there is a horrendous cloud of inconsistencies and contradictions, and when the shooting dies down and the air clears, one is impressed chiefly by the courage of the rider and by how splendid it was that somebody should have ridden in there and raised all that ruckus.

When he went to the pond, Thoreau struck an attitude and did so deliberately, but his posturing was not to draw the attention of others to him but rather to draw his own attention more closely to himself. "I learned this at least by my experiment: that if one advances confidently in the direction of his dreams, and endeavors to live the life which he has imagined, he will meet with a success unexpected in common hours." The sentence has the power to resuscitate the youth drowning in his sea of doubt. I recall my exhilaration upon reading it, many years ago, in a time of hesitation and despair. It restored me to health. And now in 1954 when I salute Henry Thoreau on the hundredth birthday of his book, I am merely paying off an old score—or an installment on it.

In his journal for May 3-4, 1838—Boston to Portland—he

wrote: "Midnight—head over the boat's side—between sleeping and waking—with glimpses of one or more lights in the vicinity of Cape Ann. Bright moonlight—the effect heightened by sea-sickness." The entry illuminates the man, as the moon the sea on that night in May. In Thoreau the natural scene was heightened, not depressed, by a disturbance of the stomach, and nausea met its match at last. There was a steadiness in at least one passenger if there was none in the boat. Such steadiness (which in some would be called intoxication) is at the heart of *Walden*—confidence, faith, the discipline of looking always at what is to be seen, un-deviating gratitude for the life-everlasting that he found growing in his front yard. "There is nowhere recorded a simple and ir-repressible satisfaction with the gift of life, any memorable praise of God." He worked to correct that deficiency. *Walden* is his acknowledgment of the gift of life. It is the testament of a man in a high state of indignation because (it seemed to him) so few ears heard the uninterrupted poem of creation, the morning wind that forever blows. If the man sometimes wrote as though all his readers were male, unmarried, and well-connected, it is be-cause he gave his testimony during the callow years, and, for that matter, never really grew up. To reject the book because of the immaturity of the author and the bugs in the logic is to throw away a bottle of good wine because it contains bits of the cork.

Thoreau said he required of every writer, first and last, a simple and sincere account of his own life. Having delivered himself of this chesty dictum, he proceeded to ignore it. In his books and even in his enormous journal, he withheld or disguised most of the facts from which an understanding of his life could be drawn. *Walden*, subtitled "Life in the Woods," is not a simple and sincere account of a man's life, either in or out of the woods; it is an account of a man's journey into the mind, a toot on the trumpet to alert the neighbors. Thoreau was well aware that no one can alert his neighbors who is not wide-awake himself, and he went to the woods (among other reasons) to make sure that he would stay awake during his broadcast. What actually took place during the years 1845-47 is largely unrecorded, and the reader is excluded from the private life of the author, who supplies almost no gossip about himself, a great deal about his neighbors and about the universe.

As for me, I cannot in this short ramble give a simple and sincere account of my own life, but I think Thoreau might find it instructive to know that this memorial essay is being written in a house that, through no intent on my part, is the same size and shape as his own domicile on the pond—about ten by fifteen, tight, plainly finished, and at a little distance from my Concord. The house in which I sit this morning was built to accommodate a boat, not a man, but by long experience I have learned that in most respects it shelters me better than the larger dwelling where my bed is, and which, by design, is a manhouse not a boathouse. Here in the boathouse I am a wilder and, it would appear, a healthier man, by a safe margin. I have a chair, a bench, a table, and I can walk into the water if I tire of the land. My house fronts a cove. Two fishermen have just arrived to spot fish from the air— an osprey and a man in a small yellow plane who works for the fish company. The man, I have noticed, is less well equipped than the hawk, who can dive directly on his fish and carry it away, without telephoning. A mouse and a squirrel share the house with me. The building is, in fact, a multiple dwelling, a semi-detached affair. It is because I am semidetached while here that I find it possible to transact this private business with the fewest obstacles.

There is also a woodchuck here, living forty feet away under the wharf. When the wind is right, he can smell my house; and when the wind is contrary, I can smell his. We both use the wharf for sunning, taking turns, each adjusting his schedule to the other's convenience. Thoreau once ate a woodchuck. I think he felt he owed it to his readers, and that it was little enough, considering the indignities they were suffering at his hands and the dressing-down they were taking. (Parts of *Walden* are pure scold.) Or perhaps he ate the woodchuck because he believed every man should acquire strict business habits, and the woodchuck was destroying his market beans. I do not know. Thoreau had a strong experimental streak in him. It is probably no harder to eat a woodchuck than to construct a sentence that lasts a hundred years. At any rate, Thoreau is the only writer I know who prepared himself for his great ordeal by eating a woodchuck; also the only one who got a hangover from drinking too much water. (He was drunk the whole time, though he seldom touched wine or coffee or tea.)

Here in this compact house where I would spend one day as deliberately as Nature if I were not being pressed by the editor of a magazine, and with a woodchuck (as yet uneaten) for neighbor, I can feel the companionship of the occupant of the pondside cabin in Walden woods, a mile from the village, near the Fitchburg right of way. Even my immediate business is no barrier between us: Thoreau occasionally batted out a magazine piece, but was always suspicious of any sort of purposeful work that cut into his time. A man, he said, should take care not to be thrown off the track by every nutshell and mosquito's wing that falls on the rails.

There has been much guessing as to why he went to the pond. To set it down to escapism is, of course, to misconstrue what happened. Henry went forth to battle when he took to the woods, and *Walden* is the report of a man torn by two powerful and opposing drives—the desire to enjoy the world (and not be derailed by a mosquito wing) and the urge to set the world straight. One cannot join these two successfully, but sometimes, in rare cases, something good or even great results from the attempt of the tormented spirit to reconcile them. Henry went forth to battle, and if he set the stage himself, if he fought on his own terms and with his own weapons, it was because it was his nature to do things differently from most men, and to act in a cocky fashion. If the pond and the woods seemed a more plausible site for a house than an in-town location, it was because a cowbell made for him a sweeter sound than a churchbell. *Walden,* the book, makes the sound of a cowbell, more than a churchbell, and proves the point, although both sounds are in it, and both remarkably clear and sweet. He simply preferred his churchbell at a little distance.

I think one reason he went to the woods was a perfectly simple and commonplace one—and apparently he thought so, too. "At a certain season of our life," he wrote, "we are accustomed to consider every spot as the possible site of a house." There spoke the young man, a few years out of college, who had not yet broken away from home. He hadn't married, and he had found no job that measured up to his rigid standards of employment, and like any young man, or young animal, he felt uneasy and on the defensive until he had fixed himself a den. Most young men, of course, casting about for a site, are content merely to draw apart from their kinfolks. Thoreau, convinced that the greater part of what his neighbors called good was bad, withdrew from a great deal more than family: he pulled out of everything for a while, to serve everybody right for being so stuffy, and to try his own prejudices on the dog.

The house-hunting sentence above, which starts the chapter called "Where I Lived, and What I Lived For," is followed by another passage that is worth quoting here because it so beautifully illustrates the offbeat prose that Thoreau was master of, a prose at once strictly disciplined and wildly abandoned. "I have surveyed the country on every side within a dozen miles of where I live," continued this delirious young man. "In imagination I have bought all the farms in succession, for all were to be bought, and I knew their price. I walked over each farmer's premises, tasted his wild apples, discoursed on husbandry with him, took his farm at his price, at any price, mortgaging it to him in my mind; even

put a higher price on it—took everything but a deed of it—took
his word for his deed, for I dearly love to talk—cultivated it, and
him too to some extent, I trust, and withdrew when I had enjoyed
it long enough, leaving him to carry it on." A copy-desk man
would get a double hernia trying to clean up that sentence for
the management, but the sentence needs no fixing, for it perfectly
captures the meaning of the writer and the quality of the
ramble.

"Wherever I sat, there I might live, and the landscape radiated
from me accordingly." Thoreau, the home-seeker, sitting on his
hummock with the entire State of Massachusetts radiating from
him, is to me the most humorous of the New England figures, and
Walden the most humorous of the books, though its humor is
almost continuously subsurface and there is nothing deliberately
funny anywhere, except a few weak jokes and bad puns that rise
to the surface like the perch in the pond that rose to the sound of
the maestro's flute. Thoreau tended to write in sentences, a feat
not every writer is capable of, and *Walden* is, rhetorically speaking, a collection of certified sentences, some of them, it would now
appear, as indestructible as they are errant. The book is distilled
from the vast journals, and this accounts for its intensity: he
picked out bright particles that pleased his eye, whirled them in
the kaleidoscope of his content, and produced the pattern that
has endured—the color, the form, the light.

On this its hundredth birthday, Thoreau's *Walden* is pertinent
and timely. In our uneasy season, when all men unconsciously
seek a retreat from a world that has got almost completely out of
hand, his house in the Concord woods is a haven. In our culture
of gadgetry and the multiplicity of convenience, his cry "Simplicity, simplicity, simplicity!" has the insistence of a fire alarm.
In the brooding atmosphere of war and the gathering radioactive
storm, the innocence and serenity of his summer afternoons are
enough to burst the remembering heart, and one gazes back upon
that pleasing interlude—its confidence, its purity, its deliberate-

ness—with awe and wonder, as one would look upon the face of a child asleep.

"This small lake was of most value as a neighbor in the intervals of a gentle rain-storm in August, when, both air and water being perfectly still, but the sky overcast, midafternoon had all the serenity of evening, and the wood-thrush sang around, and was heard from shore to shore." Now, in the perpetual overcast in which our days are spent, we hear with extra perception and deep gratitude that song, tying century to century.

I sometimes amuse myself by bringing Henry Thoreau back to life and showing him the sights. I escort him into a phone booth and let him dial Weather. "This is a delicious evening," the girl's voice says, "when the whole body is one sense, and imbibes delight through every pore." I show him the spot in the Pacific where an island used to be, before some magician made it vanish. "We know not where we are," I murmur. "The light which puts out our eyes is darkness to us. Only that day dawns to which we are awake." I thumb through the latest copy of *Vogue* with him. "Of two patterns which differ only by a few threads more or less of a particular color," I read, "the one will be sold readily, the other lie on the shelf, though it frequently happens that, after the lapse of a season, the latter becomes the most fashionable." Together we go outboarding on the Assabet, looking for what we've lost—a hound, a bay horse, a turtledove. I show him a distracted farmer who is trying to repair a hay baler before the thunder shower breaks. "This farmer," I remark, "is endeavoring to solve the problem of a livelihood by a formula more complicated than the problem itself. To get his shoestrings he speculates in herds of cattle."

I take the celebrated author to Twenty-One for lunch, so the waiters may study his shoes. The proprietor welcomes us. "The gross feeder," remarks the proprietor, sweeping the room with his arm, "is a man in the larva stage." After lunch we visit a classroom in one of those schools conducted by big corporations to teach their superannuated executives how to retire from business without serious injury to their health. (The shock to men's systems these days when relieved of the exacting routine of amassing wealth is very great and must be cushioned.) "It is not necessary," says the teacher to his pupils, "that a man should earn his living by the sweat of his brow, unless he sweats easier than I do. We are determined to be starved before we are hungry."

I turn on the radio and let Thoreau hear Winchell beat the red hand around the clock. "Time is but the stream I go a-fishing in," shouts Mr. Winchell, rattling his telegraph key. "Hardly a man takes a half hour's nap after dinner, but when he wakes he holds up his head and asks, 'What's the news?' If we read of one man robbed, or murdered, or killed by accident, or one house burned, or one vessel wrecked, or one steamboat blown up, or one cow run over on the Western Railroad, or one mad dog killed, or one lot of grasshoppers in the winter—we need never read of another. One is enough."

I doubt that Thoreau would be thrown off balance by the fantastic sights and sounds of the twentieth century. "The Concord nights," he once wrote, "are stranger than the Arabian nights." A four-engined airliner would merely serve to confirm his early views on travel. Everywhere he would observe, in new shapes and sizes, the old predicaments and follies of men—the desperation, the impedimenta, the meanness—along with the visible capacity for elevation of the mind and soul. "This curious world which we inhabit is more wonderful than it is convenient; more beautiful than it is useful; it is more to be admired and enjoyed than used." He would see that today ten thousand engineers are busy making sure that the world shall be convenient even if it is destroyed in the process, and others are determined to increase its usefulness even though its beauty is lost somewhere along the way.

At any rate, I'd like to stroll about the countryside in Thoreau's company for a day, observing the modern scene, inspecting today's snowstorm, pointing out the sights, and offering belated apologies for my sins. Thoreau is unique among writers in that those who admire him find him uncomfortable to live with—a regular hairshirt of a man. A little band of dedicated Thoreauvians would be a sorry sight indeed: fellows who hate compromise and have compromised, fellows who love wildness and have lived tamely, and at their side, censuring them and chiding them, the ghostly figure of this upright man, who long ago gave corroboration to impulses they perceived were right and issued warnings against the things they instinctively knew to be their enemies. I should hate to be called a Thoreauvian, yet I wince every time I walk into the barn I'm pushing before me, seventy-five feet by forty, and the author of *Walden* has served as my conscience through the long stretches of my trivial days.

Hairshirt or no, he is a better companion than most, and I would not swap him for a soberer or more reasonable friend even if I could. I can reread his famous invitation with undiminished excitement. The sad thing is that not more acceptances have been received, that so many decline for one reason or another, pleading some previous engagement or ill health. But the invitation stands. It will beckon as long as this remarkable book stays in print— which will be as long as there are August afternoons in the intervals of a gentle rainstorm, as long as there are ears to catch the faint sounds of the orchestra. I find it agreeable to sit here this morning, in a house of correct proportions, and hear across a century of time his flute, his frogs, and his seductive summons to the wildest revels of them all.

HOME-COMING

Allen Cove, December 10, 1955

On the day before Thanksgiving, toward the end of the afternoon, having motored all day, I arrived home, and lit a fire in the living room. The birch logs took hold briskly. About three minutes later, not to be outdone, the chimney itself caught fire. I became aware of this development rather slowly. Rocking contentedly in my chair, enjoying the stupor that follows a day on the road, I thought I heard the dull, fluttering roar of a chimney swift, a sound we who live in this house are thoroughly accustomed to. Then I realized that there would be no bird in residence in my chimney at this season of the year, and a glance up the flue made it perfectly plain that, after twenty-two years of my tenure, the place was at last afire.

The fact that my chimney was on fire did not greatly surprise or depress me, as I have been dogged by small and large misadventures for the past ten years, the blows falling around my head day and night, and I have learned to be ready for anything at any hour. I phoned the Fire Department as a matter of routine, dialling a number I had once forehandedly printed in large figures on the edge of the shelf in the telephone closet, so that I would be able to read it without my glasses. (We keep our phone in a closet here, as you might confine a puppy that isn't fully house-trained. The dial system is unpopular anyway in this small rural Maine community, and as far as I am concerned, the entire New England Telephone & Telegraph Co. deserves to be shut up in a closet for having saddled us with dials and deprived us of our beloved operators, who used to know where everybody was and just what to do about everything, including chimney fires.)

My call was answered promptly, but I had no sooner hung up than I observed that the fire appeared to be out, having exhausted itself, so I called back to cancel the run, and was told that the Department would like to come anyway. In the country, one excuse is as good as another for a bit of fun, and just because a fire has grown cold is no reason for a fireman's spirits to sag. In a very short time, the loud, cheerful apparatus, its red signal light blinking rapturously, careened into the driveway, and the living room filled rapidly with my fire-fighting friends. My fire chief is also my barber, so I was naturally glad to see him. And he had with him a robust accomplice who had recently been up on my roof installing a new wooden gutter, dry and ready to receive the first sparks from a chimney fire, so I was glad to see *him*. And there was still a third fire-eater, and everyone was glad to see everyone else, as near as I could make out, and we all poked about learnedly in the chimney for a while, and then the Department left. I have had dozens and dozens of home-comings at the end of an all-day ride on U.S. 1, but strangely enough this was one of the pleasantest.

Shortly before he died, Bernard DeVoto gave the Maine coast a brisk going over in his *Harper's* column, using some four-letter words that raised the hackles of the inhabitants. Mr. DeVoto used the word "slum" and the word "neon." He said that the highway into Maine was a sorry mess all the way to Bucksport, and that the whole strip was overpopulated and full of drive-ins, diners, souvenir stands, purulent amusement parks, and cheap-Jack restaurants. I was thinking about this indictment at lunch the other day, trying to reconstruct my own cheap-Jack impressions

of the familiar route after my recent trip over it. As I sat at table,
gnawing away at a piece of pie, snow began falling. At first it was
an almost imperceptible spitting from the gray sky, but it soon
thickened and came driving in from the northeast. I watched it
catch along the edge of the drive, powder the stone wall, dust
the spruce cover on the flower borders, coat the plowed land,
and whiten the surface of the dark frozen pond, and I knew that
all along the coast, from Kittery on, the worst mistakes of men
were being quietly erased, the lines of their industrial temples
softened, and U.S. 1 crowned with a cold, inexpensive glory that
DeVoto unhappily did not live to see.

Even without the kindly erasures of the snow, the road into
Maine does not seem a slum to me. Like highways everywhere, it
is a mixed dish: Gulf and Shell, bay and gull, neon and sunset,
cold comfort and warm, the fussy façade of a motor court right
next door to the pure geometry of an early-nineteenth-century
clapboard house with barn attached. You can certainly learn
to spell "moccasin" while driving into Maine, and there is often
little else to do, except steer and avoid death. Woods and fields
encroach everywhere, creeping to within a few feet of the neon
and the court, and the experienced traveller into this land is always conscious that just behind the garish roadside stand, in its
thicket of birch and spruce, stands the delicate and well-propor-
tioned deer; just beyond the overnight cabin, in the pasture of
granite and juniper, trots the perfectly designed fox. This is still
our triumphant architecture, and the Maine man does not have
to penetrate in depth to be excited by his coastal run; its flavor
steals into his consciousness with the first ragged glimpse of
properly textured woodland, the first whiff of punctually drained
cove.

Probably a man's destination (which is ever in the motorist's
thoughts) colors the highway, enlarges or diminishes its defects.
Gliding over the tar, I was on my way home. DeVoto, travelling
the same route, was on his way to what he described rather warily

as "professional commitments," by which he probably meant that he was on his way somewhere to make a speech or get a degree. Steering a car toward home is a very different experience from steering a car toward a rostrum, and if our findings differ, it is not that we differed greatly in powers of observation but that we were headed in different emotional directions. I sometimes suspect that when I am headed east, my critical faculties are retarded almost to the vanishing point, like a frog's heartbeat in winter.

What happens to me when I cross the Piscataqua and plunge rapidly into Maine at a cost of seventy-five cents in tolls? I cannot describe it. I do not ordinarily spy a partridge in a pear tree, or three French hens, but I do have the sensation of having received a gift from a true love. And when, five hours later, I dip down across the Narramissic and look back at the tiny town of Orland, the white spire of its church against the pale-red sky stirs me in a way that Chartres could never do. It was the Narramissic that once received as fine a lyrical tribute as was ever paid to a river—a line in a poem by a schoolboy, who wrote of it, "It flows through Orland every day." I never cross that mild stream without thinking of his testimonial to the constancy, the dependability of small, familiar rivers.

Familiarity is the thing—the sense of belonging. It grants exemption from all evil, all shabbiness. A farmer pauses in the doorway of his barn and he is wearing the right boots. A sheep stands under an apple tree and it wears the right look, and the tree is hung with puckered frozen fruit of the right color. The spruce boughs that bank the foundations of the homes keep out the only true winter wind, and the light that leaves the sky at four o'clock automatically turns on the yellow lamps within, revealing to the soft-minded motorist interiors of perfect security, kitchens full of a just and lasting peace. (Or so it seems to the homing traveller.)

Even journalism in Maine has an antic quality that gives me the feeling of being home. The editorial in our weekly paper, after taking DeVoto to task for his disparaging remarks, ended on a note of delirious maladroitness. The editorialist strongly urged DeVoto to return—come back and take a second look, see the *real* Maine. Then he added, "Note: DeVoto has died since this article was written."

Benny DeVoto, a good fighter in all good causes, would enjoy that one thoroughly if he could indeed return for one more look around.

The deer season is all over for 1955. One day last week, half the hunters in town converged on the swamp south of here, between the road and the shore, for a final drive. As I rode into the village that afternoon, there was a rifleman at every crossing, and the cries of the beaters could be heard from the woods, the voice of one of them much louder and clearer than the others—a bugle-like sound that suggested the eagerness of a hound. During November, a deer can't move anywhere in this community without having its whereabouts flashed via the grapevine. As the season draws to a close, a sort of desperateness infects the male population. That afternoon it was almost as though the swamp contained an escaped convict. I heard two shots just before dark, but I learned later that neither of them took effect, and was secretly glad. Still, this business of favoring the deer over the hunter is a perplexing one; some of my best friends are deerslayers, and I never wish a man bad luck. As a spectator at the annual contest between deer and man, I am in the same fix as at the Harvard-Yale game—I'm not quite sure which club I'm rooting for.

In the village, I found three big trucks loading fir-balsam wreaths for Boston. They were lined up in formation, headed out, ready for the starter's gun. The loads were already built high in the air. Fir balsam is like no other cargo; even a workaday truck is exalted and wears a consecrated look when carrying these aromatic dumplings to the hungry dwellers in cities. This is the link that must not be broken. The head man in charge of wreaths was standing in front of his platoon, directing operations. He was one of those who had officiated at my chimney fire. His cheeks were red with cold. I asked him if he would be going to Boston himself with one of the trucks, and he said no, he couldn't go, because he had pneumonia.

"You really got pneumonia?" I asked as the wicked wind tugged at our shirts.

"Yes, indeed," he replied cheerfully. "Can't seem to shake it."

I report this conversation so the people of Boston will not take their Christmas greens for granted. Wreaths do not come out of our wood lots and roll up to Boston under their own steam; they must be pried out and boosted on their way by a man with pneumonia. I noted that several of the crew were fellows whom I had last seen a few weeks ago shingling the roof of my ell in Indian summer. Hereabouts a man must know every trade. First he tacks cedar shingles to a neighbor's roof, then he's off to Boston to shingle the front doors of Beacon Hill with the living green.

Maine sends about a million Christmas trees out of the state every year, according to my latest advices. It is an easy figure to remember, and an easy one to believe as you drive about the county and see the neatly tied bundles along the road, waiting to be picked up, their little yellow butts so bright and round against the darkling green. The young fir balsam is a standard cash crop, just like the middle-aged clam. The price paid for trees "at the side of the road" ranges from a dollar a bundle (four or five trees) to three-seventy-five. A man can be launched, or catapulted, into the Christmas-tree business quite by surprise. I wandered across the road the other day and up into the maple woods beyond my hayfield, and discovered that a miracle had taken place while my back was turned: the grove was alive with young firs, standing as close together as theatregoers between the acts.

The Christmas-tree harvest is hard on the woods, though. People tend to cut wastefully, hacking away wherever the going is good. And the enemy is always at our gates in the form of bugs and blights. I have just read a report on the forest-insect situation, sent me by the County Agent. We have all sorts of picturesque plagues. The balsam woolly aphid. Birch dieback. Dutch elm disease. Spruce budworm. (A spruce "bud" in Maine parlance is a spruce cone—the thing a red squirrel eats the seeds of, sitting on a rock, and the thing Boston and New York celebrants like to put on their mantelpieces. The budworm comes into the state in the form of a moth, on the northeast wind, in summertime. I don't know whether a squirrel or a wood-lot owner has more at stake in this particular crisis.)

There are only a few small items of news to report at this season. Canada jays have been observed in the vicinity, and they managed to get into the paper, under the headline "UNUSUAL BIRD SEEN." I felt pretty good about this, because I had spotted two of these whiskey-jacks (not to be confused with cheap-Jacks) way back in October. The liquor store in the county seat was held up by a masked gunman recently and robbed of $2,672.45, which turned out to be the day's receipts and, of course, gave a much clearer picture of the amount of drinking done around here than any previous event. It would appear that the whiskey-jacks are here advisedly; they just like the sound of the place. Under the big shade trees in front of the house, the lawn is littered with dozens of half-eaten apples. I studied these, wondering what had been going on. Then I discovered that it was the work of crows. The crows pick little yellow apples from the old tree by the shed and carry them to some high perch before rifling them for seeds. In this respect they are no different from the people of San Francisco, who like to drink at the Top of the Mark, where they can really see what they are doing.

Here in New England, each season carries a hundred foreshadowings of the season that is to follow—which is one of the things I love about it. Winter is rough and long, but spring lies all round about. Yesterday, a small white keel feather escaped from my goose and lodged in the bank boughs near the kitchen porch, where I spied it as I came home in the cold twilight. The minute I saw the feather, I was projected into May, knowing that a barn swallow would be along to claim the prize and use it to decorate the front edge of its nest. Immediately, the December air seemed full of wings of swallows and the warmth of barns. Swallows, I have noticed, never use any feather but a white one in their nest-building, and they always leave a lot of it showing, which makes me believe that they are interested not in the feather's insulating power but in its reflecting power, so that when they skim into the dark barn from the bright outdoors they will have a beacon to steer by.

P.S. (April 1962).   A trip home over the highway still warms me in the same indescribable way, but the highway itself changes from year to year. The seductive turnpike, which used to peter out conveniently at Portland, introducing the traveller to the pleasures of Route 1, now catapults him clear through to Augusta and will soon shoot him to Bangor if he isn't careful. The Narramissic still flows through Orland every day, but the last time I drove home I did not "dip down across" the river; instead I found myself hustling along on a new stretch of improved highway that cut out around Orland to the north and rushed me across the stream on a new bridge. The steep hill and sharp turns had been ironed out by the ironers, effecting a saving of probably three minutes in running time. So I was home three minutes earlier, but have no idea how I spent those three extra minutes, or whether they profited me as much as the old backward glance at Orland—its church spire, its reliable river, its nestling houses, its general store, and its bouquet of the flowering of New England.

The whiskey-jack showed up again around here a couple of

years ago. I encountered one down in the cedar swamp in the pasture, where I had gone to look for a fox's den. The bird, instead of showing alarm at my intrusion, followed me about, jumping silently from branch to branch in the thick woods, seemingly eager to learn what I was up to. I found it spooky yet agreeable to be tailed by a bird, and a disreputable one at that. The Canada jay looks as though he had slept in his clothes.

BEDFELLOWS

Turtle Bay, February 6, 1956

I am lying here in my private sick bay on the east side of town between Second and Third avenues, watching starlings from the vantage point of bed. Three Democrats are in bed with me: Harry Truman (in a stale copy of the *Times*), Adlai Stevenson (in *Harper's*), and Dean Acheson (in a book called *A Democrat Looks at His Party*). I take Democrats to bed with me for lack of a dachshund, although as a matter of fact on occasions like this I am almost certain to be visited by the ghost of Fred, my dash-hound everlasting, dead these many years. In life, Fred always attended the sick, climbing right into bed with the patient like some lecherous old physician, and making a bad situation worse. All this dark morning I have reluctantly entertained him upon the rumpled blanket, felt his oppressive weight, and heard his fraudulent report. He was an uncomfortable bedmate when alive; death has worked little improvement—I still feel crowded, still wonder why I put up with his natural rudeness and his pretensions.

The only thing I used to find agreeable about him in bed was his smell, which for some reason was nonirritating to my nose and evocative to my mind, somewhat in the way that a sudden whiff of the cow barn or of bone meal on a lawn in springtime carries sensations of the richness of earth and of experience. Fred's aroma

37

has not deserted him; it wafts over me now, as though I had just removed the stopper from a vial of cheap perfume. His aroma has not deserted the last collar he wore, either. I ran across this great, studded strap not long ago when I was rummaging in a cabinet. I raised it cautiously toward my nose, fearing a quill stab from his last porcupine. The collar was extremely high—had lost hardly ten percent of its potency.

Fred was sold to me for a dachshund, but I was in a buying mood and would have bought the puppy if the storekeeper had said he was an Irish Wolfschmidt. He was only a few weeks old when I closed the deal, and he was in real trouble. In no time at all, his troubles cleared up and mine began. Thirteen years later he died, and by rights *my* troubles should have cleared up. But I can't say they have. Here I am, seven years after his death, still sharing a fever bed with him and, what is infinitely more burdensome, still feeling the compulsion to write about him. I sometimes suspect that subconsciously I'm trying to revenge myself by turning him to account, and thus recompensing myself for the time and money he cost me.

He was red and low-posted and long-bodied like a dachshund, and when you glanced casually at him he certainly gave the quick impression of being a dachshund. But if you went at him with a tape measure, and forced him onto scales, the dachshund theory collapsed. The papers that came with him were produced hurriedly and in an illicit atmosphere in a back room of the pet shop, and are most unconvincing. However, I have no reason to unsettle the Kennel Club; the fraud, if indeed it was a fraud, was ended in 1948, at the time of his death. So much of his life was given to shady practices, it is only fitting that his pedigree should have been (as I believe it was) a forgery.

I have been languishing here, looking out at the lovely branches of the plane tree in the sky above our city back yard. Only starlings and house sparrows are in view at this season, but soon other birds will show up. (Why, by the way, doesn't the *Times* publish an "Arrival of Birds" column, similar to its famous "Arrival of Buyers"?) Fred was a window gazer and bird watcher, particularly during his later years, when hardened arteries slowed him up and made it necessary for him to substitute sedentary pleasures for active sport. I think of him as he used to look on our bed in Maine—an old four-poster, too high from the floor for him to reach unassisted. Whenever the bed was occupied during the daylight hours, whether because one of us was sick or was napping, Fred would appear in the doorway and enter without knocking. On his big gray face would be a look of quiet amusement (at having caught somebody in bed during the daytime) coupled with his usual look of fake respectability. Whoever occupied the bed would reach down, seize him by the loose folds of his thick neck, and haul him painfully up. He dreaded this maneuver, and so did the occupant of the bed. There was far too much dead weight involved for anybody's comfort. But Fred was always willing to put up with being hoisted in order to gain the happy heights, as, indeed, he was willing to put up with far greater discomforts—such as a mouthful of porcupine quills—when there was some prize at the end.

Once up, he settled into his pose of bird-watching, propped luxuriously against a pillow, as close as he could get to the window, his great soft brown eyes alight with expectation and scientific knowledge. He seemed never to tire of his work. He watched steadily and managed to give the impression that he was a secret agent of the Department of Justice. Spotting a flicker or a starling on the wing, he would turn and make a quick report.

"I just saw an eagle go by," he would say. "It was carrying a baby."

This was not precisely a lie. Fred was like a child in many ways, and sought always to blow things up to proportions that satisfied his imagination and his love of adventure. He was the Cecil B. deMille of dogs. He was also a zealot, and I have just been reminded of him by a quote from one of the Democrats sharing my bed—Acheson quoting Brandeis. "The greatest dangers to liberty," said Mr. Brandeis, "lurk in insidious encroachment by men of zeal, well-meaning but without understanding." Fred saw in every bird, every squirrel, every housefly, every rat, every skunk, every porcupine, a security risk and a present danger to his republic. He had a dossier on almost every living creature, as well as on several inanimate objects, including my son's football.

Although birds fascinated him, his real hope as he watched the big shade trees outside the window was that a red squirrel would show up. When he sighted a squirrel, Fred would straighten up from his pillow, tense his frame, and then, in a moment or two, begin to tremble. The knuckles of his big forelegs, unstable from old age, would seem to go into spasm, and he would sit there with his eyes glued on the squirrel and his front legs alternately collapsing under him and bearing his weight again.

I find it difficult to convey the peculiar character of this ignoble old vigilante, my late and sometimes lamented companion. What was there about him so different from the many other dogs I've owned that he keeps recurring and does not, in fact, seem really dead at all? My wife used to claim that Fred was deeply devoted to me, and in a certain sense he was, but his was the devotion of an opportunist. He knew that on the farm I took the over-all view and travelled pluckily from one trouble spot to the next. He dearly loved this type of work. It was not his habit to tag along faithfully behind me, as a collie might, giving moral support and sometimes real support. He ran a trouble-shooting business of his own and was usually at the scene ahead of me, compounding the trouble and shooting in the air. The word "faithful" is an adjective I simply never thought of in connection with Fred. He differed from most dogs in that he tended to knock down, rather than build up, the master's ego. Once he had outgrown the capers of puppyhood, he never again caressed me or anybody else during his life. The only time he was ever discovered in an attitude that suggested affection was when I was in the driver's seat of our car and he would lay his heavy head on my right knee. This, I soon perceived, was not affection, it was nausea. Drooling always followed, and the whole thing was extremely inconvenient, because the weight of his head made me press too hard on the accelerator.

Fred devoted his life to deflating me and succeeded admirably. His attachment to our establishment, though untinged with affection, was strong nevertheless, and vibrant. It was simply that he found in our persons, in our activities, the sort of complex, disorderly society that fired his imagination and satisfied his need for tumult and his quest for truth. After he had subdued six or seven porcupines, we realized that his private war against porcupines was an expensive bore, so we took to tying him, making him fast to any tree or wheel or post or log that was at hand, to keep him from sneaking off into the woods. I think of him as always at the end of some outsize piece of rope. Fred's disgust at these confinements was great, but he improved his time, nonetheless, in a thousand small diversions. He never just lay and rested. Within the range of his tether, he continued to explore, dissect, botanize, conduct post-mortems, excavate, experiment, expropriate, savor, masticate, regurgitate. He had no contemplative life, but he held as a steady gleam the belief that under the commonplace stone and behind the unlikely piece of driftwood lay the stuff of high adventure and the opportunity to save the nation.

But to return to my other bedfellows, these quick Democrats. They are big, solid men, every one of them, and they have been busy writing and speaking, and sniffing out the truth. I did not deliberately pack my counterpane with members of a single political faith; they converged on me by the slick device of getting into print. All three turn up saying things that interest me, so I make bed space for them.

Mr. Truman, reminiscing in a recent issue of the *Times*, says the press sold out in 1948 to "the special interests," was ninety percent hostile to his candidacy, distorted facts, caused his low popularity rating at that period, and tried to prevent him from reaching the people with his message in the campaign. This bold, implausible statement engages my fancy because it is a half-truth, and all half-truths excite me. An attractive half-truth in bed with a man can disturb him as deeply as a cracker crumb. Being a second-string member of the press myself, and working, as I do, for the special interests, I tend to think there is a large dollop of pure irascibility in Mr. Truman's gloomy report. In 1948, Mr. Truman made a spirited whistle-stop trip and worked five times as hard as his rival. The "Republican-controlled press and radio" reported practically everything he said, and also gave vent to frequent horselaughs in their editorials and commentaries. Millions of studious, worried Americans heard and read what he said; then they checked it against the editorials; then they walked silently into the voting booths and returned him to office. Then they listened to Kaltenborn. Then they listened to Truman do-ing Kaltenborn. The criticism of the opposition in 1948 was neither a bad thing nor a destructive thing. It was healthy and (in our sort of society) necessary. Without the press, radio, and TV, President Truman couldn't have got through to the people in anything like the volume he achieved. Some of the published news was distorted, but distortion is inherent in partisan journalism, the same as it is in political rallies. I have yet to see a piece of writing, political or nonpolitical, that doesn't have a slant. All writing slants the way a writer leans, and no man is born perpendicular, although many men are born upright. The beauty of the American free press is that the slants and the twists and the distortions come from so many directions, and the special interests are so numerous, the reader must sift and sort and check and countercheck in order to find out what the score is. This he does. It is only when a press gets its twist from a single source, as in the case of government-controlled press systems, that the reader is licked.

Democrats do a lot of bellyaching about the press being preponderantly Republican, which it is. But they don't do the one thing that could correct the situation: they don't go into the publishing business. Democrats say they haven't got that kind of money, but I'm afraid they haven't got that kind of temperament or, perhaps, nerve.

Adlai Stevenson takes a view of criticism almost opposite to Harry Truman's. Writing in *Harper's*, Stevenson says, ". . . I very well know that in many minds 'criticism' has today become an ugly word. It has become almost *lèse majesté*. It conjures up pictures of insidious radicals hacking away at the very foundations of the American way of life. It suggests nonconformity and non-conformity suggests disloyalty and disloyalty suggests treason, and before we know where we are, this process has all but identi-fied the critic with the saboteur and turned political criticism into an un-American activity instead of democracy's greatest safe-guard."

The above interests me because I agree with it and everyone is fascinated by what he agrees with. Especially when he is sick in bed.

Mr. Acheson, in his passionately partisan yet temperate book, writes at some length about the loyalty-security procedures that were started under the Democrats in 1947 and have modified our lives ever since. This theme interests me because I believe, with the author, that security declines as security machinery expands. The machinery calls for a secret police. At first, this device is used solely to protect us from unsuitable servants in sensitive positions. Then it broadens rapidly and permeates nonsensitive areas, and, finally, business and industry. It is in the portfolios of the secret police that nonconformity makes the subtle change into dis-loyalty. A secret-police system first unsettles, then desiccates, then calcifies a free society. I think the recent loyalty investigation of the press by the Eastland subcommittee was a disquieting event.

It seemed to assume for Congress the right to poke about in newspaper offices and instruct the management as to which employees were O.K. and which were not. That sort of procedure opens wonderfully attractive vistas to legislators. If it becomes an accepted practice, it will lead to great abuses. Under extreme conditions, it could destroy the free press.

The loyalty theme also relates to Fred, who presses ever more heavily against me this morning. Fred was intensely loyal to himself, as every strong individualist must be. He held unshakable convictions, like Harry Truman. He was absolutely sure that he was in possession of the truth. Because he was loyal to himself, I found his eccentricities supportable. Actually, he contributed greatly to the general health and security of the household. Nothing has been quite the same since he departed. His views were largely of a dissenting nature. Yet in tearing us apart he somehow held us together. In obstructing, he strengthened us. In criticizing, he informed. In his rich, aromatic heresy, he nourished our faith. He was also a plain damned nuisance, I must not forget that.

The matter of "faith" has been in the papers again lately. President Eisenhower (I will now move over and welcome a Republican into bed, along with my other visitors) has come out for prayer and has emphasized that most Americans are motivated (as they surely are) by religious faith. The *Herald Tribune* headed the story, "PRESIDENT SAYS PRAYER IS PART OF DEMOCRACY." The implication in such a pronouncement, emanating from the seat of government, is that religious faith is a *condition*, or even a *precondition*, of the democratic life. This is just wrong. A President should pray whenever and wherever he feels like it (most Presidents have prayed hard and long, and some of them in desperation and in agony), but I don't think a President should advertise prayer. That is a different thing. Democracy, if I understand it at all, is a society in which the unbeliever feels undisturbed and at home. If there were only half a dozen unbelievers in America, their well-being would be a test of our democracy, their tranquillity would be its proof. The repeated suggestion by the present administration that religious faith is a precondition of the American way of life is disturbing to me and, I am willing to bet, to a good many other citizens. President Eisenhower spoke of the tremendous favorable mail he received in response to his inaugural prayer in 1953. What he perhaps did not realize is that the persons who felt fidgety or disquieted about the matter were not likely to write in about it, lest they appear irreverent, irreligious, unfaithful, or even un-American. I remember the prayer very well. I didn't mind it, although I have never been able to pray electronically and doubt that I ever will be. Still, I was able to perceive that the President was sincere and was doing what came naturally, and anybody who is acting in a natural way is all right by me. I believe that our political leaders should live by faith and should, by deeds and sometimes by prayer, demonstrate faith, but I doubt that they should *advocate* faith, if only because such advocacy renders a few people uncomfortable. The concern of a democracy is that no honest man shall feel uncomfortable, I don't care who he is, or how nutty he is.

I hope that Belief never is made to appear mandatory. One of our founders, in 1787, said, "Even the diseases of the people should be represented." Those were strange, noble words, and they have endured. They were on television yesterday. I distrust the slightest hint of a standard for political rectitude, knowing that it will open the way for persons in authority to set arbitrary standards of human behavior.

Fred was an unbeliever. He worshiped no personal God, no Supreme Being. He certainly did not worship *me*. If he had suddenly taken to worshiping me, I think I would have felt as queer as God must have felt the other day when a minister in California, pronouncing the invocation for a meeting of Democrats, said, "We believe Adlai Stevenson to be Thy choice for President of the United States. Amen."

I respected this quirk in Fred, this inability to conform to conventional canine standards of religious feeling. And in the miniature democracy that was, and is, our household he lived undisturbed and at peace with his conscience. I hope my country will never become an uncomfortable place for the unbeliever, as it could easily become if prayer was made one of the requirements of the accredited citizen. My wife, a spiritual but not a prayerful woman, read Mr. Eisenhower's call to prayer in the *Tribune* and said something I shall never forget. "Maybe it's all right," she said. "But for the first time in my life I'm beginning to feel like an outsider in my own land."

Democracy is itself a religious faith. For some it comes close to being the only formal religion they have. And so when I see the first faint shadow of orthodoxy sweep across the sky, feel the first cold whiff of its blinding fog steal in from sea, I tremble all over, as though I had just seen an eagle go by, carrying a baby.

Anyway, it's pleasant here in bed with all these friendly Democrats and Republicans, every one of them a dedicated man, with all these magazine and newspaper clippings, with Fred, watching the starlings against the wintry sky, and the prospect of another Presidential year, with all its passions and its distortions and its dissents and its excesses and special interests. Fred died from a life of excesses, and I don't mind if I do, too. I love to read all these words—most of them sober, thoughtful words—from the steadily growing book of democracy: Acheson on security, Truman on the press, Eisenhower on faith, Stevenson on criticism, all writing away like sixty, all working to improve and save and maintain in good repair what was so marvelously constructed to begin with. This is the real thing. This is bedlam in bed. As Mr. Stevenson puts it: ". . . no civilization has ever had so haunting a sense of an ultimate order of goodness and rationality which can be known and achieved." It makes me eager to rise and meet the new day, as Fred used to rise to his, with the complete conviction that through vigilance and good works all porcupines, all cats, all skunks, all squirrels, all houseflies, all footballs, all evil birds in the sky could be successfully brought to account and the scene made safe and pleasant for the sensible individual—namely, him. However distorted was his crazy vision of the beautiful world, however perverse his scheme for establishing an order of goodness by murdering every creature that seemed to him bad, I had to hand him this: he really worked at it.

P.S. (June 1962).   This piece about prayer and about Fred drew a heavy mail when it appeared—heavy for me, anyway. (I call six letters a heavy mail.) Some of the letters were from persons who felt as I did about the advocacy of prayer but who had been reluctant to say anything about it. And there were other letters from readers who complained that my delineation of Fred's character (half vigilante, half dissenter) was contradictory, or at least fuzzy. I guess there is some justification for this complaint: the thing didn't come out as clear as I would have liked, but nothing I write ever does.

In the 1960 Presidential campaign, faith and prayer took a back seat and the big question was whether the White House could be occupied by a Catholic or whether that would be just too much. Again the voters studied the *Racing Form*, the *Wall Street Journal*, the *Christian Science Monitor*; they sifted the winds that blew through the Republican-controlled press; they gazed into television's crystal ball; they went to church and asked guidance; and finally they came up with the opinion that a Catholic *can* be President. It was a memorable time, a photo finish, and a healthful exercise generally.

The McCarthy era, so lately dead, has been followed by the Birch Society era (eras are growing shorter and shorter in America—some of them seem to last only a few days), and again we find ourselves with a group of people that proposes to establish a standard for political rectitude, again we have vigilantes busy compiling lists and deciding who is anti-Communist and who fails in that regard. Now in 1962, conservatism is the big, new correct thing, and the term "liberal" is a term of opprobrium. In the newspaper that arrives on my breakfast table every morning, liberals are usually referred to as "so-called" liberals, the implication being that they are probably something a whole lot worse than the name "liberal" would indicate, something really shady. The Birchers, luckily, are not in as good a position to create sensational newspaper headlines as was Senator McCarthy, who, because he was chairman of a Senate committee, managed to turn Page One into a gibbet, and hung a new fellow each day, with the help of a press that sometimes seemed to me unnecessarily cooperative in donating its space for the celebration of those grim rites.

Prayer broke into the news again with the Supreme Court's decision in the New York school prayer case. From the violence of the reaction you would have thought the Court was in the business of stifling America's religious life and that the country was going to the dogs. But I think the Court again heard clearly the simple theme that ennobles our Constitution: that no one shall be made to feel uncomfortable or unsafe because of nonconformity. New York State, with the best intentions in the world, created a moment of gentle orthodoxy in public school life, and here and there a child was left out in the cold, bearing the stigma of being different. It is this one child that our Constitution is concerned about—his tranquillity, his health, his safety, his conscience. What a kindly old document it is, and how brightly it shines, through interpretation after interpretation!

One day last fall I wandered down through the orchard and into the woods to pay a call at Fred's grave. The trees were bare; wild apples hung shamelessly from the grapevine that long ago took over the tree. The old dump, which is no longer used and which goes out of sight during the leafy months, lay exposed and candid—rusted pots and tin cans and sundries. The briers had lost some of their effectiveness, the air was good, and the little dingle, usually so mean and inconsiderable, seemed to have acquired stature. Fred's headstone, ordinarily in collapse, was bolt upright, and I wondered whether he had quieted down at last. I felt uneasy suddenly, as the quick do sometimes feel when in the presence of the dead, and my uneasiness went to my bladder. Instead of laying a wreath, I watered an alder and came away.

This grave is the only grave I visit with any regularity—in fact, it is the only grave I visit at all. I have relatives lying in cemeteries here and there around the country, but I do not feel any urge to return to them, and it strikes me as odd that I should return to the place where an old dog lies in a shabby bit of woodland next to a private dump. Besides being an easy trip (one for which I need make no preparation) it is a natural journey— I really go down there to see what's doing. (Fred himself used to scout the place every day when he was alive.) I do not experience grief when I am down there, nor do I pay tribute to the dead. I feel a sort of over-all sadness that has nothing to do with the grave or its occupant. Often I feel extremely well in that rough cemetery, and sometimes flush a partridge. But I feel sadness at All Last Things, too, which is probably a purely selfish, or turned-in, emotion—sorrow not at my dog's death but at my own, which hasn't even occurred yet but which saddens me just to think about in such pleasant surroundings.

THE RING OF TIME

Fiddler Bayou, March 22, 1956

After the lions had returned to their cages, creeping angrily through the chutes, a little bunch of us drifted away and into an open doorway nearby, where we stood for a while in semidark-ness, watching a big brown circus horse go harumphing around the practice ring. His trainer was a woman of about forty, and the two of them, horse and woman, seemed caught up in one of those desultory treadmills of afternoon from which there is no apparent escape. The day was hot, and we kibitzers were grateful to be briefly out of the sun's glare. The long rein, or tape, by which the woman guided her charge counterclockwise in his dull career formed the radius of their private circle, of which she was the revolving center; and she, too, stepped a tiny circumfer-ence of her own, in order to accommodate the horse and allow him his maximum scope. She had on a short-skirted costume and a conical straw hat. Her legs were bare and she wore high heels, which probed deep into the loose tanbark and kept her ankles in a state of constant turmoil. The great size and meekness of the horse, the repetitious exercise, the heat of the afternoon, all exerted a hypnotic charm that invited boredom; we spectators were experiencing a languor—we neither expected relief nor felt entitled to any. We had paid a dollar to get into the grounds, to be sure, but we had got our dollar's worth a few minutes before, when the lion trainer's whiplash had got caught around a toe of one of the lions. What more did we want for a dollar?

Behind me I heard someone say, "Excuse me, please," in a low voice. She was halfway into the building when I turned and saw her—a girl of sixteen or seventeen, politely threading her way through us onlookers who blocked the entrance. As she emerged in front of us, I saw that she was barefoot, her dirty little feet fighting the uneven ground. In most respects she was like any of two or three dozen showgirls you encounter if you wander about the winter quarters of Mr. John Ringling North's circus, in Sarasota—cleverly proportioned, deeply browned by the sun, dusty, eager, and almost naked. But her grave face and the naturalness of her manner gave her a sort of quick distinction and brought a new note into the gloomy octagonal building where we had all cast our lot for a few moments. As soon as she had squeezed through the crowd, she spoke a word or two to the older woman, whom I took to be her mother, stepped to the ring, and waited while the horse coasted to a stop in front of her. She gave the animal a couple of affectionate swipes on his enormous neck and then swung herself aboard. The horse immediately resumed his rocking canter, the woman goading him on, chanting something that sounded like "Hop! Hop!"

In attempting to recapture this mild spectacle, I am merely acting as recording secretary for one of the oldest of societies—the society of those who, at one time or another, have surrendered, without even a show of resistance, to the bedazzlement of a circus rider. As a writing man, or secretary, I have always felt charged with the safekeeping of all unexpected items of worldly or unworldly enchantment, as though I might be held personally responsible if even a small one were to be lost. But it is not easy to communicate anything of this nature. The circus comes as close to being the world in microcosm as anything I know; in a way, it puts all the rest of show business in the shade. Its magic is universal and complex. Out of its wild disorder comes order; from

its rank smell rises the good aroma of courage and daring; out of
its preliminary shabbiness comes the final splendor. And buried in
the familiar boasts of its advance agents lies the modesty of most
of its people. For me the circus is at its best before it has been
put together. It is at its best at certain moments when it comes to
a point, as through a burning glass, in the activity and destiny of a
single performer out of so many. One ring is always bigger than
three. One rider, one aerialist, is always greater than six. In short,
a man has to catch the circus unawares to experience its full impact and share its gaudy dream.

The ten-minute ride the girl took achieved—as far as I was concerned, who wasn't looking for it, and quite unbeknownst to
her, who wasn't even striving for it—the thing that is sought by
performers everywhere, on whatever stage, whether struggling
in the tidal currents of Shakespeare or bucking the difficult motion
of a horse. I somehow got the idea she was just cadging a ride,
improving a shining ten minutes in the diligent way all serious
artists seize free moments to hone the blade of their talent and
keep themselves in trim. Her brief tour included only elementary
postures and tricks, perhaps because they were all she was capable
of, perhaps because her warmup at this hour was unscheduled and
the ring was not rigged for a real practice session. She swung
herself off and on the horse several times, gripping his mane.
She did a few knee-stands—or whatever they are called—dropping to her knees and quickly bouncing back up on her feet
again. Most of the time she simply rode in a standing position,
well aft on the beast, her hands hanging easily at her sides, her
head erect, her straw-colored ponytail lightly brushing her
shoulders, the blood of exertion showing faintly through the tan
of her skin. Twice she managed a one-foot stance—a sort of ballet
pose, with arms outstretched. At one point the neck strap of her
bathing suit broke and she went twice around the ring in the
classic attitude of a woman making minor repairs to a garment.
The fact that she was standing on the back of a moving horse

while doing this invested the matter with a clownish significance that perfectly fitted the spirit of the circus—jocund, yet charming. She just rolled the strap into a neat ball and stowed it inside her bodice while the horse rocked and rolled beneath her in dutiful innocence. The bathing suit proved as self-reliant as its owner and stood up well enough without benefit of strap.

The richness of the scene was in its plainness, its natural condition—of horse, of ring, of girl, even to the girl's bare feet that gripped the bare back of her proud and ridiculous mount. The enchantment grew not out of anything that happened or was performed but out of something that seemed to go round and around and around with the girl, attending her, a steady gleam in the shape of a circle—a ring of ambition, of happiness, of youth. (And the positive pleasures of equilibrium under difficulties.) In a week or two, all would be changed, all (or almost all) lost: the girl would wear makeup, the horse would wear gold, the ring would be painted, the bark would be clean for the feet of the horse, the girl's feet would be clean for the slippers that she'd wear. All, all would be lost.

As I watched with the others, our jaws adroop, our eyes alight, I became painfully conscious of the element of time. Everything in the hideous old building seemed to take the shape of a circle, conforming to the course of the horse. The rider's gaze, as she peered straight ahead, seemed to be circular, as though bent by force of circumstance; then time itself began running in circles, and so the beginning was where the end was, and the two were the same, and one thing ran into the next and time went round and around and got nowhere. The girl wasn't so young that she did not know the delicious satisfaction of having a perfectly behaved body and the fun of using it to do a trick most people can't do, but she was too young to know that time does not really move in a circle at all. I thought: "She will never be as beautiful as this again"—a thought that made me acutely unhappy—and in a flash my mind (which is too much of a busybody to suit me) had projected her twenty-five years ahead, and she was now in the center of the ring, on foot, wearing a conical hat and high-heeled shoes, the image of the older woman, holding the long rein, caught in the treadmill of an afternoon long in the future. "She is at that enviable moment in life [I thought] when she believes she can go once around the ring, make one complete circuit, and at the end be exactly the same age as at the start." Everything in her movements, her expression, told you that for her the ring of time was perfectly formed, changeless, predictable, without beginning or end, like the ring in which she was travelling at this moment with the horse that wallowed under her. And then I slipped back into my trance, and time was circular again—time, pausing quietly with the rest of us, so as not to disturb the balance of a performer.

Her ride ended as casually as it had begun. The older woman stopped the horse, and the girl slid to the ground. As she walked toward us to leave, there was a quick, small burst of applause. She smiled broadly, in surprise and pleasure; then her face suddenly regained its gravity and she disappeared through the door.

It has been ambitious and plucky of me to attempt to describe what is indescribable, and I have failed, as I knew I would. But I have discharged my duty to my society; and besides, a writer, like an acrobat, must occasionally try a stunt that is too much for him. At any rate, it is worth reporting that long before the circus comes to town, its most notable performances have already been given. Under the bright lights of the finished show, a performer need only reflect the electric candle power that is directed upon him; but in the dark and dirty old training rings and in the makeshift cages, whatever light is generated, whatever excitement, whatever beauty, must come from original sources—from internal fires of professional hunger and delight, from the exuberance and gravity of youth. It is the difference between planetary light and the combustion of stars.

The South is the land of the sustained sibilant. Everywhere, for the appreciative visitor, the letter "s" insinuates itself in the scene: in the sound of sea and sand, in the singing shell, in the heat of sun and sky, in the sultriness of the gentle hours, in the siesta, in the stir of birds and insects. In contrast to the softness of its music, the South is also cruel and hard and prickly. A little striped lizard, flattened along the sharp green bayonet of a yucca, wears in its tiny face and watchful eye the pure look of death and violence. And all over the place, hidden at the bottom of their small sandy craters, the ant lions lie in wait for the ant that will stumble into their trap. (There are three kinds of lions in this region: the lions of the circus, the ant lions, and the Lions of the Tampa Lions Club, who roared their approval of segregation at a meeting the other day—all except one, a Lion named Monty Gurwit, who declined to roar and thereby got his picture in the paper.)

The day starts on a note of despair: the sorrowing dove, alone on its telephone wire, mourns the loss of night, weeps at the bright perils of the unfolding day. But soon the mockingbird wakes and begins an early rehearsal, setting the dove down by force of character, running through a few slick imitations, and trying a couple of original numbers into the bargain. The redbird takes it from there. Despair gives way to good humor. The Southern dawn is a pale affair, usually, quite different from our northern daybreak. It is a triumph of gradualism; night turns to day imperceptibly, softly, with no theatrics. It is subtle and undisturbing. As the first light seeps in through the blinds I lie in bed half awake, despairing with the dove, sounding the A for the brothers Alsop. All seems lost, all seems sorrowful. Then a mullet jumps in the bayou outside the bedroom window. It falls back into the water with a smart smack. I have asked several people why the mullet incessantly jump and I have received a variety of answers. Some say the mullet jump to shake off a parasite that annoys them. Some say they jump for the love of jumping—as the girl on the horse seemed to ride for the love of riding (although she, too, like all artists, may have been shaking off some parasite that fastens itself to the creative spirit and can be got rid of only by fifty turns around a ring while standing on a horse).

In Florida at this time of year, the sun does not take command of the day until a couple of hours after it has appeared in the east. It seems to carry no authority at first. The sun and the lizard keep the same schedule; they bide their time until the morning has advanced a good long way before they come fully forth and strike. The cold lizard waits astride his warming leaf for the perfect moment; the cold sun waits in his nest of clouds for the crucial time.

On many days, the dampness of the air pervades all life, all living. Matches refuse to strike. The towel, hung to dry, grows wetter by the hour. The newspaper, with its headlines about integration, wilts in your hand and falls limply into the coffee and the egg. Envelopes seal themselves. Postage stamps mate with one another as shamelessly as grasshoppers. But most of the time the days are models of beauty and wonder and comfort, with the kind sea stroking the back of the warm sand. At evening there are great flights of birds over the sea, where the light lingers; the gulls, the pelicans, the terns, the herons stay aloft for half an hour after land birds have gone to roost. They hold their ancient formations, wheel and fish over the Pass, enjoying the last of day like children playing outdoors after suppertime.

To a beachcomber from the North, which is my present status, the race problem has no pertinence, no immediacy. Here in Florida I am a guest in two houses—the house of the sun, the house of the State of Florida. As a guest, I mind my manners and do not criticize the customs of my hosts. It gives me a queer feeling, though, to be at the center of the greatest social crisis of my time and see hardly a sign of it. Yet the very absence of signs seems to increase one's awareness. Colored people do not come to the public beach to bathe, because they would not be made welcome there; and they don't fritter away their time visiting the circus, because they have other things to do. A few of them turn up at the ballpark, where they occupy a separate but equal section of the left-field bleachers and watch Negro players on the visiting Braves team using the same bases as the white players, instead of separate (but equal) bases. I have had only two small encounters with "color." A colored woman named Viola, who had been a friend of my wife's sister years ago, showed up one day with some laundry of ours that she had consented to do for us, and with the bundle she brought a bunch of nasturtiums, as a sort of natural accompaniment to the delivery of clean clothes. The flowers seemed a very acceptable thing and I was touched by them. We asked Viola about her daughter, and she said she was at Kentucky State College, studying voice.

The other encounter was when I was explaining to our cook, who is from Finland, the mysteries of bus travel in the American Southland. I showed her the bus stop, armed her with a time-table, and then, as a matter of duty, mentioned the customs of the Romans. "When you get on the bus," I said, "I think you'd better sit in one of the front seats—the seats in back are for colored people." A look of great weariness came into her face, as it does when we use too many dishes, and she replied, "Oh, I know—isn't it silly!"

Her remark, coming as it did all the way from Finland and landing on this sandbar with a plunk, impressed me. The Supreme Court said nothing about silliness, but I suspect it may play more of a role than one might suppose. People are, if anything, more touchy about being thought silly than they are about being thought unjust. I note that one of the arguments in the recent manifesto of Southern Congressmen in support of the doctrine of "separate but equal" was that it had been founded on "common sense." The sense that is common to one generation is uncommon to the next. Probably the first slave ship, with Negroes lying in chains on its decks, seemed commonsensical to the owners who operated it and to the planters who patronized it. But such a vessel would not be in the realm of common sense today. The only sense that is common, in the long run, is the sense of change —and we all instinctively avoid it, and object to the passage of time, and would rather have none of it.

The Supreme Court decision is like the Southern sun, laggard in its early stages, biding its time. It has been the law in Florida for two years now, and the years have been like the hours of the morning before the sun has gathered its strength. I think the decision is as incontrovertible and warming as the sun, and, like the sun, will eventually take charge.

But there is certainly a great temptation in Florida to duck the passage of time. Lying in warm comfort by the sea, you receive gratefully the gift of the sun, the gift of the South. This is true seduction. The day is a circle—morning, afternoon, and night. After a few days I was clearly enjoying the same delusion as the girl on the horse—that I could ride clear around the ring of day, guarded by wind and sun and sea and sand, and be not a moment older.

P.S. (April 1962).   When I first laid eyes on Fiddler Bayou, it was wild land, populated chiefly by the little crabs that gave it its name, visited by wading birds and by an occasional fisherman. Today, houses ring the bayou, and part of the mangrove shore has been bulkheaded with a concrete wall. Green lawns stretch from patio to water's edge, and sprinklers make rainbows in the light. But despite man's encroachment, Nature manages to hold her own and assert her authority: high tides and high winds in the Gulf sometimes send the sea crashing across the sand barrier, depositing its wrack on lawns and ringing everyone's front door bell. The birds and the crabs accommodate themselves quite readily to the changes that have taken place; every day brings herons to hunt around among the roots of the mangroves, and I have discovered that I can approach to within about eight feet of a Little Blue Heron simply by entering the water and swimming slowly toward him. Apparently he has decided that when I'm in the water, I am without guile—possibly even desirable, like a fish.

The Ringling circus has quit Sarasota and gone elsewhere for its hibernation. A few circus families still own homes in the town, and every spring the students at the high school put on a circus, to let off steam, work off physical requirements, and provide a promotional spectacle for Sarasota. At the drugstore you can buy a postcard showing the bed John Ringling slept in. Time has not stood still for anybody but the dead, and even the dead must be able to hear the acceleration of little sports cars and know that things have changed.

From the all-wise *New York Times*, which has the animal kingdom ever in mind, I have learned that one of the creatures most acutely aware of the passing of time is the fiddler crab himself. Tiny spots on his body enlarge during daytime hours, giving him the same color as the mudbank he explores and thus protecting him from his enemies. At night the spots shrink, his color fades, and he is almost invisible in the light of the moon. These changes are synchronized with the tides, so that each day they occur at a different hour. A scientist who experimented with the crabs to learn more about the phenomenon discovered that even when they are removed from their natural environment and held in confinement, the rhythm of their bodily change continues uninterrupted, and they mark the passage of time in their laboratory prison, faithful to the tides in their fashion.

COON TREE

Allen Cove, June 14, 1956

The temperature this morning, here in the East, is sixty-eight degrees. The relative humidity is sixty-four percent. Barometer 30.02, rising. Carol Reed is nowhere in sight. A light easterly breeze ruffles the water of the cove, where a seine boat lies at anchor, her dories strung out behind like ducklings. Apple blossoms are showing, two weeks behind schedule, and the bees are at work—all six of them. (A bee is almost as rare a sight these days as a team of horses.) The goldfinch is on the dandelion, the goose is on the pond, the black fly is on the trout brook, the Northeast Airliner is on course for Rockland. As I write these notes, the raccoon is nursing one of her hangovers on the branch outside the hole where her kittens are.

My doctor has ordered me to put my head in traction for ten minutes twice a day. (Nobody can figure out what to do with my head, so now they are going to give it a good pull, like an exasperated mechanic who hauls off and gives his problem a smart jolt with the hammer.) I have rigged a delightful traction center in the barn, using a canvas halter, a length of clothesline, two galvanized pulleys, a twelve-pound boat anchor, a milking stool, and a barn swallow. I set everything up so I could work the swallow into the deal, because I knew he would enjoy it, and he does. While his bride sits on the eggs and I sit on the milking stool, he sits on a harness peg a few feet away, giggling at me throughout the ten-minute period and giving his mate a play-by-play account of Man's fantastic battle with himself, which in my case must look like suicide by hanging.

I think this is the fourth spring the coon has occupied the big tree in front of the house, but I have lost count, so smoothly do the years run together. She is like a member of our family. She has her kittens in a hole in the tree about thirty-five feet above the ground, which places her bedchamber a few feet from my bedchamber but at a slightly greater elevation. It strikes me as odd (and quite satisfactory) that I should go to sleep every night so close to a litter of raccoons. The mother's comings and goings are as much a part of my life at this season of the year as my morning shave and my evening drink. Being a coon, she is, of course, a creature of the night; I am essentially a creature of the day, so we Cox and Box it very nicely. I have become so attuned to her habits—her departure as the light fades at quarter past eight, her return to the hungry kittens at about 3 A.M., just before daylight, after the night's adventures —that I have taken to waking at three to watch her home-coming and admire her faint silhouette against the sky as she carefully sniffs the bark all around the hole to learn if anything has been along during her absence and if any child of hers has disobeyed the instructions about *not* venturing out of the hole.

My introduction to raccoons came when, as a child, I read in a book by the late Dr. William J. Long a chapter called "A Little Brother to the Bear." I read all the books of William J. Long with a passionate interest, and learned the Milicete Indian names for the animals. (Dr. Long always called a bear Mooween; he always called a chickadee Ch'geegee-lokh-sis. This device stimulated me greatly, but if I remember right, it annoyed Theodore Roosevelt, who was also interested in nature.) I must have read the raccoon story twenty times. In those days, my imagination was immensely stirred by the thought of wild life, of which I knew absolutely nothing but for which I felt a kind of awe. Today, after a good many years of tame life, I find myself in the incredibly rich situation of living in a steam-heated, electrically lit dwelling on a tarred highway with a raccoon dozing in her penthouse while my power lawn mower circles and growls noisily below. At last I am in a position to roll out the green carpet for a little sister to the bear. (I have even encountered Dr. Long's daughter Lois in my travels, but it was not among raccoons that we met, and she seemed to have no mark of the Milicete Indian about her whatsoever, and never in my presence has she referred to a great horned owl as Kookooskoos, which saddens me.)

There are two sides to a raccoon—the arboreal and the terrestrial. When a female coon is in the tree, caring for young, she is one thing. When she descends and steps off onto solid earth to prowl and hunt, she is quite another. In the tree she seems dainty and charming; the circles under her eyes make her look slightly dissipated and deserving of sympathy. The moment she hits the ground, all this changes; she seems predatory, sinister, and as close to evil as anything in Nature (which contains no evil) can be. If I were an Indian, naming animals, I would call the raccoon He Who Has the Perpetual Hangover. This morning, conditions inside the hole are probably unbearable. The kittens are quite big now, the sun is hot, and the hole is none too roomy anyway—it's nothing but a flicker hole that time has enlarged. So she has emerged, to lie in full view on the horizontal limb just under her doorway. Three of her four legs are draped lifelessly over the limb, the fourth being held in reserve to hang on with. Her coat is rough, after the night of hunting. In this state she presents a picture of utter exhaustion and misery, unaccompanied by remorse. On the rare occasions when I have done a little hunting myself at night, we sleep it off together, she on her pallet, I on mine, and I take comfort in her nearness and in our common suffering.

I guess I have watched my coon descend the tree a hundred times; even so, I never miss a performance if I can help it. It has a ritualistic quality, and I know every motion, as a ballet enthusiast knows every motion of his favorite dance. The secret of its enchantment is the way it employs the failing light, so that when the descent begins, the performer is clearly visible and is a part of day, and when, ten or fifteen minutes later, the descent is complete and the coon removes the last paw from the tree and takes the first step away, groundborne, she is almost indecipherable and is a part of the shadows and the night. The going down of the sun and the going down of the coon are interrelated phenomena; a man is lucky indeed who lives where sunset and coonset are visible from the same window.

The descent is prefaced by a thorough scrub-up. The coon sits on her high perch, undisturbed by motorcars passing on the road below, and gives herself a complete going over. This is cat-like in its movements. She works at the tail until it is well bushed out and all six rings show to advantage. She washes leg and foot and claw, sometimes grabbing a hind paw with a front paw and pulling it closer. She washes her face the way a cat does, and she rinses and sterilizes her nipples. The whole operation takes from five to fifteen minutes, according to how hungry she is and according to the strength of the light, the state of the world below the tree, and the mood and age of the kittens within the hole. If the kittens are young and quiet, and the world is young and still, she finishes her bath without delay and begins her downward journey. If the kittens are restless, she may return and give them another feeding. If they are well grown and anxious to escape (as they are at this point in June), she hangs around in an agony of indecision. When a small head appears in the opening, she seizes it in her jaws and rams it back inside. Finally, like a mother with no baby-sitter and a firm date at the theater, she takes her leave, regretfully, hesitantly. Sometimes, after she has made it halfway down the tree, if she hears a stirring in the nursery she hustles back up to have another look around.

A coon comes down a tree headfirst for most of the way. When she gets within about six feet of the ground, she reverses herself, allowing her hind end to swing slowly downward. She then finishes the descent tailfirst; when, at last, she comes to earth, it is a hind foot that touches down. It touches down as cautiously as though this were the first contact ever made by a mammal with the flat world. The coon doesn't just let go of the tree and drop to the ground, as a monkey or a boy might. She steps off onto my lawn as though in slow motion—first one hind paw, then the other hind paw, then a second's delay when she stands erect, her two front paws still in place, as though the tree were her partner in the dance. Finally, she goes down on all fours and strides slowly off, her slender front paws reaching ahead of her to the limit, like the hands of an experienced swimmer.

I have often wondered why the coon reverses herself, starting headfirst, ending tailfirst. I believe it is because although it comes naturally to her to descend headfirst, she doesn't want to arrive on the ground in that posture, lest an enemy appear suddenly and catch her at a disadvantage. As it is, she can dodge back up without unwinding herself if a dog or a man should appear.

Because she is a lover of sweet corn, the economic status of my raccoon is precarious. I could shoot her dead with a .22 any time I cared to. She will take my corn in season, and for every ear she eats she will ruin five others, testing them for flavor and ripeness. But in the country a man has to weigh everything against everything else, balance his pleasures and indulgences one against another. I find that I can't shoot this coon, and I continue to plant corn—some for her, what's left for me and mine—surrounding the patch with all sorts of coon baffles. It is an arrangement that works out well enough. I am sure of one thing: I like the taste of corn, but I like the nearness of coon even better, and I cannot recall ever getting the satisfaction from eating an ear of corn that I get from watching a raccoon come down a tree just at the edge of dark.

Today I've been rereading a cheerful forecast for the coming century, prepared by some farsighted professors at the California Institute of Technology and published not long ago in the *Times*. Man, it would appear, is standing at the gateway to a new era of civilization. Technology will be king. Everything man needs (the report says) is at hand. All we require is air, sea water, ordinary rock, and sunlight. The population of the earth will increase and multiply, but that'll be no problem—the granite of the earth's crust contains enough uranium and thorium to supply an abundance of power for everybody. If we just pound rock, we're sitting pretty.

It is a splendid vision: technology the king, Jayne Mansfield the queen. (It is also the same old conflict.) Right in the middle of the forecast, the professors paused long enough to let drop a footnote. Their prediction, they said, applies *only* if world catastrophe is avoided. At any rate, the civilization at whose gateway I am said to be standing will pose one rather acute problem for me: *What position am I going to take in the matter of rock?* I have taken my stand on raccoon; now I have to take my stand on rock. These acres on which I live are well supplied and underlaid with rock. The pasture is full of granite, the vegetable garden has some splendid rocks in it, the foundation of the house is granite, the doorstone is granite, there is a granite outcropping in the lawn where the whippoorwill comes to sit and repeat himself in the hour before daybreak, several of the fields are ledgy in places, and if you wander into the woods, you come on old stone walls made of tons and tons of rock. A ton of granite, according to my advices, contains about four grams of uranium and twelve grams of thorium. Is my next move to extract this stuff, or can I leave my stones be? I assume that if I am to dwell contentedly and adjust to the new era, I must pick the uranium and thorium from my rocks and convert them into power, but I'm not sure I am ready to fall in with any such harebrained scheme. The only time I ever fooled with rocks in a big way on this place, I simply made a lot of noise, created a memorable era of confusion, and ended up about where I started. (I got fooling with rocks because I had bought a cow, and in the country one thing leads to another.) The only place for a nuclear reactor here would be the brooder house, and I need the brooder house for my chicks. If the modern way to get electric power to run my brooder stove is to tap the energy in my pasture rocks, I may very well consider returning to the old natural method of raising chicks, using a couple of broody hens—in which case I am standing at the gateway to the long past rather than the long future. There is one big boulder down in the pasture woods where I sometimes go to sit when I am lonely or sick or melancholy or disenchanted or frightened, and in combination with sweet fern, juniper, and bayberry this old rock has a remarkably restorative effect on me. I'm not sure but that this is the true energy, the real source of man's strength. I'm not sure rocks would work out so well for me if I were to drag them up out of the pasture and pry the fissionable materials out of them.

I am not convinced that atomic energy, which is currently said to be man's best hope for a better life, is his best hope at all, or even a good bet. I am not sure energy is his basic problem, although the weight of opinion is against me. I would feel more optimistic about a bright future for man if he spent less time proving that he can outwit Nature and more time tasting her sweetness and respecting her seniority. Almost every bulletin I receive from my county agent is full of wild schemes for boxing Nature's ears and throwing dust in her eyes, and the last issue of the *Rural New-Yorker* contained a tiny item saying that poultry-men had "volunteered" to quit feeding diphenyl-para-phenylene-diamine to chickens, because it can cause illness in "persons"—one of the tardiest pieces of volunteer activity I ever heard of. Yesterday, it was reported in the news that atomic radiation is cumulative and that no matter how small the dose, it harms the person receiving it and all his descendants. Thus, a lifetime of dental X-rays and other familiar bombardments and fallouts may finally spell not better teeth and better medicine but no teeth and no medicine, and a chicken dinner may become just another word for bellyache. The raccoon, for all her limitations, seems to me better adjusted to life on earth than men are; she has never taken a tranquillizing pill, has never been X-rayed to see whether she is going to have twins, has never added DPPD to the broiler mash, and is not out at night looking for thorium in rocks. She is out looking for frogs in the pond.

Dr. Fritz Zwicky, the astrophysicist, has examined the confused situation on this planet, and his suggestion is that we create one hundred *new* planets. Zwicky wants to scoop up portions of Neptune, Saturn, and Jupiter and graft them onto smaller planets, then change the orbits of these enlarged bodies to make their course around the sun roughly comparable to that of our earth. This is a bold, plucky move, but I would prefer to wait until the inhabitants of *this* planet have learned to live in political units that are not secret societies and until the pens on the writing desks in banks are not chained to the counter. Here we are, busily preparing ourselves for a war already described as "unthinkable," bombarding our bodies with gamma rays that everybody admits are a genetical hazard, spying on each other, rewarding people on quiz programs with a hundred thousand dollars for knowing how to spell "cat," and Zwicky wants to make a hundred *new* worlds. Maybe he gained confidence to go ahead when he heard that in Florida they had succeeded in putting an elephant on water skis. Any race of creatures that can put an elephant on water skis is presumably ready to construct new worlds.

Dr. Vannevar Bush, who is in a far better position to discuss science and progress than I am, once said, "Man may, indeed, have evolved from the primordial ooze, and this may be accepted as good if we assume that it is good to have complex life on earth, but this again is an arbitrary assumption." Many of the commonest assumptions, it seems to me, are arbitrary ones: that the new is better than the old, the untried superior to the tried, the complex more advantageous than the simple, the fast quicker than

the slow, the big greater than the small, and the world as re-
modelled by Man the Architect functionally sounder and more
agreeable than the world as it was before he changed everything
to suit his vogues and his conniptions.

I have made a few private tests of my own, and my findings
differ somewhat from those of the Cal Tech men. We have two
stoves in our kitchen here in Maine—a big black iron stove that
burns wood and a small white electric stove that draws its strength
from the Bangor Hydro-Electric Company. We use both. One
represents the past, the other represents the future. If we had to
give up one in favor of the other and cook on just one stove,
there isn't the slightest question in anybody's mind in my household which is the one we'd keep. It would be the big black Home
Crawford 8-20, made by Walker & Pratt, with its woodbox that
has to be filled with wood, its water tank that has to be replen-
ished with water, its ashpan that has to be emptied of ashes, its
flue pipe that has to be renewed when it gets rusty, its grates that
need freeing when they get clogged, and all its other foibles and
deficiencies. We would choose this stove because of the quality of
its heat, the scope of its talents, the warmth of its nature (the
place where you dry the sneakers, the place where the small dog
crawls underneath to take the chill off, the companionable sounds
it gives forth on cool nights in fall and on zero mornings in winter). The electric stove is useful in its own way, and makes a
good complementary unit, but it is as cold and aseptic as a doctor's
examining table, and I can't imagine our kitchen if it were the
core of our activity.

The American kitchen has come a long way, and it has a long
way to return before it gets to be a good room again. Last fall,
the American Society of Industrial Designers met in Washington
and kicked the kitchen around a bit. One of the speakers, I remember, said that we will soon get to the point of eating "simply
and fast." He said we would push a button and peas would
appear on a paper plate. No preparation at all.

It really comes down to what a man wants from a plate of peas, and to what peas have it in their power to give. I'm not much of an eater, but I get a certain amount of nourishment out of a seed catalogue on a winter's evening, and I like to help stretch the hen wire along the rows of young peas on a fine morning in June, and I feel better if I sit around and help with the shelling of peas in July. This is all a part of the pageantry of peas, if you happen to like peas. Our peas didn't get planted until May 9th this spring—about three weeks later than the normal planting time. I shall hardly know what day in July to push the button and watch them roll out onto the paper plate.

Another speaker at the designers' conference said, "The kitchen as we know it today is a dead dodo." (One solution this man offered for the house of the future is to have a place called a "dirty room." This would be equipped with appliances for all cleaning problems, and into it would be dumped everything dirty. But in most American homes the way to have a dirty room is to have a small boy; that's the way *we* worked it for a number of happy years.) I think the kitchen, like the raccoon, is a dead dodo only if you choose to shoot it dead. Years ago, at the time I bought this house, I examined my kitchen with a wondering and skeptical eye and elected to let it live. The decision stands as one of the few sensible moves I've made on this place. Our kitchen today is a rich, intoxicating blend of past, present, and future; basically it belongs to the past, when it was conceived and constructed. It is a strange and implausible room, dodolike to the modern eye but dear to ours, and far from dead. In fact, it teems with life of all sorts—cookery, husbandry, horticulture, canning, planning. It is an arsenal, a greenhouse, a surgical-dressing station, a doghouse, a bathhouse, a lounge, a library, a bakery, a cold-storage plant, a factory, and a bar, all rolled up into one gorgeous ball, or ballup. In it you can find the shot gun and shell for shooting up the whole place if it ever should get obsolete; in it you can find the molasses cookie if you decide just to sit down and leave everything the way it is. From morning till night, sounds drift from the kitchen, most of them familiar and comforting, some of them surprising and worth investigating. On days when warmth is the most important need of the human heart, the kitchen is the place you can find it; it dries the wet sock, it cools the hot little brain. During heat waves, the wood fire is allowed to go out, and with all doors open the kitchen sucks a cool draft through from one side of the house to the other, and General Electric is king for a day.

Our kitchen contains such modern gadgets as an electric re- frigerator, a Macy cabinet, and a Little Dazey ice smasher, and it contains such holdovers from the past as the iron stove, the roller towel, the iron sink, the wooden drainboard, and the set tubs. (You can wash a dog in my kitchen without any trouble except from the dog.) It is remarkably free of the appliances that you see in exhibits whose name ends in "ama." It *does* have an egg beater, an electric mixer, and a garbage can that opens miracu- lously at a slight pressure from the toe. It also has the electric stove, with the dials that you turn. I can't read these dials without my glasses, and it is usually more practical for me to build a fire in the wood stove than to hunt up my glasses. For that matter, the wood stove almost always has steam up, our climate being what it is, and is all ready to go without any fire-building. You just add a stick of wood, open the draft, and shove the kettle a few inches to the left, toward the heat.

I don't think I am kidding myself about this stove. If I had to go to the woods myself, cut the wood, haul it out, saw it, and split it, I wouldn't be able to afford a wood stove, because I lack the strength and the skill for such adventures. In a way, the stove is my greatest luxury. But I'm sure I've spent no more on it than many a man has spent on more frivolous or complex devices. A wood stove is like a small boat; it costs something to keep, but it satisfies a man's dream life. Mine even satisfies all the cooks in this family—and there are half a dozen of them—which is a more telling argument and a more substantial reward.

I read a statement by Jim Bailey not long ago, after he had run his mile in 3:58.6. "I have no sensation of speed when I run," he said, "and I never know how fast I'm going." Such is the case with most of us in this queer century of progress. Events carry us rapidly in directions tangential to our true desires, and we have almost no sensation of being in motion at all—except at odd moments when we explode an H-bomb or send up a hundred new planets or discard an old stove for a new one that will burn thorium instead of spruce.

My stove, which I'm sure would be impractical in many American homes, is nevertheless a symbol of my belief. The technologists, with their vision of happiness at the core of rock, see only half the rock—half of man's dream and his need. Perhaps success in the future will depend partly on our ability to generate cheap power, but I think it will depend to a greater extent on our ability to resist a technological formula that is sterile: peas without pageantry, corn without coon, knowledge without wisdom, kitchens without a warm stove. There is more to these rocks than uranium; there is the lichen on the rock, the smell of the fern whose feet are upon the rock, the view from the rock.

Last night, to amuse the grandson who is presently handling the problem of our "dirty room," we read the first chapter of *The Peterkin Papers*, and I was amazed to discover what a perfect fable it is for these times. You recall that Mrs. Peterkin poured herself a delicious cup of coffee and then, just as she was ready to drink it, realized that she had put salt in it instead of sugar. Here was a major crisis. A family conference was held, and the chemist was called in on the case. The chemist put in a little chlorate of potassium, but the coffee tasted no better. Then he added some tartaric acid and some hypersulphate of lime. It was no better. The chemist then tried ammonia and, in turn, some oxalic, cyanic, acetic, phosphoric, chloric, hyperchloric, sulphuric, boracic, silicic, nitric, formic, nitrous nitric, and carbonic acid. Mrs. Peterkin tasted each, but it still wasn't coffee. After another unsuccessful round of experimentation, this time with herbs, Elizabeth Eliza took the problem to the lady from Philadelphia, who said, "Why doesn't your mother make a fresh cup of coffee?"

The lady's reply is arresting. Certainly the world's brew is bitter today, and we turn more and more to the chemist and the herbwoman to restore its goodness. But every time I examine those Cal Tech elements—sun, sea, air, and rock—I am consumed with simple curiosity, not about whether there is thorium in the rock but whether there is another cup of coffee in the pot.

P.S. (March 1962).   Six years have elapsed. It is a pleasure to report that the coon tree is still in business and so is our black iron stove. When I wrote that a coon comes down a tree head-first and then reverses herself when near the ground, touching down with one hind foot, I had observed only one coon in the act of leaving a tree. The coon I wrote about is no longer with us; she was ousted by another female (probably a younger one and perhaps her own daughter) after a fierce battle high in the tree at the entrance to the hole, both females being pregnant and ready to lie in. The new young coon, the one we have now, descends the tree headfirst but does not reverse when near the ground. She continues headfirst and steps off onto the lawn with one front foot. Moral: a man should not draw conclusions about raccoons from observing one individual. The day may come when we'll have a coon that completes the descent of the tree with a half gainer.

Every year the coon hole gets larger, from wear and tear and from the tendency of balm-of-Gilead trees to grow hollow in their old age. The chamber, or nursery, now boasts two openings, the big one that serves as entrance in the south face of the tree and a smaller one higher up in the northeast face. The smaller hole is of occasional interest to woodpeckers—hairies and pileateds—who stop by and inspect it. They peer in, and soon become agitated. If the chamber contains a raccoon with kittens, the visiting bird is jolted by the unexpected sight of live animals inside a tree. If no coons are there, I think the bird is surprised and disappointed by the light that enters from the larger aperture, making the chamber unnaturally bright and unsuitable for woodpecker occupancy.

Last spring, when the young coons were about three weeks old, we had a torrential three-day rainstorm. It was so bad, even the coon hole shipped water. The mother made the hard decision to evacuate the young ones, which she did by carrying them, one by one, in her mouth down the tree and depositing them a few hundred yards down the road in a drier location under the floor of a neighbor's house. Three days later in broad daylight she brought them all back and reinstated them—a monumental job of planning and execution over an obstacle course bristling with dogs, men, and vehicles. There were four kittens, which meant for her a total of fourteen trips over the road, all told.

As for my kitchen, it is really two kitchens—the front one and the back one. The front kitchen, where the black stove is, has survived the pressures of time; it is the same as ever, warm, comfortable, convenient, and unimproved. The back kitchen, however, fell on evil days and modern appliances, as I knew it would eventually. It now looks like the setting for a television commercial. We removed the old black iron sink and substituted a shiny stainless one. We rebuilt the counters, covering them with Formica, or Micarta, or something that ends in "a," I forget what. We threw out the old wooden drainboard, which had grown almost as soft as a sponge, and replaced it with a yellow rubber mat that has no pitch. We tore out the set tubs; in their place is an automatic washing machine that goes on the blink every five weeks and an automatic drier that blows lint into the woodshed through an exhaust pipe every time it is used. Next to the new sink, under the counter, we installed an automatic dishwasher. This machine works quite nicely, but it celebrates each new phase of the wash with a great clanking noise; it grunts and groans incessantly at its labors, and it leaves a hot smell of detergent in the wake of its toil, so that when you pass it on your way out to the woodshed the air in the room tickles the inside of your nose. It takes the design off the china and leaves ring marks on the glassware. Strong detergents have replaced weak soaps in the back kitchen, vibration has replaced quietude, sanitation broods over all, the place smells of modernity and Ajax, and there is no place to wash the dog. (I give our current dachshund one bath a year now, in an old wash boiler, outdoors, finishing him off with a garden-hose rinse. He then rolls in the dirt to dry himself and we are where we started.)

I liked the back kitchen better the way it was before we improved it, but I knew it was doomed. I will have to admit that the old wooden drainboard had quite an impressive accumulation of gurry in its seams. Germs must have loved it. I know *I* did. Incidentally, I was pleased to learn, not long ago, that children in unsanitary homes acquire a better resistance to certain diseases (polio and hepatitis among them) than children in homes where sanitation is king. Whether or not our old drainboard was a guardian of our health I will never know; but neither my wife nor I have enjoyed as good health since the back kitchen got renovated. I would hate to think that it's just a coincidence.

SOOTFALL AND FALLOUT

Turtle Bay, October 18, 1956

This is a dark morning in the apartment, but the block is gay
with yellow moving vans disgorging Mary Martin's belongings in
front of a house a couple of doors east of here, into which (I
should say from the looks of things) she is moving. People's lives
are so exposed at moments like this, their possessions lying naked
in the street, the light of day searching out every bruise and mark
of indoor living. It is an unfair exposé—end tables with nothing
to be at the end of, standing lamps with their cords tied up in
curlers, bottles of vermouth craning their long necks from cartons
of personal papers, and every wastebasket carrying its small cargo
of miscellany. The vans cause a stir in the block. Heads appear
in the windows of No. 230, across the way. Passers-by stop on
the sidewalk and stare brazenly into the new home through the
open door. I have a mezzanine seat for the performance; like a
Peeping Tom, I lounge here in my bathrobe and look down,
held in the embrace of a common cold, before which scientists
stand in awe although they have managed to split the atom,
infect the topsoil with strontium 90, break the barrier of sound,
and build the Lincoln Tunnel.

What a tremendous lot of stuff makes up the cumulus called
"the home"! The trivet, the tiny washboard, the fire tools, the big
copper caldron large enough to scald a hog in, the metal filing

77

cabinets, the cardboard filing cabinets, the record player, the glass and the china invisible in their barrels, the carpet sweeper. (I wonder whether Miss Martin knows that she owns an old-fashioned carpet sweeper in a modern shade of green.) And here comes a bright little hacksaw, probably the apple of Mr. Halliday's eye. When a writing desk appears, the movers take the drawers out, to lighten the load, and I am free to observe what a tangle Mary Martin's stationery and supplies are in—like my wife's, everything at sixes and sevens. And now the bed, under the open sky above Forty-eighth Street. And now the mattress. A wave of decency overtakes me. I avert my gaze.

The movers experience the worst trouble with two large house plants, six-footers, in their great jars. The jars, on being sounded, prove to be a third full of water and have to be emptied into the gutter. Living things are always harder to lift, somehow, than inanimate objects, and I think any mover would rather walk up three flights with a heavy bureau than go into a waltz with a rubber plant. There is really no way for a man to put his arms around a big house plant and still remain a gentleman.

Out in back, away from the street, the prospect is more pleasing. The yellow cat mounts the wisteria vine and tries to enter my bedroom, stirred by dreams of a bullfinch in a cage. The air is hazy, smoke and fumes being pressed downward in what the smog reporter of the *Times* calls "a wigwam effect." I don't know what new gadget the factories of Long Island are making today to produce such a foul vapor—probably a new jet appli-cator for the relief of nasal congestion. But whatever it is, I would swap it for a breath of fresh air. On every slight stirring of the breeze, the willow behind Mary Martin's wigwam lets drop two or three stylish yellow leaves, and they swim lazily down like golden fish to where Paul, the handyman, waits with his broom. In the ivy border along the wall, watchful of the cat, three thrushes hunt about among the dry leaves. I can't pronounce "three thrushes," but I can see three thrushes from this window, and this is the first autumn I have ever seen three at once. An October miracle. I think they are hermits, but the visibility is so poor I can't be sure.

This section of Manhattan boasts the heaviest sootfall in town, and the United States of America boasts the heaviest fallout in the world, and when you take the sootfall and the fallout and bring smog in on top of them, I feel I am in a perfect position to discuss the problem of universal pollution. The papers, of course, are full of the subject these days, as they follow the Presidential campaigners around the nation from one contaminated area to another.

I have no recent figures on sootfall in the vicinity of Third Avenue, but the *Times* last Saturday published some figures on fallout from Dr. Willard F. Libby, who said the reservoir of radioactive materials now floating in the stratosphere from the tests of all nations was roughly twenty-four billion tons. That was Saturday. Sunday's *Times* quoted Dr. Laurence H. Snyder as saying, "In assessing the potential harm [of weapons-testing], statements are always qualified by a phrase such as 'if the testing of weapons continues at the present rate . . .' This qualification is usually obsolete by the time the statement is printed." I have an idea the figure twenty-four billion tons may have been obsolete when it appeared in the paper. It may not have included, for instance, the radioactive stuff from the bomb the British set off in Australia a week or two ago. Maybe it did, maybe it didn't. The point of Dr. Snyder's remark is clear; a thermonuclear arms race is, as he puts it, self-accelerating. Bomb begets bomb. A begets H. Anything you can build, I can build bigger.

"Unhappily," said Governor Harriman the other night, "we are still thinking in small, conventional terms, and with unwarranted complacency."

The habit of thinking in small, conventional terms is, of course, not limited to us Americans. You could drop a leaflet or a Hubbard squash on the head of any person in any land and you would almost certainly hit a brain that was whirling in small, conventional circles. There is something about the human mind that keeps it well within the confines of the parish, and only one outlook in a million is nonparochial. The impression one gets from campaign oratory is that the sun revolves around the earth, the earth revolves around the United States, and the United States revolves around whichever city the speaker happens to be in at the moment. This is what a friend of mine used to call the Un-Copernican system. During a Presidential race, candidates sometimes manage to create the impression that their thoughts are ranging widely and that they have abandoned conventional thinking. I love to listen to them when they are in the throes of these quadrennial seizures. But I haven't heard much from either candidate that sounded unconventional—although I have heard some things that sounded sensible and sincere. A candidate could easily commit political suicide if he were to come up with an unconventional thought during a Presidential tour.

I think Man's gradual, creeping contamination of the planet, his sending up of dust into the air, his strontium additive in our bones, his discharge of industrial poisons into rivers that once flowed clear, his mixing of chemicals with fog on the east wind add up to a fantasy of such grotesque proportions as to make everything said on the subject seem pale and anemic by contrast. I hold one share in the corporate earth and am uneasy about the management. Dr. Libby said there is new evidence that the amount of strontium reaching the body from topsoil impregnated by fallout is "considerably less than the seventy per cent of the topsoil concentration originally estimated." Perhaps we should all feel elated at this, but I don't. The correct amount of strontium with which to impregnate the topsoil is *no* strontium. To rely on "tolerances" when you get into the matter of strontium 90, with three sovereign bomb testers already testing, independently of one another, and about fifty potential bomb testers ready to enter the stratosphere with their contraptions, is to talk with unwarranted complacency. I belong to a small, unconventional school that believes that *no* rat poison is the correct amount to spread in the kitchen where children and puppies can get at it. I believe that *no* chemical waste is the correct amount to discharge into the fresh rivers of the world, and I believe that if there is a way to trap the fumes from factory chimneys, it should be against the law to set these deadly fumes adrift where they can mingle with fog and, given the right conditions, suddenly turn an area into another Donora, Pa.

"I have seen the smoky fury of our factories—rising to the skies," said President Eisenhower pridefully as he addressed the people of Seattle last night. Well, I can see the smoky fury of our factories drifting right into this room this very minute; the fury sits in my throat like a bundle of needles, it explores my nose, chokes off my breath, and makes my eyes burn. The room smells like a slaughterhouse. And the phenomenon gets a brief mention in the morning press.

One simple, unrefuted fact about radioactive substances is that scientists do not agree about the "safe" amount. All radiation is harmful, all of it shortens life, all is cumulative, nobody keeps track of how much he gets in the form of X-rays and radiotherapy, and all of it affects not only the recipient but his heirs. Both President Eisenhower and Governor Stevenson have discussed H-bomb testing and the thermonuclear scene, and their views differ. Neither of them, it seems to me, has quite told the changing facts of life on earth. Both tend to speak of national security as though it were still capable of being dissociated from universal well-being; in fact, sometimes in these political addresses it sounds as though this nation, or any nation, through force of character or force of arms, could damn well rise *above* planetary considerations, as though we were greater than our environment, as though the national verve somehow transcended the natural world.

"Strong we shall stay free," said President Eisenhower in Pittsburgh. And Governor Stevenson echoed the statement in Chicago: ". . . only the strong can be free."

This doctrine of freedom through strength deserves a second

look. It would have served nicely in 1936, but nobody thought of it then. Today, with the H-bomb deterring war, we are free and we are militarily strong, but the doctrine is subject to a queer, embarrassing amendment. Today it reads, "Strong we shall stay free, *provided we do not have to use our strength.*" That's not quite the same thing. What was true in 1936, if not actually false today, is at best a mere partial, or half, truth. A nation wearing atomic armor is like a knight whose armor has grown so heavy he is immobilized; he can hardly walk, hardly sit his horse, hardly think, hardly breathe. The H-bomb is an extremely effective deterrent to war, but it has little virtue as a *weapon* of war, because it would leave the world uninhabitable.

For a short while following the release of atomic energy, a strong nation was a secure nation. Today, no nation, whatever its thermonuclear power, is a strong nation in the sense that it is a fully independent nation. All are weak, and all are weak from the same cause: each depends on the others for salvation, yet none likes to admit this dependence, and there is no machinery for interdependence. The big nations are weak because the strength has gone out of their arms—which are too terrifying to use, too poisonous to explode. The little nations are weak because they have always been relatively weak and now they have to breathe the same bad air as the big ones. Ours is a balance, as Mr. Stevenson put it, not of power but of terror. If anything, the H-bomb rather favors small nations that don't as yet possess it; they feel slightly more free to jostle other nations, having discovered that a country can stick its tongue out quite far these days without provoking war, so horrible are war's consequences.

The atom, then, is a proper oddity. It has qualified the meaning of national security, it has very likely saved us from a third world war, it has given a new twist to the meaning of power, and it has already entered our bones with a cancer-producing isotope. Furthermore, it has altered the concept of personal sacrifice for moral principle. Human beings have always been willing to shed their blood for what they believed in. Yesterday this was clear and simple; we would pay in blood because, after the price was exacted, there was still a chance to make good the gain. But the modern price tag is not blood. Today our leaders and the leaders of other nations are, in effect, saying, "We will defend our beliefs not alone with our blood—by God, we'll defend them, if we have to, with our genes." This is bold, resolute talk, and one can't help admiring the spirit of it. I admire the spirit of it, but the logic of it eludes me. I doubt whether any noble principle—or any ignoble principle, either, for that matter—can be preserved at the price of genetic disintegration.

The thing I watch for in the speeches of the candidates is some hint that the thermonuclear arms race may be bringing people nearer together, rather than forcing them farther apart. I suspect that because of fallout we may achieve a sort of universality sooner than we bargained for. Fallout may compel us to fall in. The magic-carpet ride on the mushroom cloud has left us dazed—we have come so far so fast. There is a passage in Anne Lindbergh's book *North to the Orient* that captures the curious lag between the mind and the body during a plane journey, between the slow unfolding of remembered images and the swift blur of modern flight. Mrs. Lindbergh started her flight to the Orient by way of North Haven, her childhood summer home. "The trip to Maine," she wrote, "used to be a long and slow one. There was plenty of time in the night, spattered away in the sleeper, in the morning spent ferrying across the river at Bath, in the afternoon syncopated into a series of calls on one coast town after another— there was plenty of time to make the mental change coinciding with our physical change. . . . But on this swift flight to North Haven in the *Sirius* my mind was so far behind my body that when we flew over Rockland Harbor the familiar landmarks below me had no reality."

Like the girl in the plane, we have arrived, but the familiar scene lacks reality. We cling to old remembered forms, old definitions, old comfortable conceptions of national coziness, national self-sufficiency. The Security Council meets solemnly and takes up Suez, eleven sovereign fellows kicking a sovereign ditch around while England threatens war to defend her "lifelines," when modern war itself means universal contamination, universal death-lines, and the end of ditches. I would feel more hopeful, more *secure*, if the Councilmen suddenly changed their tune and began arguing the case for mud turtles and other ancient denizens of ponds and ditches. That is the thing at stake now, and it is what will finally open the Canal to the world's ships in perfect concord.

Candidates for political office steer clear of what Mrs. Luce used to call "globaloney," for fear they may lose the entire American Legion vote and pick up only Norman Cousins. Yet there are indications that supranational ideas are alive in the back of a few men's minds. Through the tangle of verbiage, the idea of "common cause" skitters like a shy bird. Mr. Dulles uses the word "interdependent" in one sentence, then returns promptly to the more customary, safer word "independent." We give aid to Yugoslavia to assure her "independence," and the very fact of the gift is proof that neither donor nor recipient enjoys absolute independence any more; the two are locked in mortal *inter*-dependence. Mr. Tito says he is for "new forms and new laws." I haven't the vaguest notion of what he means by that, and I doubt whether he has, either. Certainly there are no *old* laws, if by "laws" he means enforceable rules of conduct by which the world community is governed. But I'm for new forms, all right. Governor Stevenson, in one of his talks, said, "Nations have become so accustomed to living in the dark that they find it hard to learn to live in the light." What light? The light of government? If so, why not say so? President Eisenhower ended a speech the other day with the phrase "a peace of justice in a world of law." Everything else in his speech dealt with a peace of justice in a world of anarchy.

The riddle of disarmament, the riddle of peace, seems to me to hang on the interpretation of these conflicting and contradictory phrases—and on whether or not the men who use them really mean business. Are we independent or interdependent? We can't possibly be both. Do we indeed seek a peace of justice in a world of law, as the President intimates? If so, when do we start, and how? Are we for "new forms," or will the old ones do? In 1945, after the worst blood bath in history, the nations settled immediately back into old forms. In its structure, the United Nations reaffirms everything that caused World War II. At the end of a war fought to defeat dictators, the U.N. welcomed Stalin and Péron to full membership, and the Iron Curtain quickly descended to put the seal of authority on this inconsistent act. The drafters of the Charter assembled in San Francisco and defended their mild, inadequate format with the catchy phrase "Diplomacy is the art of the possible." Meanwhile, a little band of physicists met in a squash court and said, "The hell with the art of the possible. Watch this!"

The world organization debates disarmament in one room and, in the next room, moves the knights and pawns that make national arms imperative. This is not justice and law, and this is not light. It is not new forms. The U.N. is modern in intent, old-fashioned in shape. In San Francisco in 1945, the victor nations failed to create a constitution that placed a higher value on principle than on sovereignty, on common cause than on special cause. The world of 1945 was still a hundred percent parochial. The world of 1956 is still almost a hundred percent parochial. But at last we have a problem that is clearly a community problem, devoid of nationality—the problem of the total pollution of the planet.

We have, in fact, a situation in which the deadliest of all weapons, the H-bomb, together with its little brother, the A-bomb, is the latent source of great agreement among peoples. The bomb is universally hated, and it is universally feared. We cannot escape it with collective security; we shall have to face it with united action. It has given us a few years of grace without war, and now it offers us a few millenniums of oblivion. In a paradox of unbelievable jocundity, the shield of national sovereignty suddenly becomes the challenge of national sovereignty. And, largely because of events beyond our control, we are able to sniff the faint stirring of a community ferment—something every man can enjoy.

The President speaks often of "the peaceful uses of atomic energy," and they are greatly on his mind. I believe the peaceful use of atomic energy that should take precedence over all other uses is this: stop it from contaminating the soil and the sea, the rain and the sky, and the bones of man. That is elementary. It comes ahead of "good-will" ships and it comes ahead of cheap power. What good is cheap power if your child already has an incurable cancer?

The hydrogen-garbage-disposal program unites the people of the earth in a common anti-litterbug drive for salvation. Radioactive dust has no nationality, is not deflected by boundaries; it falls on Turk and Texan impartially. The radio-strontium isotope finds its way into the milk of Soviet cow and English cow with equal ease. This simple fact profoundly alters the political scene and calls for political leaders to echo the physicists and say, "Never mind the art of the possible. Watch this!"

To me, living in the light means an honest attempt to discover the germ of common cause in a world of special cause, even against the almost insuperable odds of parochialism and national fervor, even in the face of the dangers that always attend political growth. Actually, nations are already enjoying little pockets of unity. The European coal-steel authority is apparently a success. The U.N., which is usually impotent in political disputes, has nevertheless managed to elevate the world's children and the world's health to a community level. The trick is to encourage and hasten this magical growth, this benign condition—encourage it and get it on paper, while children still have healthy bones and before we have all reached the point of no return. It will not mean the end of nations; it will mean the true beginning of nations.

Paul-Henri Spaak, addressing himself to the Egyptian government the other day, said, "We are no longer at the time of the absolute sovereignty of states." We are not, and we ought by this time to know we are not. I just hope we learn it in time. In the beautiful phrase of Mrs. Lindbergh's, there used to be "plenty of time in the night." Now there is hardly any time at all.

Well, this started out as a letter and has turned into a discourse. But I don't mind. If a candidate were to appear on the scene and come out for the dignity of mud turtles, I suppose people would hesitate to support him, for fear he had lost his reason. But he would have my vote, on the theory that in losing his reason he had kept his head. It is time men allowed their imagination to infect their intellect, time we all rushed headlong into the wilder regions of thought where the earth again revolves around the sun instead of around the Suez, regions where no individual and no group can blithely assume the right to sow the sky with seeds of mischief, and where the sovereign nation at last begins to function as the true friend and guardian of sovereign man.

P.S. (May 1962).   The dirty state of affairs on earth is getting worse, not better. Our soil, our rivers, our seas, our air carry an ever-increasing load of industrial wastes, agricultural poisons, and military debris. The seeds of mischief are in the wind—in the warm sweet airs of spring. Contamination continues in greater force and new ways, and with new excuses: the Soviet tests last autumn had a double-barrelled purpose—to experiment and to intimidate. This was the first appearance of the diplomacy of dust; the breaking of the moratorium by Russia was a high crime, murder in the first degree. President Kennedy countered with the announcement that he would reply in kind unless a test-ban agreement could be reached by the end of April. None was reached, and our tests are being conducted. One more nation, France, has joined the company of testers. If Red China learns the trick, we will probably see the greatest pyrotechnic display yet, for the Chinese love fireworks of all kinds.

I asked myself what I would have done, had I been in the President's shoes, and was forced to admit I would have taken the same course—test. The shattering of the moratorium was for the time being the shattering of our hopes of good nuclear conduct. In a darkening and dirt-ridden world the course of freedom must be maintained even by desperate means, while there is a time of grace, and the only thing worse than being in an arms race is to be in one and not compete. The President's decision to resume testing in the atmosphere was, I believe, a correct decision, and I think the people who protest by lying down in the street have not come up with an alternative course that is sensible and workable. But the time of grace will run out, sooner or later, for all nations. We are in a vast riddle, all of us—dependence on a strength that is inimical to life—and what we are really doing is fighting a war that uses the lives of future individuals, rather than the lives of existing young men. The President did his best to lighten the blow by pointing out that fallout isn't as bad as it used to be, that our tests would raise the background radiation by only one percent. But this is like saying that it isn't dangerous to go in the cage with the tiger because the tiger is taking a nap. I am not calmed by the news of fallout's mildness, or deceived by drowsy tigers. The percentages will increase, the damage will mount steadily unless a turn is made somehow. Because our adversary tests, we test; because we test, they test. Where is the end of this dirty habit? I think there is no military solution, no economic solution, only a political solution, and this is the area to which we should give the closest attention and in which we should show the greatest imaginative powers.

These nuclear springtimes have a pervasive sadness about

them, the virgin earth having been the victim of rape attacks. This is a smiling morning; I am writing where I can look out at our garden piece, which has been newly harrowed, ready for planting. The rich brown patch of ground used to bring delight to eye and mind at this fresh season of promise. For me the scene has been spoiled by the maggots that work in the mind. Tomorrow we will have rain, and the rain falling on the garden will carry its cargo of debris from old explosions in distant places. Whether the amount of this freight is great or small, whether it is measurable by the farmer or can only be guessed at, one thing is certain: the character of rain has changed, the joy of watching it soak the waiting earth has been diminished, and the whole meaning and worth of gardens has been brought into question.

THE SHAPE OF THE U.N.

Turtle Bay, December 1, 1956

My most distinguished neighbor in Turtle Bay, as well as my most peculiar one, is the U.N., over on the East River. Its fame has soared in the past month, on the wings of its spectacular deeds, and its peculiarities have become more and more apparent. Furthermore, the peculiarities have taken on an added importance, because of President Eisenhower's determination to make United States foreign policy jibe with the U.N. Charter. In many respects, I would feel easier if he would just make it jibe with the Classified Telephone Directory, which is clear and pithy.

The Charter was a very difficult document to draft and get accepted. The nations were still at war and the founding fathers were doubtful about whether a world organization could be made to work at all, so they inserted a clause or two to cover themselves in case it didn't. Every member went in with his fingers crossed, and the Charter reflects this. It derives a little from the Ten Commandments, a little from the Covenant of the League of Nations, and a little from the fine print on a bill of lading. It is high in purpose, low in calories. Portions of it are sheer double-talk and, as a result, support double-dealing, but membership in a league is an exercise in double-dealing anyway, because the stern fact is that each sovereign nation has one foot in, one foot out. When the United States, for example, found itself up to its neck in the Middle East dilemma, it subscribed to the Charter's pledge to suppress aggression in the common interest; it also issued an order to the commander of the 6th Fleet: "Take no guff from anyone!" You won't find such words in the Charter, but they are implicit in the Charter, and that is one of its peculiarities.

In shape the U.N. is like one of the very early flying machines—a breath-taking sight as it takes to the air, but full of bugs. It is obviously in the experimental stage, which is natural. Since many readers have probably never examined the Charter, I will give a quick rundown, covering merely the Preamble and Chapter One, where the gist of the political structure is to be found.

The Preamble awards honorable mention to the following: human rights, equal rights, justice, respect for treaties (the Charter itself is a treaty, so it is just whistling to keep up its courage here), tolerance, peace, neighborliness, economic and social advancement. The Preamble is *against*: war, and the use of armed force except in the common interest.

Chapter One deals with (1) Purposes, (2) Principles. The *purposes* are, in summarized form: to maintain peace; to suppress aggression; to develop friendly relations among nations on the principle of equal rights and self-determination (which I presume includes cannibalism); to cooperate; to harmonize actions of nations. The *principles* are: sovereign equality; members shall fulfill obligations in good faith; settle disputes by peaceful means; refrain from the threat or use of force against the territorial integrity or political independence of any state; cooperate; and never, never intervene in matters which are essentially within the domestic jurisdiction of any state.

As you can see, the thing has bugs. There are some truly comical ones, like Chapter I, Article 2, Paragraph 5, which, if I interpret it correctly, commands a member to help deliver a public whipping to himself. But I shall not dwell on the funny ones. Let us just stare for a few moments at two of the more serious bugs.

One: In a fluid world, the Charter affirms the *status quo*.

By its use of the word "aggression" and by other devices it makes the *status quo* the test of proper international conduct.

Two: Aimed at building a moral community, of peace, order, and justice, the Charter fails to lay down rules of conduct as a condition of membership. Any nation can enjoy the sanctuary of the Charter while violating its spirit and letter. A member, for example, is not required to allow the organization to examine its internal activities. Mr. Shepilov can come to Turtle Bay, but can Mr. Hammarskjöld go to Budapest? The world waits to see. Even if he makes it, he will arrive awfully late.

Despite its faults, the U.N. has just emerged from a great month in world history, and emerged all in one piece. It pulled England and France out of a shooting war and sent the constabulary to replace them in Egypt. It failed in Hungary, but in the General Assembly the Soviet Union took a rhetorical shellacking that really counted. The U.N. is our most useful international device, but it is built on old-fashioned ideas. The Charter is an extremely tricky treaty. Its trickiness is dangerous to the world because, for one thing, it leads idealistic nations like ours into situations that suddenly become sticky and queer. This very thing happened when, in order to "condemn aggression" in the Middle East, in conformity with our Charter obligations, we deserted England and France and took up with the dictator of the Arab world and his associate the Soviet Union.

Some people, perhaps most people, think words are not really important, but I am a word man and I attach the very highest importance to words. I even think it was dishonest to call the world organization the "United Nations," when everybody knew the name was a euphemism. Why start on a note of phonyness, or wistfulness? The newspapers, with their sloppy proofreading, sometimes call the world organization the United Notions, sometimes the Untied Nations. Neither of these typos would make a serviceable title, but curiously enough, both are pat. Dr. Luns, of the Netherlands, recently described the U.N. Charter as "the expression of an attitude of mind." He said some countries used it merely as a juke box—they put in their nickel and the box would light up and play. That is about it. The Charter is an accommodating box and can produce a remarkable variety of tunes.

When Hungary erupted, the world was shocked beyond measure at what was taking place. But under the Charter of the United Nations the Hungarian government was in a position to put up just as noisy an argument as the oppressed people who were in rebellion. "Nothing contained in the present Charter shall authorize the United Nations to intervene in matters which are essentially within the domestic jurisdiction of any state." (Chapter I, Article 2, Paragraph 7.) And when the U.N. wanted to send observers in, it received a polite no. This is palpably ridiculous, and it boils down to a deficiency in the Charter, a deficiency that is in the nature of an eleven-year-old appeasement. The Charter says that a member shall encourage "respect for human rights." That is laudable but fluffy. One way a Charter can advance human rights is to insist that the rights themselves (such as they are) remain visible to the naked eye, remain open to inspection. One of the preconditions of membership in the United Nations should be that the member himself not shut his door in the face of the Club. If the member won't agree to that, let him look elsewhere, join some other club.

Many will argue that if you are dealing with Iron Curtain countries, you have to take them on their own terms or you don't get them at all. That may be true. But who agreed to that amount of appeasement in the first place? And were they right? The appeasement was agreed to eleven years ago by charter writers who were trying to put together a world organization while a world war was still in progress. Their eye was not always on the ball, and they were looking back more than ahead. They were playing with century-old ideas: nonaggression (which is undefinable), self-determination (which includes the determination to send people to the salt mines), sovereign equality (which means that all nations are equal in the sight of God but the big ones are equal in the Security Council). The Charter bravely tries to keep these

threadbare ideas alive, but they will not stay alive in the modern
world of hydrogen and horror, and unless the Charter is brought
up to date, it may fail us.

Much has happened in eleven years. Almost everything that
has happened indicates that the United Nations should never have
admitted the Communist nations on *their* terms; that is, freedom to
operate behind a wall. If nations are to cooperate, the first condition must be that they have social and political intercourse. The
Soviet Union held out for cooperation without intercourse, which
is a contradiction in terms and which is as unworkable for nations
as for spouses. A marriage can be annulled on the ground of denial
of intercourse. A world organization can blow up on account of
it.

The subtlest joker in the Charter is the word "aggression."
There are other jokers, but none so far-reaching. When the
United States was confronted with the Middle East crisis, it was
surprised and bewildered to discover itself backing Nasser and
Russia against France and England. One reason for this queer turn
of events was that Britain and France had "aggressed," and therefore had violated the Charter of the United Nations. Actually,
our government did not take its stand solely, or even principally,
on the basis of its U.N. membership, but it did use its U.N. membership to justify its decision and lend it a high moral tone.

The word "aggression" pops up right at the very beginning
of the Charter: Chapter I, Article 1, Paragraph 1. Aggression is
the keystone of the Charter. It is what every member is pledged to
suppress. It is also what nobody has been able to define. In 1945,
the founding fathers agreed among themselves that it would be
unwise to include a definition of aggression in the Charter, on the
score that somebody would surely find a loophole in it. But in
1954 a special U.N. committee was appointed to see if it could
arrive at a definition of aggression. The committee was called the
United Nations Special Committee on the Question of Defining
Aggression. It huffed and it puffed, but it did not come up with a
definition, and around the first of last month it adjourned. So one

of the great peculiarities of the Charter is that all nations are pledged to oppose what no nation is willing to have defined. I think it can fairly be said that the one subject the seventy-nine members of the United Nations are in silent agreement on is aggression: they are agreed that each nation shall reserve the right to its own interpretation, when the time comes.

This isn't surprising. To define aggression, it is necessary to get into the realm of right and wrong, and the Charter of the United Nations studiously avoids this delicate area. It is also necessary to go back a way. Webster says of aggression, "A first or unprovoked attack." And that, you see, raises the old, old question of which came first, the hen or the egg. What, we must ask, came first in the Middle East clash between Arab and Jew? You could go back two thousand years, if you wanted to. You could certainly go back beyond October 29, 1956, when the Israelis came streaming across the Sinai desert.

Not only has no member, in eleven years, accepted a definition of aggression, no member has admitted that it has committed an aggressive act, although many members have used arms to get their way and at least one member, the U.S.S.R., employs the threat of force as a continuing instrument of national policy. The Charter of the U.N. is a treaty signed by sovereign nations, and the effect of a treaty written around the concept of aggression is to equate the use of arms with wrongdoing and to assume that the world is static, when, of course, that is not so—the world is fluid and (certainly at this point in history) riddled with revolutionary currents at work everywhere. The tendency of any document founded on the idea of nonaggression is to freeze the world in its present mold and command it to stand still.

The world has seen a lot happen lately; it hasn't been standing still. And you will get as many definitions of aggression as there are parties to the event. Ask the delegate of the Soviet Union what happened in Hungary and he will say, "Remnants of Fascist bands aggressed." And he will cite Chapter I, Article, 2, Paragraph 4: "All members shall refrain . . . from the threat or use of force against the territorial integrity or political independence of any state." Ask a citizen of Budapest what happened and he will say, "We couldn't take it any longer. We threw stones." And he will cite the Preamble on fundamental human rights and the dignity and worth of the human person. Under the Charter, it is possible to condemn both these aggressive acts—you just take your choice. Is the aggressor the man who throws stones at a tank, or is the aggressor the man who drives the tank into the angry crowd? The world was quick to form an opinion about this, but it got little help from the Charter. The Charter affirms the integrity of Hungary as a political entity, and officially designates both the Hungarian government and the Soviet government as "peace-loving." But that's not the way it looked to most of the world.

When the Israelis were asked what had happened, Eban replied, "The Israeli forces took security measures in the Sinai Peninsula in the exercise of Israel's inherent right of self-defense" (Chapter VII, Article 51). When the Arabs were asked what had happened, the heads of the Arab League issued a statement applauding Egypt's "glorious defense of the safety of her territories and sovereignty" (same chapter, same verse).

Neither England nor France has admitted to an aggression, although the two nations mounted an assault and carried it out— two permanent members of the Security Council shooting their way into Egypt before breakfast. It is, in fact, inconceivable that any nation will ever admit to having aggressed.

In the *Herald Tribune* the other morning, Walter Lippmann wrote, "In the past few days, the U.N. has been pushed into a position where its main function seems to be that of restoring conditions as they were before the explosion." That is certainly true, and one reason for it is that the Charter condemns aggression, sight unseen, and then turns over to the forum the task of studying the events leading up to the tragedy and the atmosphere in which it occurred. To condemn aggression is to decide *in advance of an event* the merits of the dispute. Since this is absurd, the subject of aggression should not be made part of a charter. The business of a charter is not to decide arguments in advance, it is to diagram the conditions under which it may be possible, with luck, to settle the argument when it arises. Surely one of those conditions is the right to observe at close hand.

Another peculiarity of the U.N. is its police. These are now famous, and rightly so. A couple of weeks ago, ninety-five Danish and Norwegian riflemen, wearing emergency blue, dropped out of the sky to keep the peace of the world. They were the advance unit of the United Nations Emergency Force. The men were reported looking "tired," and I should think they might. One editorial writer described them as "symbolic soldiers"; the label is enough in itself to tire a man. The *Times* correspondent in Abu Suweir, where the troops landed, described the policemen's task as "most delicate."

Their task is more than merely delicate; it is primeval. This force (it now numbers about two thousand) is the true dawn patrol, and these Scandinavian riflemen are dawn men. They are the police who are charged with enforcing the laws that do not yet exist. They are clothed with our universal good intentions, armed with the hopes and fears of all the years. They have been turned loose in a trouble spot with the instructions "Enforce the absence of law! Keep us all safe!" Behind them is the authority of the United Nations, all of whose members are "peace-loving" and some of whose members have just engaged in war. It is a confusing scene to a young policeman. It is confusing for people everywhere. One of the first things that happened on the arrival of UNEF was that General Burns, the commander, had to fly back to First Avenue to find out what the Chief of Police had in mind. Another thing that happened was that the Secretary General of the U.N. had to fly to Cairo to get permission from the Egyptian government to let the world be policed in its bailiwick.

It is confusing, but it is not hopeless. Police (so-called) have sometimes been known to antedate the laws that they enforce. It is again a case of the egg and the hen—law enforcers preceding law itself, like the vigilantes of our frontier West.

The U.N. has from the very start stirred people's imaginations and hopes. There seems little doubt that the very existence of a world organization is a help. I read in the *Times* magazine section the other day a good analysis of the U.N. by Ambassador Henry Cabot Lodge, who praised it because it "mobilizes world opinion" and because it shows "midnight courage." All this is certainly true. The U.N. is the shaky shape of the world's desire for order. If it is to establish order, though, it will have to muster the right words as well as the midnight courage. The words of the Charter are soft and punky. The Charter makes "aggression" synonymous with "wrongdoing" but drops the matter there, as though everyone understood the nature of sin. Yet it would appear from recent events that the users of force rarely think they are aggressing, and never admit they are. To simplify an idea this way is bad writing.

A league of sovereign nations—some of them much sovereigner than others—is not in a good position to keep order by disciplining a member in the middle of a fracas. Discipline can mean war itself, as we saw in Korea, and the U.N. is physically puny. But a league *is* in a position to do other things. One thing it can do is lay down conditions of membership. In its own house the U.N. has unlimited power and authority. Its bylaws should not appease anybody or make life easy for bad actors. The U.N. swings very little weight in Moscow or in Budapest, but it swings a lot of weight in Turtle Bay, and that's where it should start to bear down. Whether the U.N. could have been effective in Hungary is anybody's guess, but certainly its chances of operating effectively, for human rights and humankind, were diminished by the softness of the Charter and the eleven-year-old accommodation to the Communists, who from the very start showed that they intended to eat their forum and have it, too. Munich has nothing on San Francisco in this matter.

Ambassador Lodge, in his article, pointed out that the U.N., contrary to what a few Americans hope and a few Americans fear, is not a world government. He wrote, "As for the future, a world government which free men could accept is as far off as a worldwide common sense of justice—without which world government would be world tyranny."

True enough. And the world is a long way from a common sense of justice. But the way to cut down the distance is to get on the right track, use the right words. Our Bill of Rights doesn't praise free speech, it forbids Congress to make any law abridging it. The U.N. could profit from that kind of tight writing. The Charter sings the praises of the dignity of man, but what it lacks is a clause saying, "A member shall make no move abridging the right of the Secretary General to stop by for a drink at any hour of the day or night."

P.S. (May 1962).   The Goa episode was a perfect demonstration of the pleasures and paradoxes of membership in a league of nations. When India, a peace-loving member, decided the time had come to tidy up its coastline, it took Goa from Portugal by force of arms, an operation that struck other members as in violation of the Charter (Chapter I, Article 2, Paragraph 4: "All Members shall refrain in their international relations from the threat or use of force against the territorial integrity or political independence of any State."). Mr. Nehru's explanation of the Goa adventure was that it was not an aggressive act, since it was "right"—an interesting new sidelight on the meaning of aggression. The Soviet Union, another peace-lover, came to India's defense; it said the seizure of Goa wasn't aggression because it was "inevitable," it was "historic." This left Western nations, including the United States, pointing to the simple words about not using arms. It also left them in bed with colonialism for a few moments, while India and Russia waved the anticolonial flag and pretended they didn't smell gunsmoke.

Goa was "historic," all right. But everything that happens is historic, because everything that happens is a part of history. It is not unlikely that some similar episode, involving the use of guns by a lover of peace, will ignite the great fire of nuclear war. This may turn out to be so historic it won't even be remembered.

The United Nations has managed to survive for seventeen years. It is a more flexible organization than the old League—more accommodating, more ambitious, more daring. Under Dag Hammarskjöld it was sometimes breathtaking. Hammarskjöld was a sort of Paladin, roaming the world, doing good according to his lights, far, far from home. And behind it, it has a far stronger desire of people to cooperate for peace, a far greater sense of urgency. The U.N. was designed not to establish order but to prevent trouble and preserve peace. It is not, as some seem to believe, an embryo government; it is simply a pistol-packing trouble-shooter. Many groups, searching for an approach to world government, advocate "strengthening" the U.N., to make it a "limited world government," its function the control of arms; and, in a sense, this is now the avowed policy of the United States in its program for general and complete disarmament under a U.N. Peace Force. I think this is idle talk. Strengthening the U.N. would not turn it into a government. Short of knocking the whole thing apart and starting fresh, there would be, I think, no way to build the U.N. into a government, even if its members wanted that, and most of them don't.

Nevertheless, the U.N. is so useful, it should strive to strengthen itself and put its own house in better order, not in the hope of becoming a government but with the intention of improving its services, lessening its capacity to cause trouble, and promoting liberty. The Charter should be re-examined. The Charter is eloquent on the subject of human rights and fundamental freedoms, but it does not spell them out in the places where they would count, such as in Chapter II, where the question of membership is dealt with. Since 1945, the U.N. has almost doubled its membership, and the newly admitted states have been taken into the fold without presenting any credentials. They merely advertised themselves as "peace-loving" and were accepted as peace-loving by the others. Red China wants in, and the question of admitting China is as vexing as it is persistent. It would be a whole lot easier for the United States, for example, to make out a case against the admission of Red China if Chapter II offered any guidelines, but it doesn't.

Here are a few elementary matters that might well be considered for inclusion in the Charter. (1) A nation that jams the air shall not be eligible for membership. (2) A member of the U.N. that jams the air shall be expelled. (3) A nation that builds a wall to prevent people from leaving the country shall not be eligible for membership. (4) In the case of members whose press is run by the government, the privilege of using the forum shall carry with it the obligation to report fully the proceedings of the forum, in the home press. Failure to publish the proceedings revokes the privilege of the forum and is ground for suspension. (5) Member states shall grant the Secretary General and his aides free access to the country at all times.

To inject such democratic things into the Charter would require a two-thirds vote in the General Assembly. Moreover, even if an amendment that favored an open society over a closed society were to pass in the Assembly, it could be vetoed by any of the five permanent members of the Security Council. (Among its other defects, the Charter is virtually amendment-proof.) The U.N. was, of course, not created to praise liberty; yet the lovers of liberty should occasionally try to write their love into the document. Amendments ought to be proposed from time to time, if only to place the proprietors of closed societies in the unwholesome and embarrassing position of having to stand up before the crowd and defend darkness. The U.N. should do more than try to preserve the peace. If it seriously hopes to save future generations from the scourge of war, it should come out in favor of light, in favor of openness, and get it into the Charter.

THE ROCK DOVE

Turtle Bay, April 20, 1957

I wonder if anyone has ever seen a baby pigeon in New York City? Or are they hatched fully grown? . . . I wonder if the pigeons in midtown Manhattan drink water, and, if so, where do they find it? . . . I wonder where pigeons have their nests, or don't they? . . . I wonder why pigeons live in cities? . . . I wonder why pigeons are so fond of air conditioners? But, pigeons, thank you for making my life so full of wonder. Or is it Manhattan, *en toto*, that does it?
—EUGENIA BEDELL in *Promenade*

It has never been my desire to diminish by so much as a crumb of information the charming wonderment of a lady. Yet the above questions have been asked publicly. They stand plain and inquiring, crying for direct answers. I shall take them up in the order of their appearance.

Q—I wonder if anyone has ever seen a baby pigeon in New York City?

A—Yes, cases have been reported. I saw a squab this afternoon in a nest at No. 813 Fifth Avenue, third floor front, a short walk from the men's bar of Carlton House, one of the hotels that sponsor *Promenade*. The nest commands a view of the pony ride in Central Park, enjoys a fashionable address, and belongs to the baroque school of pigeons' nests (Fig. I).

Q—Are they hatched fully grown?

A—When hatched, a squab is about the size of a pigeon's egg. Except for patches of fuzz, it is as naked as a baby. It attains full stature in about four weeks, during which time the parent birds will probably have started a second nest. Pigeons, being city dwellers by choice, have caught the excitement of New York, and, like an executive who enjoys having two phones on his desk, a pair of pigeons like to keep two nests going at the same time. They deliberately place themselves under this sort of pressure. The pair at 813 Fifth Avenue, as I write, have two nests, both at

Fig. 1. Baroque

that address. Squabs are being fed in one, eggs are being incubated in the other (Fig. I). Busy days! The cock and the hen take turns sitting on the eggs and pumping pigeon's milk into the mouths of the young. Pigeon's milk is a regurgitated substance. It is made of popcorn and ice and all things nice.

Q—I wonder if the pigeons in midtown Manhattan drink water, and, if so, where do they find it?

A—Pigeons in all five boroughs drink water. They drink it not as a fowl does, by scooping a few drops up and letting them trickle down its throat, but as a child does when it sucks a soda through a straw. On wet days, pigeons find water everywhere— in gutters, depressions in the sidewalk, discarded containers. In dry spells, pigeons hunt about for water. A truck draws up to deliver shaved ice to a restaurant, a few flakes of ice fall to the pavement; pigeons swoop down to await the tiny thaw. In freezing weather, pigeons seek subway ventilators and other flues, where the warm draft creates local melting conditions. A thirsty pigeon will drink almost any sort of Manhattan cocktail: the creamy spillage from a caterer's tray blended with the drip from the tailpipe of a cross-town bus. I have watched a thirsty pigeon sip sidewalk juices that would turn the stomach of a hog. In a pinch, a pigeon can fly to the yak's yard in the zoo and drink from the fountain.

Q—I wonder where pigeons have their nests?

A—At this writing, pigeons have their nests at 18 East Fiftieth Street (Engel Furs); at 42 West Forty-fourth Street (Bar Association); at the freight entrance to 444 Madison Avenue; atop one of the trefoils of a gable in the Lady Chapel of St. Patrick's Cathedral, between Fiftieth and Fifty-first; on a window ledge in the south face of St. Thomas's, on Fifty-third just west of Fifth; under an air conditioner at 912 Fifth Avenue; on a ledge at 867 Madison Avenue, above Jean Beecher Sample Hats; in an embrasure of the Seventh Regiment Armory, about twelve feet west of Lexington Avenue; at 64 East Sixty-sixth Street, on a capital near a bowed window with stained-glass panes; and at 901 Fifth Avenue, just north of Frick's flowering magnolias. Other addresses of pigeons can be obtained by watching pigeons. I have listed only those I happen to be aware of at the moment.

Nests change from day to day. Pigeons are fast workers. Nests usually contain only two eggs and the eggs hatch in seventeen days. Squabs develop with amazing rapidity. By the time these answers to Miss Bedell's questions appear, the whole scene will have changed, for better or for worse: nests that now contain eggs will contain young birds; nests that now contain young birds will be inactive, the squabs having flown or been pushed out of the nest to join the great crew of city pigeons.

I have illustrated four common types of nests: the baroque, the modern, the Gothic, and the military. There are many others. The hen at 912 Fifth Avenue (Fig. II) has gone modern but is paying a heavy price. The air conditioner gives her a broad, protecting roof, but there is insufficient headroom. She must crouch for seventeen days. Furthermore, there is almost no room

Fig. II. Modern

for nesting material. From my vantage point across the Avenue, it appeared that the bird was forced to lay her eggs on the bare ledge, where they are in danger of rolling off. I was unable to use my binoculars on this nest, not wanting to risk arrest, so my report is not as reliable as I would wish.

The nest on the trefoil of the Lady Chapel (Fig. III) is one of several Gothic nests in that vicinity. The bird in this nest has an unobstructed view into Bennett Cerf's office in Random House. She can sit by the hour watching the publisher make his hard decisions preparatory to appearing on "What's My Line?," where all he has to do is guess that the contestant sells inner soles in the Outer Hebrides. Publishers lead lives as varied and shameless as pigeons, but are less beautiful against the sky.

The bird in Figure IV (military) has built an unusually ambitious nest for a pigeon. This bird is large and in fine plumage; the nest is well conceived, well executed. The Seventh Regiment Armory is in great

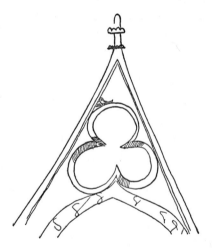

Fig. III. Gothic

demand by nesting birds. Every available
embrasure is either occupied or being fought
over. A few of the embrasures, however, have
been fitted with pigeon baffles by the military.
Here again I was handicapped by city conditions; when I found myself standing in front
of the Cosmopolitan Club, on Sixty-sixth
Street, peering at the Seventh Regiment Armory through binoculars, I felt as though I
were taking snapshots of Fort Knox. I put
the glasses away immediately, and did not see
as much as I wished.

Q—I wonder why pigeons live in cities?

A—The city pigeon is a descendant of the
wild rock dove, a bird of cliffs and ledges.
Pigeons live in cities because a city offers
cliffs and ledges. Unlike the robin and the
barn swallow, the rock dove, or "pigeon,"
has no natural talent for nest-building. What
a pigeon needs is just what the city provides
in abundance: a nook, a ledge, a recess, a
niche, a capital, an outcropping, the tin elbow

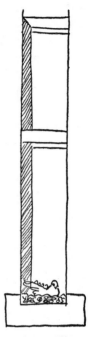

Fig. IV. Military

of a downspout, the bronze musette bag of a war hero, the
concrete beard of a saint, the narrow channel between two
buildings. (A good example of the channel nest is the one at the
freight entrance of 444 Madison, around the corner on Fiftieth.)
In April, when airs are soft, the very sight of a slot, a scroll, a
squinch, a corbiestep, a buttress, a transom, a ventilator, is enough
to send the cockbird whirling in circles and set his neck feathers
on fire. The hen, equally excited but less willing to admit it,
finally drops her defenses and picks up a few twigs. Besides
offering a pigeon a wide choice of home sites, the city gives a
pigeon a free lunch, and pigeons have taken up with men for
much the same reason cowbirds have taken up with cows—

there's a living in it. Unfortunately, the diet of city pigeons is too salty (handouts of salted nuts), and many birds suffer from salt poisoning.

Pigeons' nests are everywhere at this happy season. They go largely unobserved, however. Most nests are more than five feet above the ground (pigeons prefer second- and third-floor locations), and New Yorkers do not ordinarily lift their gaze above eye level. While studying the nest shown in Figure IV, I stood across the street from the Armory and watched the passers-by. The pigeon sat only about fifteen feet above the sidewalk, yet hundreds of people walked by without seeing the fine spectacle of a bird on eggs in springtime. Most of those who passed seemed deep in thought—scheming, worrying, hoping, dreaming, but not looking, or at any rate not looking *up*. The location of a pigeon's nest is often betrayed by the parent that is off duty at the moment. When you see a pigeon standing perfectly still and looking bored, scan the nearby ledges and you will usually discover the mate, quiet on the eggs.

Q—I wonder why pigeons are so fond of air conditioners?

A—Air conditioners form nooks with window casings (Fig. II).

Q—But, pigeons, thank you for making my life so full of wonder. Or is it Manhattan, *en toto*, that does it?

A—I am hampered in answering this question by not knowing the meaning of "*en toto*." The phrase does not turn up in my reference books. I knew a gorilla once named M'Toto, and there is a barroom in the John Ringling Hotel, in Sarasota, Florida, called the M'Toto Room, but "*en toto*" is another matter. As for the wellsprings of wonderment, they run deep. The quiet mind, the youthful heart, the perceptive eye, the racing blood —these conflow to produce wonder. Manhattan Island, entire, can sometimes cause such a confluence. For me, the nesting bird can cause it every time.

Because of the trend toward plainer façades, the city of the future may hold no charm for pigeons. Lever House offers little inducement to a nesting pair. As far as that goes, unless men cultivate the dove more successfully than they appear to be doing in this century, the city of the future may be inhospitable to men and doves alike. (The pigeon, strange to say, is closely related to the dodo.) But there are still doves among us. While they endure we must note their locations, elevate our gaze above the level of our immediate concerns, imbibe the sweet air and perfect promise: the egg miraculous upon the ledge, the bird compact upon the egg, its generous warmth, its enviable patience, its natural fortitude and grace.

A REPORT IN SPRING

Turtle Bay, May 10, 1957

I bought a puppy last week in the outskirts of Boston and drove him to Maine in a rented Ford that looked like a sculpin. There had been talk in our family of getting a "sensible" dog this time, and my wife and I had gone over the list of sensible dogs, and had even ventured once or twice into the company of sensible dogs. A friend had a litter of Labradors, and there were other opportunities. But after a period of uncertainty and waste motion my wife suddenly exclaimed one evening, "Oh, let's just get a dachshund!" She had had a glass of wine, and I could see that the truth was coming out. Her tone was one of exasperation laced with affection. So I engaged a black male without further ado.

For the long ordeal of owning another dachshund we prepared ourselves by putting up for a night at the Boston Ritz in a room overlooking the Public Garden, where from our window we could gaze, perhaps for the last time, on a world of order and peace. I say "for the last time" because it occurred to me early in the proceedings that this was our first adoption case in which there was a strong likelihood that the dog would survive the man. It had always been the other way round. The Garden had never seemed so beautiful. We were both up early the next morning for a final look at the fresh, untroubled scene; then we checked out hastily, sped to the kennel, and claimed our prize, who is the grandson of an animal named Direct Stretch of the Walls. He turned out to be a good traveller, and except for an interruption caused by my wife's falling out of the car in Gardiner, the journey went very well. At present, I am a sojourner in the city again, but here in the green warmth of Turtle Bay I see only the countenance of spring in the country. No matter what changes take place in the world, or in me, nothing ever seems to disturb the face of spring.

The smelts are running in the brooks. We had a mess for Monday lunch, brought to us by our son, who was fishing at two in the morning. At this season, a smelt brook is the night club of the town, and when the tide is a late one, smelting is for the young, who like small hours and late society.

No rain has fallen in several weeks. The gardens are dry, the road to the shore is dusty. The ditches, which in May are usually swollen to bursting, are no more than a summer trickle. Trout fishermen are not allowed on the streams; pond fishing from a boat is still permissible. The landscape is lovely to behold, but the hot, dry wind carries the smell of trouble. The other day we saw the smoke of a fire over in the direction of the mountain.

Mice have eaten the crowns of the Canterbury bells, my white-faced steer has warts on his neck (I'm told it's a virus, like everything else these days), and the dwarf pear has bark trouble. My puppy has no bark trouble. He arises at three, for tennis. The puppy's health, in fact, is exceptionally good. When my wife and I took him from the kennel, a week ago today, his mother kissed all three of us good-bye, and the lady who ran the establishment presented me with complete feeding instructions, which included a mineral supplement called Pervival and some vitamin drops called Vi-syneral. But I knew that as soon as the puppy reached home and got his sea legs he would switch to the supplement *du jour*—a flake of well-rotted cow manure from my boot, a dead crocus bulb from the lawn, a shingle from the kindling box, a bloody feather from the execution block behind the barn. Time has borne me out; the puppy was not long discovering the delicious supplements of the farm, and he now knows where every vitamin hides, under its stone, under its loose board. I even introduced him to the tonic smell of coon.

On Tuesday, in broad daylight, the coon arrived, heavy with young, to take possession of the hole in the tree, but she found another coon in possession, and there was a grim fight high in the branches. The new tenant won, or so it appeared to me, and our old coon came down the tree in defeat and hustled off into the woods to examine her wounds and make other plans for her confinement. I was sorry for her, as I am for any who are evicted from their haunts by the younger and stronger—always a sad occasion for man or beast.

The stalks of rhubarb show red, the asparagus has broken through. Peas and potatoes are in, but it is not much use putting seeds in the ground the way things are. The bittern spent a day at the pond, creeping slowly around the shores like a little round-shouldered peddler. A setting of goose eggs has arrived by parcel post from Vermont, my goose having been taken by the fox last fall. I carried the package into the barn and sat down to unpack the eggs. They came out of the box in perfect condition, each one wrapped in a page torn from the *New England Homestead*. Clustered around me on the floor, they looked as though I had been hard at it. There is no one to sit on them but me, and I had to return to New York, so I ordered a trio of Muscovies from a man in New Hampshire, in the hope of persuading a Muscovy duck to give me a Toulouse gosling. (The theme of my life is complexity-through-joy.) In reply to my order, the duck-farm man wrote saying there would be a slight delay in the shipment of Muscovies, as he was "in the midst of a forest-fire scare." I did not know from this whether he was too scared to drive to the post office with a duck or too worried to fit a duck into a crate.

By day the goldfinches dip in yellow flight, by night the frogs sing the song that never goes out of favor. We opened the lower sash of the window in the barn loft, and the swallows are already building, but mud for their nests is not so easy to come by as in most springtimes. One afternoon, I found my wife kneeling at the edge of her perennial border on the north side, trying to disengage Achillea-the-Pearl from Coral Bell. "If I could afford it," she said bitterly, "I would take every damn bit of Achillea out of this border." She is a woman in comfortable circumstances, arrived at through her own hard labor, and this sudden burst of poverty, and her inability to indulge herself in a horticultural purge, startled me. I was so moved by her plight and her unhappiness that I went to the barn and returned with an edger, and we spent a fine, peaceable hour in the pretty twilight, rapping Achillea over the knuckles and saving Coral Bell.

One never knows what images one is going to hold in memory, returning to the city after a brief orgy in the country. I find this morning that what I most vividly and longingly recall is the sight of my grandson and his little sunburnt sister returning to their kitchen door from an excursion, with trophies of the meadow clutched in their hands—she with a couple of violets, and smiling, he serious and holding dandelions, strangling them in a responsible grip. Children hold spring so tightly in their brown fists—just as grownups, who are less sure of it, hold it in their hearts.

WILL STRUNK

Turtle Bay, July 15, 1957

Mosquitoes have arrived with the warm nights, and our bed-chamber is their theater under the stars. I have been up and down all night, swinging at them with a face towel dampened at one end to give it authority. This morning I suffer from the lighthead-edness that comes from no sleep—a sort of drunkenness, very good for writing because all sense of responsibility for what the words say is gone. Yesterday evening my wife showed up with a few yards of netting, and together we knelt and covered the fireplace with an illusion veil. It looks like a bride. (One of our many theories is that mosquitoes come down chimneys.) I bought a couple of adjustable screens at the hardware store on Third Avenue and they are in place in the windows; but the window sashes in this building are so old and irregular that any mosquito except one suffering from elephantiasis has no difficulty walking into the room through the space between sash and screen. (And then there is the even larger opening between upper sash and lower sash when the lower sash is raised to receive the screen—a space that hardly ever occurs to an apartment dweller but must occur to all mosquitoes.) I also bought a very old air-conditioning machine for twenty-five dollars, a great bargain, and I like this machine. It has almost no effect on the atmosphere of the room, merely chipping the edge off the heat, and it makes a loud grinding noise reminiscent of the subway, so that I can snap off the lights, close my eyes, holding the damp towel at the ready, and imagine, with the first stab, that I am riding in the underground and being pricked by pins wielded by angry girls.

Another theory of mine about the Turtle Bay mosquito is that he is swept into one's bedroom through the air conditioner, riding the cool indraft as an eagle rides a warm updraft. It is a feeble theory, but a man has to entertain theories if he is to while away the hours of sleeplessness. I wanted to buy some old-fashioned bug spray, and went to the store for that purpose, but when I asked the clerk for a Flit gun and some Flit, he gave me a queer look, as though wondering where I had been keeping myself all these years. "We got something a lot stronger than that," he said, producing a can of stuff that contained chlordane and several other unmentionable chemicals. I told him I couldn't use it because I was hypersensitive to chlordane. "Gets me right in the liver," I said, throwing a wild glance at him.

The mornings are the pleasantest times in the apartment, exhaustion having set in, the sated mosquitoes at rest on ceiling and walls, sleeping it off, the room a swirl of tortured bedclothes and abandoned garments, the vines in their full leafiness filtering the hard light of day, the air conditioner silent at last, like the mosquitoes. From Third Avenue comes the sound of the mad builders—American cicadas, out in the noonday sun. In the garden the sparrow chants—a desultory second courtship, a subdued passion, in keeping with the great heat, love in summertime, relaxed and languorous. I shall miss this apartment when it is gone; we are quitting it come fall, to turn ourselves out to pasture. Every so often I make an attempt to simplify my life, burning my books behind me, selling the occasional chair, discarding the accumulated miscellany. I have noticed, though, that these purifications of mine—to which my wife submits with cautious grace—have usually led to even greater complexity in the long pull, and I have no doubt this one will, too, for I don't trust myself in a situation of this sort and suspect that my first act as an old horse will be to set to work improving the pasture. I may even join a pasture-improvement society. The last time I tried to purify myself by fire, I managed to acquire a zoo in the process and am still supporting it and carrying heavy pails of water to the animals, a task that is sometimes beyond my strength.

A book I have decided not to get rid of is a small one that arrived in the mail not long ago, a gift from a friend in Ithaca. It is *The Elements of Style,* by the late William Strunk, Jr., and it was known on the Cornell campus in my day as "the little book," with the stress on the word "little." I must have once owned a copy, for I took English 8 under Professor Strunk in 1919 and the book was required reading, but my copy presumably failed to survive an early purge. I'd not laid eyes on it in thirty-eight years. Am now delighted to study it again and rediscover its rich deposits of gold.

The Elements of Style was Will Strunk's *parvum opus,* his attempt to cut the vast tangle of English rhetoric down to size and write its rules and principles on the head of a pin. Will himself hung the title "little" on the book: he referred to it sardonically and with secret pride as "the *little* book," always giving the word "little" a special twist, as though he were putting a spin on a ball. The title page reveals that the book was privately printed (Ithaca, N.Y.) and that it was copyrighted in 1918 by the author. It is a forty-three-page summation of the case for cleanliness, accuracy, and brevity in the use of English. Its vigor is unimpaired, and for sheer pith I think it probably sets a record that is not likely to be broken. The Cornell University Library has one copy. It had two, but my friend pried one loose and mailed it to me.

The book consists of a short introduction, eight rules of usage, ten principles of composition, a few matters of form, a list of words and expressions commonly misused, a list of words commonly misspelled. That's all there is. The rules and principles are in the form of direct commands, Sergeant Strunk snapping orders to his platoon. "Do not join independent clauses with a comma." (Rule 5.) "Do not break sentences in two." (Rule 6.) "Use the active voice." (Rule 11.) "Omit needless words." (Rule 13.) "Avoid a succession of loose sentences." (Rule 14.) "In summaries, keep to one tense." (Rule 17.) Each rule or principle is followed by a short hortatory essay, and the exhortation is followed by, or interlarded with, examples in parallel columns—the true vs. the false, the right vs. the wrong, the timid vs. the bold, the ragged vs. the trim. From every line there peers out at me the puckish face of my professor, his short hair parted neatly in the middle and combed down over his forehead, his eyes blinking incessantly behind steel-rimmed spectacles as though he had just emerged into strong light, his lips nibbling each other like nervous horses, his smile shuttling to and fro in a carefully edged mustache.

"Omit needless words!" cries the author on page 21, and into that imperative Will Strunk really put his heart and soul. In the days when I was sitting in his class, he omitted so many needless words, and omitted them so forcibly and with such eagerness and obvious relish, that he often seemed in the position of having short-changed himself, a man left with nothing more to say yet with time to fill, a radio prophet who had outdistanced the clock. Will Strunk got out of this predicament by a simple trick: he uttered every sentence three times. When he delivered his oration on brevity to the class, he leaned forward over his desk, grasped his coat lapels in his hands, and in a husky, conspiratorial voice said, "Rule Thirteen. Omit needless words! Omit needless words! Omit needless words!"

He was a memorable man, friendly and funny. Under the remembered sting of his kindly lash, I have been trying to omit needless words since 1919, and although there are still many words that cry for omission and the huge task will never be accomplished, it is exciting to me to reread the masterly Strunkian elaboration of this noble theme. It goes:

Vigorous writing is concise. A sentence should contain no unnecessary words, a paragraph no unnecessary sentences, for the same reason that a drawing should have no unnecessary lines and a machine no unnecessary parts. This requires not that the writer make all his sentences short, or that he avoid all detail and treat his subjects only in outline, but that every word tell.

There you have a short, valuable essay on the nature and beauty of brevity—sixty-three words that could change the world. Having recovered from his adventure in prolixity (sixty-three words were a lot of words in the tight world of William Strunk, Jr.), the Professor proceeds to give a few quick lessons in pruning. The student learns to cut the deadwood from "This is a subject which . . . ," reducing it to "This subject . . . ," a gain of three words. He learns to trim ". . . used for fuel purposes" down to "used for fuel." He learns that he is being a chatterbox when he says "The question as to whether" and that he should just say "Whether"—a gain of four words out of a possible five.

The Professor devotes a special paragraph to the vile expression "the fact that," a phrase that causes him to quiver with revulsion. The expression, he says, should be "revised out of every sentence in which it occurs." But a shadow of gloom seems to hang over the page, and you feel that he knows how hopeless his cause is. I suppose I have written "the fact that" a thousand times in the heat of composition, revised it out maybe five hundred times in the cool aftermath. To be batting only .500 this late in the season, to fail half the time to connect with this fat pitch, saddens me, for it seems a betrayal of the man who showed me how to swing at it and made the swinging seem worth while.

I treasure *The Elements of Style* for its sharp advice, but I treasure it even more for the audacity and self-confidence of its author. Will knew where he stood. He was so sure of where he stood, and made his position so clear and so plausible, that his peculiar stance has continued to invigorate me—and, I am sure, thousands of other ex-students—during the years that have intervened since our first encounter. He had a number of likes and dislikes that were almost as whimsical as the choice of a necktie, yet he made them seem utterly convincing. He disliked the word "forceful" and advised us to use "forcible" instead. He felt that the word "clever" was greatly overused; "it is best restricted to ingenuity displayed in small matters." He despised the expression "student body," which he termed gruesome, and made a special trip downtown to the *Alumni News* office one day to protest the expression and suggest that "studentry" be substituted, a coinage of his own which he felt was similar to "citizenry." I am told that the *News* editor was so charmed by the visit, if not by the word, that he ordered the student body buried, never to rise again. "Studentry" has taken its place. It's not much of an improvement, but it does sound less cadaverous, and it made Will Strunk quite happy.

A few weeks ago I noticed a headline in the *Times* about Bonnie Prince Charlie: "CHARLES' TONSILS OUT." Immediately Rule 1 leapt to mind.

1. Form the possessive singular of nouns with 's. Follow this rule whatever the final consonant. Thus write,
> Charles's friend
> Burns's poems
> the witch's malice.

Clearly Will Strunk had foreseen, as far back as 1918, the dangerous tonsillectomy of a Prince, in which the surgeon removes the tonsils and the *Times* copy desk removes the final "s." He started his book with it. I commend Rule 1 to the *Times* and I trust that Charles's throat, not Charles' throat, is mended.

Style rules of this sort are, of course, somewhat a matter of individual preference, and even the established rules of grammar are open to challenge. Professor Strunk, although one of the most inflexible and choosy of men, was quick to acknowledge the fallacy of inflexibility and the danger of doctrine.

"It is an old observation," he wrote, "that the best writers sometimes disregard the rules of rhetoric. When they do so, however, the reader will usually find in the sentence some compensating merit, attained at the cost of the violation. Unless he is certain of doing as well, he will probably do best to follow the rules."

It is encouraging to see how perfectly a book, even a dusty rulebook, perpetuates and extends the spirit of a man. Will Strunk loved the clear, the brief, the bold, and his book is clear, brief, bold. Boldness is perhaps its chief distinguishing mark. On page 24, explaining one of his parallels, he says, "The left-hand version gives the impression that the writer is undecided or timid; he seems unable or afraid to choose one form of expression and hold to it." And his Rule 12 is "Make definite assertions." That was Will all over. He scorned the vague, the tame, the colorless, the irresolute. He felt it was worse to be irresolute than to be wrong. I remember a day in class when he leaned far forward in his characteristic pose—the pose of a man about to impart a secret— and croaked, "If you don't know how to pronounce a word, say it loud! If you don't know how to pronounce a word, say it loud!" This comical piece of advice struck me as sound at the time, and I still respect it. Why compound ignorance with inaudibility? Why run and hide?

All through *The Elements of Style* one finds evidences of the author's deep sympathy for the reader. Will felt that the reader was in serious trouble most of the time, a man floundering in a swamp, and that it was the duty of anyone attempting to write English to drain this swamp quickly and get his man up on dry ground, or at least throw him a rope.

"The little book" has long since passed into disuse. Will died in 1946, and he had retired from teaching several years before that. Longer, lower textbooks are in use in English classes nowadays, I daresay—books with upswept tail fins and automatic verbs. I hope some of them manage to compress as much wisdom into as small a space, manage to come to the point as quickly and illuminate it as amusingly. I think, though, that if I suddenly found myself in the, to me, unthinkable position of facing a class in English usage and style, I would simply lean far out over the desk, clutch my lapels, blink my eyes, and say, "Get the *little* book! Get the *little* book! Get the *little* book!"

P.S. (April 1962). Soon after this piece about Professor Strunk appeared in *The New Yorker*, a publisher asked me to revise and amplify *The Elements of Style* in order that it might be reissued. I agreed to do this, and did it; but the job, which should have taken about a month's time, took me a year. I discovered that for all my fine talk I was no match for the parts of speech—was, in fact, over my depth and in trouble. Not only that, I felt uneasy at posing as an expert on rhetoric, when the truth is I write by ear, always with difficulty and seldom with any exact notion of what is taking place under the hood. Some of the material in the Strunk book proved too much for me, and two or three times during my strange period of confinement I was forced to turn for help to a friend who is a grammarian and could set me straight.

When the book came out, it managed to get on the best-seller list, where it stayed for a while. The appearance of a style book on hallowed ground was considered a freak of publishing, and a couple of newspapers ran editorials about it, asking what was happening to the world, that people should show interest in English usage. I was as surprised as the next man, but I think I now understand what happened. The Strunk book, which is a "right and wrong" book, arrived on the scene at a time when a wave of reaction was setting in against the permissive school of rhetoric, the Anything Goes school where right and wrong do not exist and there is no foundation all down the line. The little book climbed on this handy wave and rode it in.

It was during the permissive years that the third edition of Webster's *New International Dictionary* was being put together, along new lines of lexicography, and it was Dr. Gove, the head man, who perhaps expressed the whole thing most succinctly when he remarked that a dictionary "should have no traffic with . . . artificial notions of correctness or superiority. It must be descriptive and not prescriptive." This approach struck many people as chaotic and degenerative, and that's the way it strikes me. Strunk was a fundamentalist; he believed in right and wrong, and so, in the main, do I. Unless someone is willing to entertain notions of superiority, the English language disintegrates, just as a home disintegrates unless someone in the family sets standards of good taste, good conduct, and simple justice.

One parting note: readers of the first edition of the book were overjoyed to discover that the phrase "the fact that" had slid by me again, landing solidly in the middle of one of my learned dissertations. It has since disappeared, but it had its little day.

GOOD-BYE TO 48TH STREET

Turtle Bay, November 12, 1957

For some weeks now I have been engaged in dispersing the contents of this apartment, trying to persuade hundreds of inanimate
objects to scatter and leave me alone. It is not a simple matter.
I am impressed by the reluctance of one's worldly goods to go
out again into the world. During September I kept hoping that
some morning, as by magic, all books, pictures, records, chairs,
beds, curtains, lamps, china, glass, utensils, keepsakes would drain
away from around my feet, like the outgoing tide, leaving me
standing silent on a bare beach. But this did not happen. My wife
and I diligently sorted and discarded things from day to day, and
packed other objects for the movers, but a six-room apartment
holds as much paraphernalia as an aircraft carrier. You can whittle
away at it, but to empty the place completely takes real ingenuity
and great staying power. On one of the mornings of disposal,
a man from a second-hand bookstore visited us, bought several
hundred books, and told us of the death of his brother, the word
"cancer" exploding in the living room like a time bomb detonated
by his grief. Even after he had departed with his heavy load,
there seemed to be almost as many books as before, and twice
as much sorrow.

Every morning, when I left for work, I would take something
in my hand and walk off with it, for deposit in the big municipal

wire trash basket at the corner of Third, on the theory that the physical act of disposal was the real key to the problem. My wife, a strategist, knew better and began quietly mobilizing the forces that would eventually put our goods to rout. A man could walk away for a thousand mornings carrying something with him to the corner and there would still be a home full of stuff. It is not possible to keep abreast of the normal tides of acquisition. A home is like a reservoir equipped with a gate valve: the valve permits influx but prevents outflow. Acquisition goes on night and day—smoothly, subtly, imperceptibly. I have no sharp taste for acquiring things, but it is not necessary to desire things in order to acquire them. Goods and chattels seek a man out; they find him even though his guard is up. Books and oddities arrive in the mail. Gifts arrive on anniversaries and fête days. Veterans send ball-point pens. Banks send memo books. If you happen to be a writer, readers send whatever may be cluttering up their own lives; I had a man once send me a chip of wood that showed the marks of a beaver's teeth. Someone dies, and a little trickle of indestructible keepsakes appears, to swell the flood. This steady influx is not counterbalanced by any comparable outgo. Under ordinary circumstances, the only stuff that leaves a home is paper trash and garbage; everything else stays on and digs in.

Lately we haven't spent our nights in the apartment; we are bivouacked in a hotel and just come here mornings to continue the work. Each of us has a costume. My wife steps into a cotton dress while I shift into midnight-blue tropical pants and bowling shoes. Then we buckle down again to the unending task.

All sorts of special problems arise during the days of disposal. Anyone who is willing to put his mind to it can get rid of a chair, say, but what about a trophy? Trophies are like leeches. The ones made of paper, such as a diploma from a school or a college, can be burned if you have the guts to light the match, but the ones made of bronze not only are indestructible but are almost impossible to throw away, because they usually carry your name, and a man doesn't like to throw away his good name, or even his bad one. Some busybody might find it. People differ in their approach to trophies, of course. In watching Edward R. Murrow's "Person to Person" program on television, I have seen several homes that contained a "trophy room," in which the celebrated pack rat of the house had assembled all his awards, so that they could give out the concentrated aroma of achievement whenever he wished to loiter in such an atmosphere. This is all very well if you enjoy the stale smell of success, but if a man doesn't care for that air he is in a real fix when disposal time comes up. One day a couple of weeks ago, I sat for a while staring moodily at a plaque that had entered my life largely as a result of some company's zest for promotion. It was bronze on walnut, heavy enough to make an anchor for a rowboat, but I didn't need a rowboat anchor, and this thing had my name on it. By deft work with a screwdriver, I finally succeeded in prying the nameplate off; I pocketed this, and carried the mutilated remains to the corner, where the wire basket waited. The work exhausted me more than did the labor for which the award was presented.

Another day, I found myself on a sofa between the chip of wood gnawed by the beaver and an honorary hood I had once worn in an academic procession. What I really needed at the moment was the beaver himself, to eat the hood. I shall never wear the hood again, but I have too weak a character to throw it away, and I do not doubt that it will tag along with me to the end of my days, not keeping me either warm or happy but occupying a bit of my attic space.

Right in the middle of the dispersal, while the mournful rooms were still loaded with loot, I had a wonderful idea: we would shut the apartment, leave everything to soak for a while, and go to the Fryeburg Fair, in Maine, where we could sit under a tent at a cattle auction and watch somebody else trying to dispose of something. A fair, of course, is a dangerous spot if a man is hoping to avoid acquisition, and the truth is I came close to ac-

quiring a very pretty whiteface heifer, safe in calf—which would
have proved easily as burdensome as a chip of wood gnawed by a
beaver. But Fryeburg is where some of my wife's ancestors lived,
and is in the valley of the Saco, looking west to the mountains,
and the weather promised to be perfect, and the premium list of
the Agricultural Society said, "Should Any Day Be Stormy, the
Exercises for That Day Will Be Postponed to the First Fair Day,"
and I would rather have a ringside seat at a cattle sale than a box
at the opera, so we picked up and left town, deliberately over-
shooting Fryeburg by a hundred and seventy-five miles in order
to sleep one night at home.

The day we spent at the Fryeburg Fair was the day the first
little moon was launched by the new race of moon-makers. Had
I known in advance that a satellite was about to be added to my
world, in this age of additives, I might have stayed in New York
and sulked instead of going to the Fair, but in my innocence I was
able to enjoy a day watching the orbiting of trotting horses—
an ancient terrestrial phenomenon that has given pleasure to un-
numbered thousands. We attended the calf scramble, the pig
scramble, and the baby-beef auction; we ate lunch in the back
seat of our flashy old 1949 automobile, parked in the infield; and
then I found myself a ringside seat with my feet in the shavings
at the Hereford sale, under the rattling tongue and inexorable
hammer of auctioneer Dick Murray, enjoying the wild look in
the whites of a cow's eyes.

The day had begun under the gray blanket of a fall overcast,
but the sky soon cleared. Nobody had heard of the Russian moon.
The wheels wheeled, the chairs spun, the cotton candy tinted the
faces of children, the bright leaves tinted the woods and hills.
A cluster of amplifiers spread the theme of love over everything
and everybody; the mild breeze spread the dust over everything
and everybody. Next morning, in the Lafayette Hotel in Portland,
I went down to breakfast and found May Craig looking solemn
at one of the tables and Mr. Murray, the auctioneer, looking

cheerful at another. The newspaper headlines told of the moon. At that hour of the morning, I could not take in the exact significance, if any, of a national heavenly body. But I was glad I had spent the last day of the natural firmament at the One Hundred and Seventh Annual Exhibition of the West Oxford Agricultural Society. I see nothing in space as promising as the view from a Ferris wheel.

But that was weeks ago. As I sit here this afternoon in this dishevelled room, surrounded by the boxes and bales that hold my undisposable treasure, I feel the onset of melancholy. I look out onto Forty-eighth Street; one out of every ten passers-by is familiar to me. After a dozen years of gazing idly at the passing show, I have assembled, quite unbeknownst to them, a cast of characters that I depend on. They are the nameless actors who have a daily walk-on part in my play—the greatest of dramas. I shall miss them all, them and their dogs. Even more, I think, I shall miss the garden out back—the wolf whistle of the starling, the summer-night murmur of the fountain; the cat, the vine, the sky, the willow. And the visiting birds of spring and fall—the small, shy birds that drop in for one drink and stay two weeks. Over a period of thirty years, I have occupied eight caves in New York, eight digs—four in the Village, one on Murray Hill, three in Turtle Bay. In New York, a citizen is likely to keep on the move, shopping for the perfect arrangement of rooms and vistas, changing his habitation according to fortune, whim, and need. And in every place he abandons he leaves something vital, it seems to me, and starts his new life somewhat less encrusted, like a lobster that has shed its skin and is for a time soft and vulnerable.

A REPORT IN WINTER

Allen Cove, January 30, 1958

Margaret Mitchell once made a remark I have treasured. Someone asked her what she was "doing," and she replied, "Doing? It's a full-time job to be the author of *Gone with the Wind.*" I remembered this cheerful statement this morning as I lay in bed, before daylight, marshalling in my head the problems and projects and arrangements of the day and wondering when I would again get a chance to "do" something—like sit at a typewriter. I felt a kinship with Miss Mitchell and comforted myself with the pleasing thought that just to live in New England in winter is a full-time job; you don't have to "do" anything. The idle pursuit of making-a-living is pushed to one side, where it belongs, in favor of living itself, a task of such immediacy, variety, beauty, and excitement that one is powerless to resist its wild embrace.

Right this minute I am making a brief show of resistance; I have resolved to keep the wolf from the door. But what I'm really trying to keep from my door is the fox—a very different proposition. A loaded gun is at my side, and my typewriter is placed strategically at a window that commands a view of the strip of woods from which the fox usually emerges. He has been thrice in our dooryard within the week. Thrice have I muffed him. He came first during a snow squall, and carried off a little buff Cochin Bantam hen who was outdoors trying her snowshoes.

I witnessed the murder from an upstairs window, feeling as help-less as I'd felt on a day years ago when I stood at a window in St. Luke's Hospital overlooking Morningside Park and watched a thief beat up a woman. Yesterday I got a shot at the fox, but I hurried the shot (in anger) and he ran off into the woods grinning.

One of the most time-consuming things is to have an enemy. The fox is mine. He wants to destroy my form of society—a society of free geese, of Bantams unconfined. So I react in the natural way, building up my defenses, improving my weapons and my aim, spending more and more time on the problem of supremacy. This morning the wolf and the fox compete for my attention; I am a hunter divided against himself. Either animal could slip easily through my guard while I am thinking about the other. When I realize what a vast amount of time the world would have for useful and sensible tasks if each country could take its mind off "the enemy," I am appalled. I shot a fox last fall—a long, lucky shot with a .22 as he drank at the pond. It was cold murder. All he wanted at that moment was a drink of water, but the list of his crimes against me was a long one, and so I shot him dead, and he fell backward and sank slowly into the mud.

The war between me and the fox is as senseless as all wars. There is no way to rationalize it. The fox is not even the biggest and meanest killer here—I hold that distinction myself. I think nothing of sending half a dozen broilers to the guillotine. Come June, heads will be rolling behind my barn. Foxes are now carry-ing a disease called hardpad, but even that is insufficient reason for shooting a fox. My puppy, I presume, could pick up hardpad from sniffing around in the dooryard, and then I would have a dachshund that was not only hard-headed but hard-footed, too, which would try my patience. But if you were to solve the prob-lem of disease by shooting the sick, you'd have to shoot Aunt Mollie when she got the flu. I have plenty of convictions but no real courage, and I find it hard to live in the country without

slipping into the role of murderer. From where I sit I can see a
piece of suet hanging on a crab-apple tree. A hairy woodpecker
is digging away at it contentedly. The suet is from a steer we
killed last fall—I gave the order for the hatchet job. Imagine
killing a steer to feed a woodpecker! (We also got three hundred
and sixty-seven pounds of beef for our freezer, but I can't see
that that changes the matter any. The fox and I are up to the
same mischief; we differ only in technique.)

Hunters in this state killed 40,142 deer during the 1957 season.
It was the third-highest kill on record. Maine is a bit touchy
about its deerslaying and prefers to break the record each year.
In 1951 the hunters tagged 41,730 deer, and that figure still stands
as the one to beat. I don't know why people feel unhappy when
the curve of a graph fails to keep going up, but they do. Even
when we find something we'd like to reduce, such as highway
fatalities, it doesn't always sound as though we had our heart in
it. On the eve of every holiday, the National Safety Council
broadcasts its prediction that such-and-such a number of motorists
are "expected" to die over the weekend, almost as though it were
a man's duty to go out and get killed in order to make the
estimate come out right. I didn't shoot a deer, but someone
brought me a hindquarter and it was good. A moose came to town
right in the middle of the battle, and somebody shot him and cut
his head off, leaving the meat to spoil. Everybody was stirred up
about the incident of the moose: there is a heavy fine for killing
a moose nowadays, but there is an even heavier resentment against
anyone's wasting good meat.

Shortly after the close of the deer season, there was a lead
editorial in the paper complaining that there had been a drop
in out-of-state hunting licenses and urging that Maine get busy
and appropriate more money for development, to attract hunters
to the state. The theory is that if you shoot forty thousand deer
one year you aren't getting ahead unless you shoot fifty thousand
the next, but I suspect there comes a point where you have shot

just exactly the right number of deer. Our whole economy hangs precariously on the assumption that the higher you go the better off you are, and that unless more stuff is produced in 1958 than was produced in 1957, more deer killed, more automatic dishwashers installed, more out-of-staters coming into the state, more heads aching so they can get the fast fast fast relief from a pill, more automobiles sold, you are headed for trouble, living in danger and maybe in squalor. If that theory is sound, Maine won't be in a solid position until we kill at least forty million deer and with a good prospect of making it fifty million the following year. But that would be the end of the wilderness, and without its wilderness Maine would feel awfully naked.

The editorial pointed to Florida as an example of a state that had sense enough to spend large sums on promotion. "Florida ads all but smother Maine's," said the editorial. I guess this is true. Another thing that is true is that Florida recently "developed" the beach where I used to swim, and as a result I no longer care about going there. Some fellow with strong promotional instincts put a bulldozer to work on the beach and levelled the sand dunes in order to improve the parking facilities and make a place for a hot-dog stand. Formerly it was very pleasant to prop yourself against a sand dune and look out at the beautiful sea, but now you have to lie perfectly flat and look out at the beautiful candy wrappers swirling in the eddies of the wind. The last time I gazed at the scene, I realized that I had lost interest in that particular strip of beach. (And if the surf hath lost its savor, wherewith shall we be surfeited?) So I am lingering in Maine this winter, to fight wolves and foxes. The sun here is less strong than Florida's, but so is the spirit of development, and I can stare at the sea without peering through the wire mesh of a trash basket. Of course, it is conceivable that Florida will get along nicely without me. But if the various state development programs are to work properly a man would have to be in all forty-eight states at the same time.

The urge to solve a problem with a bulldozer or some other piece of heavy machinery is strong. I succumbed to it last fall when I hired a man to scoop out my pasture pond with a device called a back hoe. What I was trying to do was restore the pond to the condition it was in when I first laid eyes on it, many years ago. So far, all I have accomplished is to stir the pond up. The banks look like a place where enormous children have been making enormous mud pies. The pond has a clay bottom, and when this got agitated by the back hoe the water became cloudy. On certain days, when the light is right, it looks as though someone had poured milk into the pond. Every morning, I look out to see if the pond has cleared during the night, but it stays milky. When it froze, it made cloudy ice—which is just as good for skating as clear ice, but that is no solace, because for the first time in thirty-five years I can't find my shoe hockeys. Everything points to the conclusion that when thieves entered our apartment in New York last summer they were so sore at me for not having stocked the place with mink coats they took my skates to get even.

The winter has been mild so far, and excessively wet. Snow lies on the ground today, but for the most part we have had rain and wind. Everybody says he can't remember any winter like it in all his life, but that's what you always hear, no matter what the weather is like. The rains have been almost continuous; water stands everywhere. The barnyard is the consistency of oatmeal gruel, and my two Hereford heifers slide around like a couple of otters. The geese do not have to walk clear down to the pond; they just go as far as the bottom of the lane, where a pool has formed deep enough for their carnivals, which at this season include dalliance.

Work is not plentiful here in town this winter. The Christmas-greens business, however, hit an all-time high last month. A good many people—men, women, and children—earn their Christmas-shopping money by cutting brush (spruce and fir) to be trucked to Boston for use in wreaths and other decorations. My best information is that the take was around nine thousand dollars.

Scalloping was poor in December—too much wind. Lately it has improved a bit; there have been days when the sea was quiet enough for the boats to go out. Winter fishing, even under good conditions, is hazardous, and our town has just lost a man to the sea. He fell overboard last night from the slippery deck of a dragger tied up in Rockland and was drowned. Like many a fisherman, he couldn't swim a stroke.

I heard yesterday that the school-lunch program, which has been a fixture for a number of years, had been abruptly discontinued; no two people agree on what the reason is, but it seems to be partly a lessening of government support, partly a rise in the price of food. In a nearby town, the lunch program received a tremendous shot in the arm last fall when a couple of deer were run over by motorists. The alert school board soon had venison on the menu two or three times a week, at the going rate— twenty-five cents a meal.

Until yesterday's snowfall the woods had been bare. We got out our year's supply of firewood on wheels—two old wire wheels off a Model A Ford. Years ago, people depended on sleds for bringing wood out from the wood lots, but very few do it that way any more. They use scoots, which are a sort of drag, or they use a two-wheel trailer drawn by a tractor. My tractor is quite old now, and has faded to a pretty color—zinnia pink, like a red shirt that has been much washed. When I bought it, it was fire-engine red, but now it can slink away into the woods and go out of sight as quickly as a little animal. An hour or so later it reappears, dragging a load of wood to add to the pile. Arthur Cole arrived one blustery afternoon after work, trailing his sawing machine behind his coupé, and sawed almost all of our six and a half cords before dark. Arthur is seventy-six and dearly loves to saw wood. He still has all ten fingers. He is

working on his twenty-three-thousandth cord, having been at it
—mostly at odd moments, before or after work—for forty-nine
years. He has a record of every stick of wood that has been
through his machine, and can show it to you, in cords and in
dollars—the plain accounting of a man who has never been able
to leave work alone. When he started sawing, forty-nine years
ago, he used to get fifty cents a cord. Now he gets two dollars.
"You handle a lot of big money now," he said as I handed him
thirteen dollars, "but you're no better off." He has had many
accidents, and on a couple of occasions has had to be sewn together, so that he could be out early the next morning to saw
more wood. Once, the saw threw a stick at him and caught his
upper plate, driving it into his jaw. Dry wood is more treacherous
than green wood, and sometimes Arthur wears a catcher's mask
when he finds the saw throwing knucklers at him. He does not
always take money for his work—just swings in with his machine
at the house of someone who is disabled, and starts sawing.

At this season of the year, darkness is a more insistent thing
than cold. The days are short as any dream. A new house has been
built about twenty miles from here by a man who has plenty
of money to spend, and he has equipped it with an automatic
light-boosting system, so that as soon as the sun begins losing its
strength in the afternoon, electric lights come on all through
the place, maintaining an even intensity of illumination at all times.
I wouldn't care for that one bit. I like to come in from chores
and find the early dark in the rooms, when the only gleam is a
single lamp over an amaryllis bulb on which my wife is practicing
some sort of deception. I like groping my way into the barn
cellar at six, where my two whiteface heifers are feeding at the
rack, their great white heads visible, their dark bodies invisible—
just two heads suspended in air, as neatly as John the Baptist's.
I should think a house in which the light never varies would
be as dull as a woman in whom the emotions were always the
same. I am reasonably sure, however, that the trick lighting system

will go on the blink every once in a while, and that the owner
will creep around with a flashlight, the way all the rest of us do,
to find the seat of darkness.

It's been fifteen years since we last wintered in this house. Settling in again to live steadily right around the year, as we used to
do, has been full of excitement and the sense of our changed
condition. (Anybody who is fifteen years older is in a changed
condition, no matter what his condition.) There is no schoolboy
in the house now to keep the air stirred up. The room he once
occupied now contains a television set; we sit there in stupefaction,
listening to "April Love" and learning how to set our hair. Other
gadgets have crept in, most of them in the back kitchen.

The days ahead unroll in the mind, a scroll of blessed events
in garden and in barn. Wherever you look, you see something
that advertises the future: in the heifer's sagging sides you see the
calf, in the cock's shrill crow you hear the pipping egg, in the
cache of warm topsoil down cellar next the furnace you see the
seedling, and even on the darkest day the seed catalogue gives off
a gleam from some tomato of the first magnitude. The brightness
of the dream is exceeded only by its complexity. Farming, even
my kind, is infinitely complex, and it grows more so with every
year. A few days after I had mailed my order for fifty day-old
Silver Cross chicks, I received a long letter from the hatcheryman.
(My order amounted to $9.50—nineteen cents a chick—and
must have been one of the smallest orders received by that
hatchery, so there was no obligation to write anything but a postcard of acknowledgment.) The letter said my chicks would be
shipped on Monday, March 31st, and would probably arrive the
following morning. Then it went on:

As you perhaps know, our Silver Cross is made by top-crossing a
Rhode Island Red female with a Schoonmaker White Rock male
which is pure for Silver and Restricted Black. The reciprocal of this
cross breed is the Golden (or Buff) Sex Link, which looks not unlike
the Rhode Island Red. Of the two, the Buff lays the larger egg.

Cockerel chicks in both crosses are identical in color (Columbian).
For what it is worth we have developed a Silver Rhode Island Red
from four generations of backcrosses to the Rhode Island Red. Bird
looks like a Silver Cross, but breeds true for its plumage pattern. We
also have a Canadian Columbian Rock (a yellow-skinned Sussex
segregate), which produces a remarkably pure Columbian pattern in
crosses with the Rhode Island Red female. The alleles of Silver and
Gold fascinate the geneticist, for any number of multiple crosses can
be made, using the linkage of color and sex. We are, for example,
testing three three-way crosses, made from top-crossing a "synthetic"
Rhode Island Red (unrelated to our own strain) with different Silver
cockerels. We then top-cross the Silver Cross females (derived from
this original two-way cross) with Parmenter Red cockerels. All females
come Gold (or Buff) like the sire. We expect considerable hybrid
vigor, probably expressed as good livability. . . .

This struck me as a real chatty letter. It is clear from its contents that to run a hatchery these days a man must know something more than how to carry a pail of water to a thirsty hen.
Even though I got lost in the tangle of those backcrosses, I liked
getting the letter. Livability is what I am after: I greatly admire
a live bird. But my program is to simplify, and I am not much
interested in the space-hen, which will probably be the next cross.
The other day I read a piece in the *New England Homestead* saying that of Cornell's two hundred and sixty-eight agricultural
graduates last year only twenty-five went into farming. Young
people, the article said, hesitate to go into farming because of the
low income. I think some of them may be more worried about
the high complexity than the low income.

In one respect my henpen in the barn is ahead of the most
modern egg-producing plant: from it come eggs that are ninety-
eight percent clean-shelled, with no trace of dirt. Today many
commercial egg raisers have quit worrying about dirty eggs;
they simply install a washing machine and run every egg through.
I stood in the laundry room of a large egg factory not long ago
and watched the eggs come off the assembly line by the hundred.
Each wire basket of eggs (clean and dirty mixed) was immedi-

ately placed in the washing machine that was standing there throbbing its heart out. Here, in a detergent bath at a temperature of 120 degrees, the eggs remained for three minutes. When they were removed from their hot tub, the shells had the fine patina of a cheap plastic toy. If that's an egg, I'm a rabbit.

THE MOTORCAR

A Pavilion near Jeffreys Hook, March 16, 1958

The automobile industry, according to the newspaper that usurps my bed, is facing a period of crucial decisions. On the whole, this is good news. There is always the chance that during a time of crisis some car manufacturer will shake free from the vision of stratocruisers and rockets and at last see the automobile for what it is—a handy little four-wheeled contraption that moves along the surface of the earth carrying an American family on errands of an inconsequential nature, a vehicle requiring no wings for rising into the air, no fins for diving into the sea. The determination to resist the queer, corrupting conception of the automobile as a winged thing or a finny thing should be the first crucial decision the industry makes.

For twenty-five years car makers have foolishly pursued two false and seductive ideas: first, that the stature of man is decreasing; second, that the way to create beauty is to turn the matter over to a style department after consulting a few motivational-research monkeys and a covey of social psychologists. Everyone should know that the stature of man is *not* decreasing (if anything, men and women are somewhat taller than they used to be), and anyone who has eyes in his head should know that beauty is the child of truth, not to be had by last-minute scheming and conniving. I do not recall ever seeing a properly designed boat that was not also a beautiful boat. Purity of line, loveliness, symmetry—these arrive mysteriously whenever someone who knows and cares creates something that is perfectly fitted to do its work, whether the object is a grain scoop, a suspension bridge, or a guillotine. Nobody styled the orb web of a spider, nobody styled the sixteen-foot canoe. Both are beautiful, and for a common reason: each was designed to perform a special task under special conditions. I think it would be impossible to build a thoroughly honest and capable motorcar, correctly designed to meet the conditions a car must meet, and have it turn out to be anything but good-looking. But the method used in Detroit is to turn some engineers loose in one room and some stylists in another room, while the motivational pixies scamper back and forth whispering secrets in everybody's ear, and after months of such fooling and plotting and compromising and adjusting, then out comes the new automobile, and no wonder it carries the telltale marks of monstrosity on its poor tortured body. In many cases it looks as though the final licks had been given it by a group of emotionally disturbed children.

Not only have car makers lacked faith in the essential truth of a motor vehicle but they have painted their lily so lavishly and so drunkenly that they have ruined its appearance and added greatly to its cost. A garbage scow carries a filthy cargo but it has clean lines—cleaner by far than the lines of the 1958 automobile.

The mess the car makers find themselves in today bears a strong likeness to the pickle the motion-picture industry got into ten or a dozen years ago. That, too, was the direct result of indulging in dream life and underestimating the intelligence and stature of the people. The movie makers, if you remember, got so absorbed in the work of examining the entrails of pollsters and taking everybody's pulse in America to see what the average heartbeat was, they had no time to examine their own innards for a subject worth filming. It took them a number of years to pull out of their queer preoccupation with the human circulatory system and get back into the simple creative life. Now it's the car makers whose fingers are wrapped around my wrist in what feels like the grip of death. If they really want to know the state of my health and the shape of my desires, I shall be happy to accommodate them, but I warn them it's not the way to go about designing and building an automobile.

I sit here in this pavilion, running a low fever and looking out at the world from a high window. My view includes a small slice of the West Side Highway, southbound. The cars pass in an endless parade, and there is a terrible sameness to them—a litter of lively pigs from the brood sow in Detroit. Some are slightly upswept, some are slightly downcast (like the industry itself). But almost all of them seem to have been poured from the same mold: the Cadillac is blood brother to the Ford, the Lincoln and the Plymouth could lie down together in a field of daisies and you'd hardly know they weren't twins.

My newspaper says that the atmosphere in the hub of the auto industry is one of gloom. The bedtime story I am about to tell, revealing my pulse rate, my prejudices, and the state of my dreams, is not calculated to lift the industry's spirits, but it is a true story, and it concerns a man and his search for a car, and on that account it does bear on the vexing problems of these troubled times. I'll begin at the beginning, it's so soothing to do it that way.

In the summer of 1949, being then of sound mind and in good pocket, I purchased a four-door De Soto sedan in a pleasing shade of green—a green as rich as the new growth of a spruce tree in the spring. I mention the name De Soto hesitantly, for I have no wish to send a convulsion of pain through the bodies of Harlow Curtice and Henry Ford II, and indeed the name of the car could as well be Oldsmobile or Mercury and make no difference; it's the year 1949 that is the pertinent fact here. At any rate, my new car seemed at the time a very agreeable and serviceable automobile, and so it turned out to be. For this beauty I paid the handsome sum, in cash, of two thousand four hundred and ninety-five dollars, a veritable pile. I took possession of the car in Bangor, Maine, a few blocks from the railroad station. Through the years that have intervened, having through God's grace remained of sound mind, I have managed not to lose possession of the car, although there have been a couple of narrow squeaks in recent months.

I now skip lightly over eight years and we come to the summer of 1957. Last August, when somebody else was at the wheel, my car met with a slight accident involving another vehicle. The whole affair was on a very low pitch of disaster: the other car was motionless at the time, and my own car was moving at the rate of about seven miles per hour. But despite the trivial nature of the encounter, my right front fender received a long, straight slash the whole length of it, raked fore and aft by the strong, sharp blade of the opponent's rear bumper. I was so impressed by the neatness of the stroke that I drove to a local garage and instructed the mechanic to finish the job off with his shears and then weld a temporary bracket to the frame, to support what was left of the fender; namely, its upper part. When this was accomplished, the first discovery I made was that the right, or damaged, side of my car presented a better appearance, on the whole, than the left, or undamaged, side. The right front wheel had been exposed to view by the loss of the lower half of the fender, and I noted with satisfaction that a wheel revealed is more exciting to the eye than a wheel concealed.

For a few days, neither my wife nor I paid any particular attention to the fact that our family automobile was now asymmetrical and beat up. Our minds were on other matters, and when we wanted to go somewhere we would simply get in the car and go, enjoying the same inward elegance to which we had long been accustomed. But then one day the subject came up, as it was bound to sooner or later, and the phrase "new car" escaped from our lips and went darting about the rooms like Tinker Bell. "New car"! What an intoxicating sound the words make—like the jingle of frogs! What hot thoughts course through the mind! Before embarking on the golden adventure of shopping for an auto-mobile, however, we strolled out together one morning to take a long, hard look at what we had in hand (a 1949 De Soto) and size up the true situation in a mood of cold sobriety.

The busted fender was, of course, a brilliant reality. And there was also the little matter of the torn upholstery on the front seat, which looked like the work of squirrels but was actually *my* work. I habitually carry a jackknife in my right-hand trousers pocket, and the bony structure of this useful tool, working through to the cloth of the seat, had taken its toll over the years. Also, on one occasion I had deliberately cut a swatch from the seat, to give to an upholsterer as a sample. This was during a phase when we were entertaining the idea of reupholstering the car. Nothing came of the reupholstery project at the time; it died of its own weight, leaving the front seat with its swatch-hole as a reminder of our good intentions and untapped resourcefulness.

After studying our car for a few minutes, we decided that the word for it was "shabby." Both of us knew, though, that we were looking at an automobile the likes of which (if we were to lose it) we might not see again, a car that had not given us a moment's anxiety or pain in the whole time we had owned it and that still served us in an almost perfect manner. Its paint, after eight years, compared favorably with the paint on the new crop of cars; its metal seemed somehow stronger and heavier; all the doors worked with precision; and the only rattle it had was one it had had from the very beginning—a built-in rattle caused by a small glass plate on the instrument panel framing the legend "DE LUXE." I had always rather enjoyed this rattle as a piece of audible irony; it made me chuckle to observe that the only cheap streak in the entire car was caused by the stylist's written proclamation of swank. Every now and again I'd tire of the noise and plug the glass plate with a paper match or a tiny wad of Kleenex, but sooner or later DE LUXE would sound off again. DE LUXE was all that ever broke the silence of De Soto.

The upshot of our conference was this: Because of "shabbiness" we would look for a new car, but we would take our time about it. We were not faced with a crisis in transportation (the car ran fine), and we agreed that we would trade in our old automobile on a new one only if we could find a new one that seemed to be at least as good as what we had. We would not buy a new car merely because it bore the label "1957" or the label "1958." We would not let shabbiness embarrass us into doing anything foolish. That was the way we talked in our pride.

My wife is the sort of woman who does not notice automobiles except during the infrequent periods when we are in the process of selecting one. She has never counted on an automobile to invest her with prestige. (She was a distinguished woman at birth and needed no help from Detroit.) Motorcars simply do not attract her attention or excite her fancy, and I knew well enough that it was eight years since she'd last examined an automobile with eyes that see, and that she was in for a number of surprises, most of them unpleasant. The three things that especially interest her in a car are whether she can see out when at the wheel, whether she can ride in the front seat for any length of time without getting a pain in her back, and whether she can enter the car in a forthright manner, without turning around and going in backwards. She has never been willing to slink into an automobile fanny first, as millions of spineless and adjustable American women have learned to do, and I greatly respect this quality in her.

To prepare for what lay ahead I went to my workbench, got a spirit level and a two-foot rule, and carefully measured the height of the driver's seat from the floor. It measured fourteen and three-quarters inches.

From the end of August till the middle of January, whenever we could find a spare hour or two, we drove about the country-side, visiting nearby towns and cities in search of a car. We would pull in to a dealer's place with our naked right front wheel gleaming in the beautiful light and illuminating the car the way a cauliflower ear illuminates the face of an old fighter, and I would watch the dealer's eye rove furtively over the injured fender and see him make a mental note to knock an extra hundred dollars off the trade-in allowance. A new car would be trotted out for our inspection, and each of us in turn would sit in the driver's seat to get the feel of the thing. In most instances my wife lasted only a fraction of a minute at the wheel and came sliding and slithering out amid little stifled cries of alarm and disgust. Front seats had sunk in eight years, some of them a few inches, many of them without a trace. In several of the cars we looked at, the front seat was little more than a tilted hassock—a hassock that answered to the touch of a button, gliding forward and back, up and down, and leaving you either with your legs stretched straight out in front of you as though you were sitting on the floor, or with your knees pinned in a vicious grip under the steering wheel as though you were in the stocks.

At first we were shown 1957 automobiles, but soon after Labor Day we began encountering cars that were called 1958, among them the Edsel of great renown. It was an autumn rich in new experience for us. Everywhere we were courteously treated and everywhere we were bitterly disappointed. We ran through General Motors, we ran through Chrysler, we ran through Ford, we rambled through Rambler, and we poked around among foreign cars. A friend of ours who runs the general store where we trade let me drive his Lincoln, and another friend, just home from Germany, let me drive the Mercedes that he had brought back with him. (This last car, incidentally, felt more like our old 1949 sedan than anything else we had tried, but its manual gearshift seemed to me so delicately selective as to require the sandpapered fingers of a lock picker, and I felt fairly certain that even if I got together enough money to buy such a car, my wife would strip the gears out of it inside of a day, unless I managed to beat her to it myself.)

I usually carried my two-foot rule with me on our excursions and would make quick measurements of the front seat when nobody was looking, hoping to run across a car that could touch the fourteen-and-three-quarters-inch mark. The little Hillman, curiously enough, came close, and we were so impressed by this single fact we almost bought the car on the spot. But the same thing happened at the Hillman place that happened at all the other agencies: we took a short ride, with me at the wheel; then we thanked the man and said we wanted time to think it over; then we climbed back into the De Soto and started for home in an easy glide. Almost immediately the subtle superiority of our 1949 car to the one we had just been testing infected us, manifesting itself in a dozen indescribable ways and stirring our blood, and we felt relieved and happy and exhilarated by the rediscovery of old familiar virtues and properties, and this made us lightheaded and gay, and I stepped down on the accelerator and gradually the old automobile responded to the surge of gasoline until we were rushing along at the speed of the wind (forty-five miles an hour), singing and clowning and admiring the wonderful sheen of the green hood that stretched out in front of us, a green as rich as the new growth of a spruce tree in the spring. Even the holes in the upholstery were in perfect concealment; I sat on the knife-hole, my bride on the swatch-hole. Not a sign of shabbiness was apparent, the missing section of the fender being well out of view over the curve of the machine.

Sometime in January we tired of the rigmarole of buying a new car and decided to wait patiently for a turn in the automotive tide. I treated our sedan to a new front fender, had a few minor dents smoothed out, installed a pair of new front springs, and commissioned our upholsterer to re-cover the seats. (He told us that he was about to leave for Cape Canaveral to visit a son who is engaged in Space but that he would tend to our car when he returned to Maine and to terrestrial affairs.) I also arranged for another coat of Turtle Wax to be applied to the surface of Old Shabby. And that is where the matter stands now, and that is the end of my story.

Thirty or forty years ago, when a man wanted a car, he had a fabulous assortment to choose from—everything from a jack-rabbit to a bearcat. Big cars, small cars, medium-size cars, cheap cars, expensive cars, moderate-priced cars, high cars, low cars, open cars, closed cars, gas cars, steam cars, electric cars: it was paradise. The trend in manufacturing has been to standardize the automobile, as though the consumer were himself standard and fixed. Big cars have grown smaller, small cars have grown bigger, all cars have grown lower, all cars have gone up in price. Sales of most American cars are lagging; only the foreign cars are enjoying an active market.

My newspaper says that Detroit is reappraising the scene. Car makers are asking, "Do people want expensive chrome-covered, prestige-laden big cars, or do they want smaller and more economical basic transportation?" I think the answer to that is, there is no such thing as "people" in the sense that the word is used here. Every person is different. Some want expensive chrome-covered, prestige-laden cars; some want plain undecorated inexpensive cars that carry no more prestige than an old umbrella. Some want a car that is spacious, to carry big loads long distances. Others want a small, economical car for light going on short hauls.

For millions of men a motorcar is primarily a means of getting to and from work. For millions of wives it is primarily a means of getting to and from the nearby shops, churches, and schools. Yet from reading auto ads you would think that the primary function of the motorcar in America was to carry its owner first into a higher social stratum, then into an exquisite delirium of high adventure.

In the New England village I live in, the automobile is used chiefly for getting to and from a job and a store. The one car for which there is always a brisk demand in my town is the Model A Ford, now about thirty years old. Whenever a Model A comes on the market, it is snapped up in no time, and usually there is a waiting list. People actually advertise in the papers, wanting to buy a Model A. The reason the A is going strong today is simple: the car is a triumph of honest, unfussy design and superior materials. It doesn't look like a turbojet or like an elephant's ear, it drinks gasoline in moderation, it puts on no airs, and when something gets out of adjustment the owner can usually tinker it back to health himself. The car is not long, it is not low, but it works and it is extremely durable. It wouldn't fill the bill today for high-speed travel over superhighways, but I am quite sure of one thing—if Ford could suddenly produce a new batch of Model A's and put them up for sale some morning, at about double what they cost originally, they'd be gone by nightfall. I'd be strongly tempted to buy one myself. It isn't *exactly* what I'm looking for, but it's close. And the price would be so favorable I wouldn't have to turn in my old car but could keep it and become a two-car American, using the Ford for dashing to the store for a box of soap flakes and the De Soto for long-distance de-luxe occasions, such as running out to San Francisco to see the Giants play ball.

Whenever the automobile industry is in trouble, it's a serious matter for the country. The motorcar is really our No. 1 consumer item; when it languishes, everything languishes. I have contributed my tiny bit to the sickness in Detroit, because I haven't bought a car in nine years—an un-American way to act. But the fault is not mine. I think manufacturers should take a deep breath and start over, on new principles. They should regard the American motorist as an individual, not a type. They should respect his honesty and his intellect and his physical stature. They should abandon the cult of "lowness," as though lowness were synonymous with beauty and performance. (Every car should have a low center of gravity, but it isn't hard to come by. Virtually everything that's heavy about an automobile is in a naturally low position—engine, wheels, axles, frame, drive shaft, transmission, differential.)

The architect and his brother the engineer are perhaps the most valuable citizens we have. When they fail us, it affects our health and our purse. I believe that in motordom architects and engineers are not permitted to work undisturbed; their elbow is constantly being jiggled by tipsters, pollsters, motivationalists, and dream-mongers. To design a car is a responsible job, like designing a railroad bridge or a skyscraper. The motorcar is a killer and will always be a killer, but the death rate will always respond to re-sponsible work at the drawing board. Where there are honesty and sincerity and technical skill and belief in the good traits of human beings, there is never any problem about beauty of form and line. The reason women's clothes are hideous this season is that the bag or sack is a betrayal of anatomy, and fails to trans-late the figure of a woman, merely caricaturing it. But it's one thing to pander to human foibles when creating a dress and quite another when creating a car. A car is a matter of life and death.

I didn't carry a two-foot rule around the countryside in order to annoy dealers. I did it because I was afraid we might have a terrible accident if my wife was obliged to sit almost at floor level while driving a high-powered car. This was a more compelling consideration than the slight increment of prestige I might gain by owning a vehicle my neighbors would think was smart because it was low. I'd rather stay down on a low level of society with a living wife than be up with the best of them as a widower. During our days of searching, I noticed that although dealers don't like two-foot rules, many of the ones I encountered were sympathetic to my cry. None of them gave me much of an argument, and several of them said they agreed.

I'll promise Detroit one thing: build me a car that's as comfortable, as safe, as durable, and as handsome as the one I have today, and I'll swap cars.

P.S. (May 1962).   The tide did turn, and I kept my promise to Detroit. The air in that city has changed; gloom has been dispersed, sales are brisk, and this spring is jubilee. Sylvia Porter says it will last eleven months.

Cars are no longer uniform in size and shape. Today a man can find almost anything he wants—big, little, medium, fancy, plain, foreign, sporting, sedate. And if a conventional body fails to satisfy his needs, he can buy a minibus and sit well forward over the front wheels, while the children sit behind and leave the driving to him. The automotive scene is far healthier than it was in that grim springtime of 1958. There is real vigor in it.

Instead of trading in my old De Soto for a new car, I bought a new car outright and sold my De Soto to a friend who lives about a mile up the road and who had had his eye on my buggy for quite a while. I knew about his interest in the car, but he himself had never mentioned it to me. One afternoon, having made my mind up, I turned in at his place and stopped the car just short of the barn door and got out, and he came out of his kitchen and we stood together for a long while, leaning against the car and chinning. I am sure he knew perfectly well what the purpose of my visit was, and under the circumstances I felt as conspicuous coming into his yard with the De Soto as I would have felt if I had come in leading a Holstein bull. But although each of us knew what was in the other's mind, we both carefully avoided the subject, in the manner of traders the world over, as though the subject were indecent, or distasteful. Instead of discussing cars, we discussed bees. My friend is the foremost beeman in town: he loves to hunt wild honey in the fall of the year by tracking bees, and if you suddenly find yourself with a swarm of bees on your porch and are in trouble, he's the man you call on for help.

After we had covered the subject of bees thoroughly, and several other subjects, I remarked casually that I had heard he might be interested in buying a car. "I might," he replied. "What price have you got on it?" All this without looking at the automobile. I named a figure. "I'll go in and write you a check," he said, as though he were saying, "Looks as though it might turn warmer tomorrow." The whole transaction was over in less time than it takes a bee to rifle a flower.

It is nice to have my old car so close by. The new owner and I pass each other several times a week on the road and always exchange a small salute. When I go past his place, I often catch a glimpse of the car's voluptuous green posterior through the open barn door.

For myself, after much hunting, I found a car with a front seat that is well up off the floor, thirteen inches exactly—a 1960 Lark, to mention no names. I have driven this car two years and am a satisfied customer. By American standards it is already an old automobile, ready for the used-car lot; but from the looks of things, it is going to be around for a while yet. Maybe not eleven years (I can't break Detroit's heart twice in one lifetime), but at any rate for a while.

THE RAILROAD

Allen Cove, January 28, 1960

> What's the railroad to me?
> I never go to see
> Where it ends.
> It fills a few hollows,
> And makes banks for the swallows,
> It sets the sand a-blowing,
> And the blackberries a-growing.

Henry Thoreau, who wrote those lines, was a student of railroading. He was a devotee, though seldom a passenger. He lived, of course, in the morningtime of America's railroads. He was less concerned with where the railroad ended than with what the railroad meant, and his remarks on the Fitchburg seem fadeproof in the strong light of this century, their liturgical quality still intact.

And what's the railroad to me? I have to admit that it means a great deal to me. It fills more than a few hollows. It is the link with my past, for one thing, and with the city, for another—two connections I would not like to see broken. The railroads of Maine are eager to break these connections, having found them to be unprofitable, and are already at work on the problem. They hope to discontinue all passenger service within the state, and although they failed in their first try, in 1959, they may do better in the year ahead.

155

Bangor is the second-oldest railroad town in New England; a steam train pulled out of Bangor, bound upriver for Old Town, on November 6, 1836. The running time for the twelve-mile trip was two and a half hours, the conductor's name was Sawyer, passengers were aboard, and the fare was thirty-seven and a half cents. That was the first steam train to roll in Maine, the second to roll in New England. Soon Bangor may set another mark in rail history; it may watch the departure of the Last Train, and as this sad hulk moves off down the track (if it ever does), Maine will become the first state in the Union, except for Hawaii, to have no rail passenger service between its major cities.

What's the railroad to me? It is a lingering pain in the heart, an old friend who has tired of me and my antics. Unlike Thoreau, whose rail adventures were largely intellectual, I do go to see where the railroad ends. On some occasions—as on next Monday, for instance—I have no choice but to go; I will pay the tariff cheerfully and stare at the bare blackberry vines with affection. But the sleeper I had planned to take, the sleeper out of Bangor, has been pulled off, and I will have to find another one, a hundred and forty miles to the westward. (The distance to the depot gets longer and longer.) I live in the twilight of railroading, the going down of its sun. For the past few months I've been well aware that I am the Unwanted Passenger, one of the last survivors of a vanishing and ugly breed. Indeed, if I am to believe the statements I see in the papers, I am all that stands between the Maine railroads and a bright future of hauling fast freight at a profit. It makes me feel like a spoilsport.

But I have other sensations, too. I bought this house almost thirty years ago, confident that whatever else happened to me, the railroad would always pick me up and carry me here and there, to and fro. This morning our village lies under several thicknesses of snow. Snow has fallen almost without interruption for a week, beginning with a northeast storm, tapering off to dull weather in which the low clouds spat snow day and night, and today another storm from the northeast. The highway is a ready cake mix of snow, ice, sand, salt, and trouble. Within the fortnight there has been the greatest rash of air disasters in my memory. And on top of everything the railroad, which is my old love, is sick of me and the likes of me, and I feel that my connections have been broken, as sharply as by the man in coveralls who crawls between the cars and knocks apart the steam line with his hammer. My thoughts, as they sometimes do on sad occasions, revert to Concord and another railroad in another century.

"On this morning of the Great Snow, perchance," wrote Thoreau, "which is still raging and chilling men's blood, I hear the muffled tone of their engine bell from out the fog bank of their chilled breath, which announces that the cars *are coming*, without long delay, notwithstanding the veto of a New England north-east snowstorm. . . ." How different my village from his village, my century from his century! The only bell that is audible to me in this snowstorm is the one that rings inside my head, which announces that the cars *are going*—soon, perhaps, to be gone for good. For although the passengers' dilemma here in Maine is still unresolved, there is a strong suspicion that we are living on borrowed time; the railroads would like to chop my head off instanter and be done, but the Public Utilities Commission, after looking at all sides of the matter, has given me a stay of execution, on good behavior. It stipulates that I must travel more often and that I must not go first class.

Maine has two railroads—the Bangor & Aroostook and the Maine Central. One serves the north country, hauling potatoes and newsprint from field and forest; the other serves the midsection, hauling mail and packages of bonbons between Portland and Bangor, with an occasional sortie to Vanceboro. Both roads carry passengers when any show up. A third road, the Boston & Maine, dips into the state as far as Portland. A fourth, the Canadian Pacific, comes in briefly across the border.

Several months ago, the two principal railroads petitioned the Commission to be allowed to quit carrying passengers and thus free their talents for the exciting and rewarding task of moving freight and mail. Public hearings were held; for the most part they were poorly attended. While the Commissioners listened, the railroad men told grim tales of ruin and utter desolation. At one hearing in Portland, a lawyer for the Maine Central summed up the disjointed times when he said, "We are right now engaged in the diagnosis of a very sick patient." At another hearing, a man speaking for a cat-food factory in Lubec—makers of Puss 'n Boots cat food—rose to say that unless the Maine Central could wriggle free from the stifling grip of its passengers, Puss 'n Boots might have to move on to a happier and more progressive territory. The future of America's cats seemed suddenly at stake.

All in all, the year 1959 was a schizophrenic time for Maine's railroads. On Monday you would open your morning paper and find a display ad seeking your patronage and describing the rapturous experience of riding the rails. On Tuesday you would open the same paper and get a tongue-lashing from an impatient spokesman for the line, pointing out that the railroad would be bringing prosperity right this minute if only you, the passenger, would stand to one side and allow the freights to roll. "I am refreshed and expanded when the freight train rattles past me," wrote Thoreau. So, without any question, is E. Spencer Miller, president of the Maine Central. And so, for that matter, are all of us refreshed, though for a different reason, when, after a long wait in a motionless car on a silent siding, we hear a freight train at last rattle past us, hauling its cartons of food to faraway cats and releasing us hungry passengers for the continuance of our journey.

To the lay passenger, or to the travelling layman, the book-keeping of railroads is as mysterious as the backing up of a train in the night. Even to a public-utilities commission the account books of railroads are something less than perfectly transparent.

The Maine railroads' books were, of course, opened to the Commission, and some of the figures got into the papers. Every railroad, I gather, keeps two sets of books, one on its freight operation, the other on its passenger operation; and every once in a while the books themselves manage to draw close together and a sort of seepage takes place from one set to the other, so that to the unpracticed eye, it is hard to tell how deeply a profitable sack of potatoes is being eaten into by those rats, the passengers. But there is no question that we passengers, of late years, have *been* gnawing away at the potatoes. Some of us do it in desperation, because we are starving to death between station stops. No food is carried on the train that brings me up the Kennebec, and a passenger must live by his wits and off the land. At Waterville, on the eastbound run of the State of Maine, there is a midmorning pause, and while mail sacks are being tossed about in the genial and relaxed way that has characterized the handling of mail since the beginning of time, the engineer and the passengers (all six of us) gather at the snack counter in the depot, where we huddle over coffee and doughnuts, some of us passengers breaking a thirteen-hour fast that began 456.6 miles to the westward in the cornucopia civilization of Grand Central. These late breakfasts in Waterville come to an end as ritualistically as does the President's press conference in Washington when one of the reporters rises and says "Thank you, Mr. President." In Waterville, it is the engine driver himself who breaks up the party. He simply steps down from his stool, adjusts his cap, and walks away, which is the signal for us passengers to climb back into our places behind him in the train.

I suppose the very quality in railroads that has endeared them to me all my life, their traditionalism, has helped bring them (and me) to our present plight. England is about the most traditional institution I know of, but American railroads run a close second. "What has always been shall always be" is their motto. For almost a hundred years the Iron Horse was America's mount; the continent was his range, and the sound his hoofs made in the land was the sound of stability, majesty, punctuality, and success. "Far through unfrequented woods on the confines of towns, where once only the hunter penetrated by day, in the darkest night dart these bright saloons without the knowledge of their inhabitants; this moment stopping at some brilliant station-house in town or city, where a social crowd is gathered, the next in the Dismal Swamp, scaring the owl and fox. The startings and arrivals of the cars are now the epochs in the village day. They go and come with such regularity and precision, and their whistle can be heard so far, that the farmers set their clocks by them, and thus one well-conducted institution regulates a whole country." It was all true. And gradually the railroads fell in love with the sound of their own whistle, with the brightness of the saloons and the brilliance of the station houses, and even after the whistle dwindled to little more than a faint pooping in the hills and the saloons were withdrawn from service and the lights in the station houses went out, the railroads stubbornly stuck to their accustomed ways and to the ways of the horse. Some of the station houses were so solidly built they still stand, monuments to darkness and decay. The depot in Bangor, built in 1907, is a notable example of a railroad's addiction to the glorious past. Give it bars at the windows and it could as well be a federal penitentiary. Give it a moat with a drawbridge and it could be the castle where the baron lives. (On wet days it actually acquires a sort of moat, through which we surviving passengers wade and plunge with our luggage to gain the platform.) Reduce it to miniature size and it could be a model-railroad station built out of beautiful tiny blocks by yesterday's child. It is, in short, everything except what it ought to be—a serviceable shelter for arriving and departing passengers—and any railroad that hopes to attract customers and survive as a profitable carrier would certainly have to raze it as a first step toward the new day. Come to think of it, the depot at Bangor, although fit for a baron, was at one time the property of a hustling railroad called the European & North American, whose dream was to bring Europe closer by rushing people by rail to St. John, where an ocean liner would speed them on their way. The property in Bangor on which the present station stands fell into the hands of the Maine Central in 1882, when that railroad leased the European & North American. The lease was to run for nine hundred and ninety-nine years, and although the European was dissolved a while back, there seems a good likelihood that the depot will still be standing in the year 2881, its men's room still well patronized and its freight office ablaze with lights.

I made my first rail journey into Maine in the summer of 1905, and have been riding to and fro on the cars every since. On that first trip, when I was led by the hand into the green sanctuary of a Pullman drawing room and saw spread out for my pleasure its undreamed-of facilities and its opulence and the porter holding the pillow in his mouth while he drew the clean white pillowcase up around it and the ladder to the upper and the three-speed electric fan awaiting my caprice at the control switch and the little hammock slung so cunningly to receive my clothes and the adjoining splendor of the toilet room with its silvery appointments and gushing privacy, I was fairly bowled over with childish admiration and glee, and I fell in love with railroading then and there and have not been the same boy since that night.

We were a family of eight, and I was the youngest member. My father was a thrifty man, and come the first of August every summer, he felt that he was in a position to take his large family on a month's vacation. His design, conceived in 1905 and carried out joyously for many summers, was a simple one: for a small sum he rented a rough camp on one of the Belgrade lakes, then turned over the rest of his savings to the railroad and the Pullman Company in return for eight first-class round-trip tickets and plenty of space on the sleeper—a magnificent sum, a magnificent gesture. When it came to travel, there was not a second-class bone in my father's body, and although he spent thousands of hours of his life sitting bolt upright in dusty day coaches, commuting between Mount Vernon and Grand Central, once a year he put all dusty things aside and lay down, with his entire family, in Pullman perfection, his wife fully dressed against the possibility of derailment, to awake next morning in the winy air of a spruce-clad land and to debouch, surrounded by his eager children and full of the solemnity of trunk checks, onto the platform of the Belgrade depot, just across the tracks from Messalonskee's wild, alluring swamp. As the express train pulled away from us in Belgrade on that August morning of 1905, I got my first glimpse of this benign bog, which did not seem dismal to me at all. It was an inseparable part of the first intoxication of railroading, and, of all natural habitats, a swamp has ever since been to me the most beautiful and most seductive.

Today, as my thoughts wander affectionately back over fifty-five years of railroading, the thing that strikes me as most revealing about that first rail trip in 1905 is the running time of the train. We left New York at eight o'clock in the evening and arrived at Belgrade next morning at half past nine—a thirteen-and-a-half-hour run, a distance of four hundred and fifteen miles, a speed of thirty-one miles an hour. And what is the speed of our modern Iron Horse in this decade as he gallops through the night? I timed him from New York to Bangor not long ago, divided the mileage by the number of hours, and came up with the answer: thirty-four miles an hour. Thus, in fifty-five years, while the motorcar was lifting its road speed to the dazzling rate of seventy miles an hour on the thruways, and the airplane was becoming a jet in the sky, the railroad steadfastly maintained its accustomed gait, between thirty and thirty-five miles an hour. This is an impressive record. It's not every institution that can hold to an ideal through fifty-five years of our fastest-moving century. It's not every traveller who is content to go thirty-four, either. I am not sure that even I, who love the rails, am content. A few of us visionaries would like to see the railroad step up the pace from thirty-four to forty, so we could leave New York after dinner at night and get home in time for lunch next day. (I've just learned that the Maine Central has a new schedule, effective early next month. Soon I can leave New York after dinner and be home the following *afternoon* in time for dinner. There's to be a four-hour layover in Portland, an eighteen-hour trip all told. Thus the speed of my Horse has just dropped from thirty-four miles an hour to twenty-eight. He's a very sick horse.)

The slowness of rail travel is not because the Horse is incapable of great speed but because the railroad is a gossip; all along the line it stops to chat at back porches, to exchange the latest or borrow a cup of sugar. A train on its leisurely course often reminds me of a small boy who has been sent on an errand; the train gets there eventually, and so does the boy, but after what adventures, what amusing distractions and excursions, what fruitful dawdling! A railroad has a thousand and one things on its mind, all of them worthy, many of them enchanting, but none of them conducive to swift passage for a seated customer. I think if a railroad is to profit from a passenger run, it will have to take the word "run" seriously and conquer its insatiable curiosity about what is happening along the route. Some railroads manage to do this, and I notice that when they do, their cars are usually well filled, and their pockets, too.

There are other reasons the Horse is so slow-paced. The State of Maine leaves Portland in the evening and trots along briskly till it gets to Lowell Junction, around midnight. Here it leaves the main line of the Boston & Maine and goes adventuring on a stretch of single track toward Worcester, fifty miles away. This piece of track is well known to sleepy passengers snug in their beds. It was built by a Girl Scout troop while on maneuvers. The girls felled the trees for the ties, collected gravel from abandoned guppy tanks for the fill, and for rails they got hold of some twisted I-beams from condemned buildings. Even the engine driver has a healthy respect for this remarkable section of roadbed; he slows the train to a walk, obeying his instinct for self-preservation as well as the strict safety rules of the railroad. For about an hour, the creeping train is contorted in the most violent way, and the patient passenger slats back and forth in his berth, drugged with sleep, fear, and pain.

Tomorrow night, the last sleeping car leaves Bangor for New York. I shall not be aboard but shall be thinking of it and wishing it well as it rolls through Etna and skirts the swamp. When, the other day, the news broke that the through sleeping car was to be dropped, the papers carried a statement from Harold J. Foster, our traffic manager: "The service was, we hoped, one which would build railroad patronage between Maine points and New York City on an overnight basis. The sleeper has been poorly patronized, although we advertised its convenience in a consistent program in newspapers and on radio." Mr. Foster's words are true; the sleeper was poorly patronized, except on the occasions when bad weather grounded the planes, and except by a few eccentrics like me, who enjoy railroading and patronized it well. The *convenience* of the service was advertised, but not, of course, its inconveniences, which the travelling public was familiar with anyway—its high tariff, its low speed, its luggage problems, and (in my case) its depot fifty miles from home.

Not all sick railroads die; some have been known to make a startling recovery. The Long Island recovered when New York State forgave it its taxes. (I don't know whether its sins were forgiven, too, but at least its taxes were.) The Chicago & Northwestern recovered when someone thoughtfully equipped it with comfortable cars and modern conveniences, and when it was permitted to drop a few unprofitable trains. In Philadelphia, a nonprofit corporation formed for the purpose of improving passenger service is even now blowing new life into the rails that carry people to the city. This amounts to a municipal subsidy, and may easily benefit the community far in excess of its cost. About a year ago, the Rock Island Lines tried an experiment; it reduced first-class fares instead of raising them. The test lasted several months, and during that time there was a twenty-five percent increase in passengers carried.

Several other roads reduced fares and found that business picked up. I believe that a number of things are happening that will bring passenger trains back into favor and into the profit column, which is where everyone wants them to be. America's growth is phenomenal, its habits are changeable and unpredictable, its people are always on the move. Railroads, which commonly look backward, should look ahead. Already some cities are experiencing death by motorcar; Los Angeles is the most noticeable one, where the fast-breeding automobile has had a population explosion comparable to the lemming's and will soon have to rush into the sea to make room for oncoming generations of fertile automobiles and to save the people from stagnation and asphyxiation. Railroad men should take heart when they gaze at the Automobile in its area of greatest concentration and its hour of greatest triumph.

As for planes, planes have broken the speed of sound and are reaching for the speed of light to see if they can't smash that, too, and soon we will fly to the Coast and get there before we start and so will be cheated of the journey—a dreamlike transportation system that gradually gets to be nightmarish, with people whipped so rapidly from point to point that they are in danger of becoming a race of waltzing mice. (I see that 1960, according to the Chinese calendar, is the Year of the Mouse, but I think it may turn out to be the Year of the Waltzing Mouse, so feverish have our lives become.) If our future journeys are to be little different from flashes of light, with no interim landscape and no interim thought, I think we will have lost the whole good of journeying and will have succumbed to a mere preoccupation with getting there. I believe journeys have value in themselves, and are not just a device for saving time—which never gets

saved in the end anyway. Railroad men should take courage when
they look at a jet plane, or even at a poky old airliner circling at
two hundred miles an hour over an airport waiting for the fog
to lift or for its nose wheel to lock into position. The railroad has
qualities none can take away, virtues that have never been sur-
passed. A well-driven train moving smoothly and strongly over a
well-laid roadbed offers a traveller advantages and conveniences
not to be had in any other form of transportation. Unlike the
motorcar, the train does not have to be steered. Unlike the plane,
the train can slow down in thick weather. Unlike the bus, the
train does not have to pull over to the left every few minutes to
pass what is up ahead.

Maine's railroad men are perhaps more downhearted than most,
because this state is relatively unpopulous and is for that reason a
tough nut for a passenger line to crack. Even Maine's largest cities
are not yet large enough to show much urban sprawl, and a
motorist does not ordinarily encounter serious traffic delays in the
outskirts. In good weather, it is usually more convenient for a
resident of Bangor to drive to Portland than go by rail. In my
own case, I can drive from my house to Portland in four hours,
assuming that I can drive at all, but to get to Portland by train I
must first spend an hour and a half getting to the depot in Bangor,
then four hours on the train—a total of five hours and a half.

One of the jokers of railroading in Maine is the mail contract.
In this neck of the woods, passengers and mail are usually found
riding the rails together, and the schedule of a train is geared to
the delivery of letters, not of people. The Bangor & Aroostook
has just been working on a schedule designed to satisfy both the
Public Utilities Commission, which insists that passengers be carried during 1960, and the Post Office Department, which insists
that any letter posted in one part of Maine before five o'clock in
the afternoon be able to reach any other part of Maine in time
for the morning delivery next day. Today the new schedule was
announced; a passenger northbound for Caribou will take his

departure at twenty minutes past one in the morning from a rendezvous called Northern Maine Junction, just outside of Bangor, presumably clutching an alarm clock in one hand and snowshoes in the other. I suppose this is the best train the Bangor & Aroostook could work out under existing conditions, but I doubt whether it will attract customers to the rails in great numbers, although I'd like to make the trip once myself just for the richness of the experience.

The railroads want and need mail contracts, but the job of carrying the mail turns a railroad into the creature of the federal government. Uncle Sam can put the finger on any train in America and order it to carry the mail. He pays for this, of course, but he also runs his own show. A train's scheduled departure can be delayed indefinitely by the mail. Furthermore, the postal department determines *how* the mail is to be handled; the railroad has no say in the matter. A train stop becomes an interlude for mail sorting—sorting of sacks, that is. The reason my engine driver can take a coffee break at Waterville is that each mail sack is thrown out separately, and the pitcher keeps filling in the catcher. Twenty-five sacks of mail, if they were palletized, could be removed from a mail car in twenty-five seconds, but that's not the way the government wants it. Instead of twenty-five seconds, the operation takes twenty-five minutes. It seems to me that if the government has the power to immobilize some trains for the benefit of the mail, it has an obligation to speed up other trains for the benefit of the passengers.

If Maine's railroads are to stay alive and haul passengers, they will need help from villages, cities, the state, and the federal government, and I think they should get it. A state without rail service is a state that is coming apart at the seams, and when a train stops at a village depot anywhere in America and a passenger steps off, I think that village is in an enviable condition, even if the lone passenger turns out to be a bank robber who does nothing better than stir the air up for a little while. But I think railroads will have to help themselves, too. They should raise their sights, not their fares. And they should stop sulking in their tent, and, instead, try to beat the motorcar at its own game, which, if I do not misread the signs, should get easier as the years go on. There may even be a way to divorce the rail passenger from that fat wife of his, the mail sack—a marriage that has been unhappy all along. I believe that if railroads would improve their services by ten percent, they would increase their business by twenty. They must tidy things up. "This closed car smells of salt fish," wrote Thoreau, sniffing the air as the train rushed by, and his words were echoed by several Maine citizens at the recent hearings when they got on the subject of the untidiness of day coaches.

Railroads are immensely complex, and they seem to love complexity, just as they love ritual and love the past. Not all sick roads die, as I have pointed out, but a road can sometimes put on a pretty good show of dying, and then its ritual seems to be part of the scheme of dying. During 1959, because of some sickness of my own, and of my wife's, and of other members of our two families, she and I patronized the railroad more often than usual, observing its agony while using what remained of its facilities. There was one memorable night last fall, when, sitting forlorn in the deserted waiting room of the Portland depot, waiting to take the sleeper for New York, we seemed actually to be the principal actors in the deathbed scene of railroading in America; no Hollywood director could have improved on the thing. For reasons too dull to go into, we were taking our departure from Portland instead of Bangor. The old station hung tomblike above and around our still forms, drear and drafty. (No social crowd was gathered here.) The only other persons in the place were the ticket agent, at ease behind his counter, and a redcap in slow conversation with two friends. Now and then the front door would open and a stray would enter, some fellow to whom all railroad stations are home. Shortly before train time, a porter appeared, dragging a large wooden table and two chairs, and set the stage

for the rites of ticket-taking. The table looked to be the same age
as the depot and to have been chewed incessantly by porcupines.
Two conductors in faded blue now walked stiffly onto the set
and seated themselves at the table. My wife and I, catching the
cue, rose and approached the oracle, and I laid our tickets down
in front of one of the men. He grasped them, studied them
closely, as though he had never seen anything quite like them in
all his life, then turned to his companion and shouted, for all to
hear in the room where no one was, "B in the Twenty-three!"
To which the other replied, in a tremendous voice, "B in the
Twenty-three!" (and seemed to add, "*for the last two passengers
on earth*"). Then he tore off the stub and handed it to me.

The words of the ceremony, spoken so loudly, although
familiar to us seemed unnaturally solemn and impressive, and we
felt more as though we were taking marriage vows than taking
a train. After the ceremony was over, we followed the redcap
with our luggage, walking slowly out, the last two passengers,
into the cold train shed, and picked our way across the tracks
toward our waiting sleeper. Halfway there, we passed an ancient
trainman, his arms full of kerosene lanterns, on his way to harness
the Horse with the honored trappings of the past. There was
something ineffably sad about the departure of this train; death
seemed in the air.

When I came to live in Maine, the depot was twenty-three
miles away, in Ellsworth. Then the depot got to be fifty miles
away, in Bangor. After tomorrow night, it will be a hundred and
forty miles away (for a sleeping car), in Portland. A year from
now, there may be no depot in the whole state—none with a
light burning, that is. I cannot conceive of my world without a
rail connection, and perhaps I shall have to pull up stakes and
move to some busier part of the swamp, where the rails have not
been abandoned. Whether I move away or stay put, if the trains
of Maine come to a standstill I will miss them greatly. I will miss
cracking the shade at dawn—and the first shafts of light in the

tinted woods, and the old excitement. I'll miss the Canada geese in the Kennebec in the seasons of migration, and the breakfast in bed, drinking from the punctured can of grapefruit juice as we proceed gravely up the river, and the solid old houses of Gardiner, and Augusta's little trackside glade with the wooden staircase and the vines of the embankment and the cedar waxwing tippling on berries as I tipple on juice. I'll miss the peaceful stretches of the river above Augusta, with the stranded sticks of pulpwood along the banks; the fall overcast, the winter brightness; the tiny block-house of Fort Halifax, at Winslow, mighty bastion of defense; and at Waterville the shiny black flanks of Old No. 470, the Iron Horse that has been enshrined right next to what used to be the Colby campus—the steam locomotive that pulled the cars on the last prediesel run from Portland to Bangor.

Early last spring, as my train waited on a siding for another train to go through, I looked out of the window and saw our conductor walking in the ditch, a pocketknife in his hand. He passed out of sight and was gone ten minutes, then reappeared. In his arms was a fine bunch of pussy willows, a gift for his wife, I don't doubt. It was a pleasing sight, a common episode, but I recall feeling at the time that the scene was being overplayed, and that it belonged to another century. The railroads will have to get on with the action if they are to boost that running speed from twenty-eight to forty and lure customers.

Perhaps the trains will disappear from Maine forever, and the conductor will then have the rest of his life to cut pussies along the right of way, with the sand a-blowing and the blackberries a-growing. I hope it doesn't happen in my lifetime, for I think one well-conducted institution may still regulate a whole country.

P.S. (May 1962).   Death came quickly to the railroads of Maine. The passenger trains not only disappeared "in my lifetime," they disappeared in what seemed like a trice. The trains are gone, the station houses are gone. I was watching television one day and saw the tower of Portland's Union Station fall over, struck down by a large steel ball swinging from the boom of a crane. I could feel the blow in the pit of my stomach.

The freights are running as usual, and at higher speeds, but the expected spurt in business and profits has not occurred. At the annual meeting of the Maine Central a few weeks ago, the president of the line told the stockholders that "sunshine and shadow" lay ahead for them. The cat-food factory in Lubec has decided to close down, and this event casts a long shadow over the stockholders by jeopardizing the branch line that runs from Ayer's Junction to Eastport; it may have to be abandoned unless some business can be taken away from the truckers. I don't know why the cat-food plant is quitting; perhaps Puss has lost her appetite, or possibly the people who operate the cannery would prefer to live where there is passenger rail service.

Waterville, home of Hathaway Shirts and Colby College, has not only lost its trains, it has lost its planes, too. Northeast Airlines recently decided to skip Waterville, and was permitted to do so by the Civil Aeronautics Board. Lewiston, where Bates College is located, may be the next city to be dropped from the flying schedule. Northeast is heavily in debt; a CAB examiner describes it as "on the brink of collapse." Around the state, voices that were silent when the railroads were in trouble are now raised in alarm about the disappearance of the flying machine.

A lady in North Belgrade wrote me not long ago and said, "Though the great change has been made, it is still the freight train that we depend on to warn us about the weather. If we can hear the freight come through Oakland at nine in the evening, we know that the wind is the wrong way and there will be rain." I still believe the wind is the wrong way and there will be rain; a land without rail service is a land in decline, or in suspension.

Although I knew the railroads might die, I did not foresee

that my family would almost immediately become a hardship case. Early in January 1961, my wife was taken suddenly ill at home, and during the twelve-month period that followed, she was hospitalized five times in three widely separated hospitals— once in our local hospital for surgery, three times in a Manhattan hospital for tests, once in a hospital in Rochester, New York, for surgery. My job was to take her where the doctors ordered her to go, at the times they said to go. Our family physician said not to fly. The only other way she could have travelled in reasonable comfort and safety was by rail, but because Maine had lost its trains, we went and returned each time by car, in all weathers, she sitting upright when she was too sick for that, I at the wheel when I was too worried for that. The two trips that went well, in the whole period, were the trips to and from Rochester, when we parked the car in New York and travelled in a room on the Empire State Express. The other trips were nightmares for both of us. (Note to the solicitous reader: the patient survived both operations and all motor journeys, and is recovered.) I mention this private adventure only because the Maine Supreme Court, during the last illness of the railroads, observed that opposition to the discontinuance of passenger service came from "uninformed" numbers of the public who, "for nostalgic reasons, or reasons of occasional convenience," chose to ignore the facts. In 1961, neither "nostalgia" nor "convenience" was the word for me. The lack of a passenger train was a plain, simple hardship, and I will never forget it, and neither will my wife.

In the West, railroading is still enjoying good health, and a few of the Eastern trains are rolling at a profit, notably the trains that connect Florida with the cities of the North. But in the East generally, the sickness spreads. The New Haven, in a bankrupt condition, filed for reorganization last summer; the Boston & Maine is in hard shape; the merged Erie-Lackawanna is poorly despite the merger; and the B. & O. doesn't feel good at all.

In Europe, railroads are doing a brisk business. The Europeans have made it easy to put one's car on the train, and motorists have discovered the delights and advantages of this procedure. In Chicago, commuters are riding in clean trains and on time, and are returning a profit to the company. In San Francisco, plans are being drawn for a modern transit facility in the Bay area, to serve the residents of the counties of Alameda, San Francisco, and Contra Costa. This thing is still in the study stage, but San Franciscans have their eye on the horrid fate of Los Angeles and hope to avoid a similar fate, with (to quote from the brochure) "trains speeding alternately along exclusive surface routes, graceful aerial lines, underground subways, as well as a trans-Bay tube." In Seattle, visitors to the Fair are riding a monorail.

Railroading in America enjoyed its monopoly status much too long for its own good, and the characteristic American genius for new shapes, new ideas, new ways to exploit demand, although it infects every other business, has been lacking in railroading. Inflexibility is still the trouble with the Iron Horse. I am reasonably sure that there are thousands of car owners who would like to go to Florida or California by train if without any fuss they could drive their car, fully loaded, on board the train, as onto a ferryboat, and drive it off when they reached their destination. This kind of piggyback ride would eliminate the long, arduous drive through what one of my correspondents calls a "homogenized" landscape, it would save spending nights in motels and eating meals along the way, and it would save general wear and tear on man and machine. If it works in Europe, perhaps it could be made to work here, where distances are much greater. The *Bluenose*, a car-carrying ship plying between Nova Scotia and Bar Harbor, is a sellout every summer; people are willing to pay to avoid the long drive around.

A legislator who dreams of healthy railroads is Senator Claiborne Pell, of Rhode Island. Pell has come forward with a broad-scale scheme for pulling the roads of the Northeast out of the fire. He proposes that the lines serving the populous area from

Boston to Washington, D.C., an area where thirty-seven million people live and where almost a third of America's factories are located, be acquired by and operated by a public rail authority, through interstate agreement. Private railroad companies would continue to manage and enjoy the freight operation, but the public authority, paying no tax to state or federal government, would finance and run the passenger business. Pell envisions a light, flexible, fast system, utilizing new principles of design. His cars (which already have entered my dreams) will "speed along at approximately seventy miles per hour and with the new technological advances including the possibility that these modern cars might well be monorails, ride on pneumatic tires or a cushion of air or, even, be rocket-propelled." It would be, he says, a smooth ride and a pleasant trip.

In those last days of the rails in Maine, I remember most clearly the remark of a Bangor citizen, which I read in the paper. This fellow walked downtown on the day after the razing of the depot; he stared in surprise at the new vista. "Hey!" he said. "You can see Brewer from Exchange Street!" (Brewer is Bangor's twin, a few hundred yards distant across the river.)

In the old days, when the railroads were in their prime, you couldn't see Brewer from Exchange Street, but you could close your eyes and see the continent of America stretched out in front of you, with the rails running on endlessly into the purple sunset, as in an overwritten novel. I loved it when I couldn't see Brewer from Exchange Street, the rest of the view was so good.

UNITY

Avenue of the Americas, June 4, 1960

In 1899, the year I was born, a peace conference was held at The Hague. I don't remember how it came out, but there have been two memorable wars since then, and I am now sixty, and peace parleys, some of them tackling the subject of disarmament, have been held at intervals all my life. At this writing, five nations of the East and five of the West are studying disarmament, hopeful of achieving peace. When last heard from, they were deadlocked, which is the natural condition of nations engaged in arms negotiations. The Soviet Union has suggested that they "start all over again."

The West has a real genius for doing approximately what the East wants it to do. We go to Paris and sit in stunned surprise while Khrushchev bangs a cat against a wall. We go to Geneva and listen solemnly while Russia presents herself as the author of total disarmament and peace. We hasten to the Security Council room at the United Nations and earnestly defend ourselves against a charge that we have "aggressed." We join England for Princess Margaret's wedding, and next day we separate from England again, to return our trust to last-minute diplomatic conformity. We use the word "peace" the way the East likes to see it used—in the last paragraph of the President's formal speeches, and preceded by the adjectives "just" and "lasting," as though peace were some sort of precious stone that, once discovered, would put an end to trouble for all time. I am beginning to tire of running the East's errands and dropping into the East's traps, and I wish I could set off on a different journey, under good auspices.

Senator McClellan, in a speech at Valley Forge quite a while back, said that "the only hope for freedom's survival" was moral, spiritual, political, economic, and military strength. (He should have added "intellectual strength.") Happily, freedom, if there is such an entity, is well fixed for four out of five of the Senator's ingredients. Freedom has great moral strength; this is its principal advantage over Communism. Freedom has the strength of the spirit. Freedom is strong economically—in the United States and in many other capitalist countries. It is strong in military power. But it is sadly lacking in political strength, because it does not enjoy the benefits of political unity and, unlike Communism, does not lay a course for it. Two free nations, though they may pull together in a crisis, are almost as far apart diplomatically as a free nation and a Communist nation. The two free nations are obliged to conduct their affairs as though they were fencing with each other, as indeed they are, with parries and thrusts, occasionally unmasking to smile and shake hands and test each other for popularity and good will. After the recent events in Paris, and the bruises of the night, it is not at all certain that the West should indulge itself longer in the pleasures of perfect political disunity.

Soviet arms, terrible as they are, seem less fearsome to me than the Soviet's dedication to its political faith, which includes the clear goal of political unity. Russia openly proclaims her intention of Communizing the world and announces that she is on the march. Not all her cronies present the face of unity—Mao's China, Tito's Yugoslavia, Gomulka's Poland—but at least the idea of unity is implicit in the religion of Communism. Must we in the West leave all the marching to our opponent? I hope not. Not until free men get up in the morning with the feeling that they, too, are on the march will the danger to Western Society

begin to subside. But marching is futile unless there is a destination, and the West's destination is fuzzy. Perhaps I should merely
say that it is not clear to *me*. I do not think that it is discernible in
the utterances of our statesmen.

Lately, I have been browsing among the books and published
speeches of some of the candidates for the Presidency. Here are
some of the themes against which the contestants knock their
heads: disarmament, nuclear testing, foreign aid, civil liberties, a
farm program, trade expansion, payola, race relations, admission
of Red China to the U.N., peace with honor, peace with justice,
peace with safety, peace under the rule of law, peace through
détente, better housing, better education, the missile gap, a
strengthened defense, the exploration of space. I have read Kennedy, Bowles, Nixon, Stevenson, Rockefeller, and others. They
speak of new principles for a new age, but for the most part I
find old principles for a time that is past. Most of the special
matters they discuss are pressing, but taken singly, or added
together, they do not point in a steady direction, they do not name
a destination that gets me up in the morning to pull on my
marching boots. Once in a while I try a little march on my own,
stepping out briskly toward a reputable hill, but when I do I
feel that I am alone, and that I am on a treadmill. The way things
are now, we could all march for the rest of our days and still
not advance perceptibly. This is not true of the Soviets. They
know perfectly well where they want to be. Lately, it has seemed
that they might get there.

Life magazine, I see, has raised the question of the free world's
destiny with a series of pieces on "National Purpose." The title
of the series is revealing. America's purpose, everyone's purpose
in the West, is still painted in the national frame. When we aid a
friend, it is "foreign" aid. And when the aided country emerges,
it gains "independence," thus adding one more sovereign political
unit to the ever-growing list of destiny seekers. When we establish a military base in some indispensable location outside our

borders, we call it a base on "foreign" soil, and so it is. The U-2 plane incident disclosed an American pilot taking off from an American nook in Turkey and heading for an American nook in Norway. This famous flight illustrated the queer conditions we and our Western associates are compelled to face—a world grown so small that other people's airfields are essential to our own safety, and ours to theirs, yet a world that has made no progress in bringing free men together in a political community and under a common roof. The West's only roof these days is the wild sky, with its flights, its overflights, and the boom of broken barriers. Our scientists long ago broke all known boundaries, yet the rest of us work sedulously to maintain them, in our pursuits, in our prayers, in our minds, and in our constitutions. We dwell in a house one wall of which has been removed, all the while pretending that we are still protected against the wind and the rain.

Most people think of peace as a state of Nothing Bad Happening, or Nothing Much Happening. Yet if peace is to overtake us and make us the gift of serenity and well-being, it will have to be the state of Something Good Happening. What is this good thing? I think it is the evolution of community, community slowly and surely invested with the robes of government by the consent of the governed. We cannot conceivably achieve a peaceful life merely by relaxing the tensions of sovereign nations; there is an unending supply of them. We may gain a breather by relaxing a tension here and there, but I think it a fallacy that a mere easement, or diplomacy triumphant, can ever be the whole base for peace. You could relax every last tension tonight and wake tomorrow morning with all the makings of war, all the familiar promise of trouble.

A popular belief these days is that the clue to peace is in disarmament. Pick a statesman of any stature in any nation and he will almost certainly tell you that a reduction in arms is the gateway to peace. Unfortunately, disarmament doesn't have much to do with peace. I sometimes wish it had, it enjoys such an excellent reputation and commands such a lot of attention. Keeping itself strong is always a nation's first concern whenever arms are up for discussion, and disarmament is simply one of the devices by which a nation tries to increase its strength relative to the strength of others. On this naked earth, a nation that approaches disarmament as though it were a humanitarian ideal is either suffering from delusions or deliberately planning a deception.

Chairman Khrushchev recently asked, "Is there any . . . way which would remove the threat of war without prejudicing the interests of states?" and then answered his own question: "We see it in the general and complete disarmament of states." Now, even if one were to believe that Mr. Khrushchev is averse to prejudicing the interests of states, one might still wonder whether any state relieved of its weapons was thereby relieved of the threat of war. I am afraid that blaming armaments for war is like blaming fever for disease. Khrushchev's total-disarmament bid was made for the same reason he makes other bids; namely, to advance the cause of international Communism. Total disarmament would not leave anyone free of the threat of war, it would simply leave everyone temporarily without the help of arms in the event of war. Disarmament talks divert our gaze from the root of the matter, which is not the control of weapons, or weapons themselves, but the creation of machinery for the solution of the problems that give rise to the use of weapons.

Disarmament, I think, is a mirage. I don't mean it is indistinct or delusive, I mean it isn't there. Every ship, every plane could be scrapped, every stockpile destroyed, every soldier mustered out, and if the original reasons for holding arms were still present, the world would not have been disarmed. Arms would simply be in a momentary state of suspension, preparatory to new and greater arms. The eyes of all of us are fixed on a shape we seem to see up ahead—a vision of a world relaxed, orderly, secure, friendly. Disarmament looks good because it sounds good, but

unhappily one does not get rid of disorder by getting rid of muni-
tions, and disarmament is not solid land containing a harbor, it
is an illusion caused by political phenomena, just as a mirage
is an illusion caused by atmospheric phenomena, a land mass that
doesn't exist.

Weapons are worrisome and expensive; they make everyone
edgy. But weapons are not and never have been the cause of the
trouble. The only weapon in this decade that is intrinsically
harmful is the nuclear weapon during its test period, and that is a
new and separate problem, which must be dealt with separately.
I think it can and will be dealt with, for although it is related
to the balance of power, and therefore is capable of being used
for national advantage, it carries a threat that is the same for all
nations, Eastern and Western, atomic and nonatomic—the threat
that the earth will eventually bear too great a residue of poison
and will no longer support life. All nations know this, though
some are reluctant to admit it. At any rate, a test ban, though full
of danger for whoever signs it, has at least a reasonable chance
of success, provided the nations signing it do not disarm. A nation
signing an agreement to quit exploding nuclear devices has a
selfish interest in honoring the agreement. The debris from tests
falls on home ground as well as on enemy territory; it covers the
earth like the dew. And although the nation might find many
attractive reasons for breaking the agreement, the selfish reason
would still be present, as a deterrent to violation. That is why we
may profitably talk about stopping nuclear tests: national self-
interest happens in this case to coincide with universal interest, and
the whole business is a simple matter of human survival on a
shaky planet. Usually, in negotiations, that isn't true. It isn't true
of a disarmament agreement, which is no sooner signed than a
thousand selfish reasons crop up for wanting to violate it.

We hold arms so that, in the event of another nation's breaking
its word, we will have something to fall back on, something by
which we can command respect, enforce our position, and have

our way. Modern arms are complicated by their very destruc-
tiveness, their ability to turn and bite whoever unleashes them.
That is why everyone is pleased by the prospect of disarming
and why there is a great hue and cry raised against arms. And
how are we to disarm? By signing a treaty. And what is a
treaty? A treaty is a document that is generally regarded as so
untrustworthy we feel we must hold arms in order to make sure
we're not disadvantaged by its being broken. In other words, we
are seriously proposing to sign an agreement to abandon the
very thing we will need in the event that the agreement itself
fails to stick. This seems a queer program to me.

In drawing up plans for disarming, the nations are making it
clear that their distrust of one another and of treaties is as strong
as ever. They're insisting that there be "controls"—they are called
"adequate" controls—and that there be "inspection." President
Eisenhower has suggested an "open-sky" system. And everyone
agrees that the treaty must be "enforceable"—some say by an
international disarmament organization free of the veto and
affiliated with the United Nations. As for control, there is no
way to control any aspect of a sovereign nation's internal life.
The U.N. designers sensibly bowed to this sticky fact when they
installed the veto and provided that the internal affairs of a member should be nobody else's business. (The Hungarian revolt
demonstrated how sad are the facts of international life.) It is
possible to *influence* a sovereign nation, through public opinion
and through pressures of one sort or another, but it is not possible
to control it, short of domination by force. In the case of arms,
which are among the most intimate of a nation's garments, and
which a nation instinctively conceals from view, we do not even
know at any given moment what we would be hoping to control
the next moment, so speedy is the evolution of weapons and
counterweapons. National life is secret life. It has always been
secret, and I think it is necessarily secret. To live openly, one
must first have a framework of open living—a political frame-

work very different from anything that now exists on the international level. A disarmament arrangement backed by controls
and inspection is not such a framework, it is simply a veiled invitation to more and greater secrecy.

Can we inspect the Soviet Union? Can it inspect us? In this
jungle world, inspection would be an attempt to license an international legion of Peeping Toms. I cannot believe that it would
work. It would probably spawn a legion of counter-Toms, fellows
to peep at the peepers. An "open-sky" system in which the
inspectors carried operator's licenses would itself be under the
surveillance of the open-*spy* system that all nations feel obliged
to maintain at all times. And the open-sky system, although a new
idea, has already been overtaken by events: the sovereign sky is
no longer top-level—space hangs above it, from which East and
West are taking pictures of each other with flying cameras.

As for "enforcement," an arms pact is by its nature unenforce-
able. It would be enforceable only if there was an authority higher
and more powerful than that of the parties involved in the deal.
The principal characteristic of life on earth today is that no such
authority exists. An international disarmament organization, created by treaty and representing the East and the West and
equipped with police powers, would not constitute such an authority. This does not mean that nations do not take their treaty
obligations seriously; it simply means that no nation takes *any*
obligation seriously if it begins to threaten the national safety or
obstruct the national will. In the case of a disarmament "authority," any attempt to invoke it might easily result in a riot or a
war. National arms would quickly resume their ascendancy over
pooled arms, because national forces are responsive to the will of
the nation, and this is a fluid, living thing; whereas international
arms would be the servant of the signatory powers and of a
status quo—the conditions that prevailed on the day the treaty
was signed. The Soviet Union wants this police force to be under
the Security Council, where it would be subject to the veto—

in short, a cop who would swing his club or fail to swing it according to the whim of one of the parties.

Many statesmen feel that weapons are in themselves evil, and that they should be eliminated, as you would crush a snake. They feel that vast stores of arms create tension and threaten the peace by the mere fact of their existence. This is perfectly true. I doubt, though, whether the tension created by the existence of arms is as great as the tension that would arise if there were no arms, or too few arms. President Eisenhower has said that war in this day and age would yield "only a great emptiness." So, I think, would disarmament in this day and age. An arms race is a frightening thing, but eighty sovereign nations suddenly turning up without arms is truly terrifying. One may even presume that Russia came forward with the most sensational of the disarmament proposals—total disarmament in four years—just because it *is* terrifying. A dictator dearly loves a vacuum, and he loves to rattle people. Disarmament in this day would increase, not diminish, the danger of war. Today's weapons are too destructive to use, so they stand poised and quiet; this is our strange climate, when arms are safer than no arms. If modern weapons make war unlikely, had we not better keep them until we have found the political means of making war unnecessary?

In a letter to Dag Hammarskjöld, Khrushchev said, "General and complete disarmament cannot result in advantage to any side." This is nonsense. The side that enjoys numerical superiority stands to gain by disarmament, the side that does not have any intention of remaining unarmed for more than a few minutes stands to gain, and the side that uses the lie as an instrument of national policy stands to gain. If disarmament carried no chance of advantage, Mr. Khrushchev would not be wasting his breath on it. He likes it because of its propaganda value and because it gives him a chance to oust us from our advanced military bases —which is the Soviet's precondition of an arms agreement.

Perhaps the most valuable clues to peace nowadays are to be

found in the Soviet Union's own fears, and these are many. Russia's greatest fear, apparently, is that Western democracies will act in a united and constructive way. Russia is constantly on the alert to divide us and drive the wedge that we read about every day in the papers. Mr. Khrushchev's March visit to Paris was designed primarily to arouse France against West Germany. His conniptions at the summit and his vilification of President Eisenhower were designed to stir up irritation and allow him to threaten the countries that had accidentally got involved in the spy-plane affair. If it's so very important to Russia that the West be a house divided against itself, then it should be equally important to the free nations that they stand together, not simply as old friends who have a common interest but as a going political concern. A successful attempt to open discussions on this subject has yet to be made, and the matter is seldom referred to in exact terms. The Western nations are still content to put their trust in what they know—the techniques of diplomacy, of alliance, of collective security, of bargaining, of last-ditch solidarity. A few months ago, when the United States and Great Britain were faced with a decision about nuclear-test arrangements, Macmillan had to duck over here at the eleventh hour for a quick talk. This kind of hasty tucking up should be unnecessary. It is appalling that at this late date the two great English-speaking countries, both equipped with atomic weapons, both desirous of presenting a solid front to the world, each wholly dependent on the other for survival and neither sure that it will survive, should have no political machinery for translating the wishes of their peoples and should still be obliged to go philandering to gain a decision on some vital point. England and America in this fateful decade remind me of a fabulous two-headed sheep I encountered in a book by Laurie Lee: "It could sing harmoniously in a double voice and cross-question itself for hours."

While studying the words of the candidates, I watched for signs that any of them felt favorably disposed toward a more positive and orderly political structure for the West. The signs are there, but the words are thin, guarded, hesitant, as was to be expected. Few public men are ready to state the thing unconditionally and with enthusiasm. But here, for what they are worth, are a few hints, a few promising sprouts:

Adlai Stevenson: "Should we not at least attempt a political inventiveness which in some way matches the horrific inventiveness of our scientists? . . . We do not pursue the general welfare. We pursue our separate national interests and hope that the selfish good of the parts will add up—against the witness of all social history—to the wider good of the whole. We do not urgently seek a world under law."

And again Mr. Stevenson: "A working cooperative Atlantic system would do more than enhance the basic strength of the West. It would demonstrate to other areas . . . methods by which political autonomy can be combined with supranational cooperation. In any case, the alternative is to see the centrifugal forces which are always at work between separate national entities pull us ever farther apart. One thing is sure—we cannot deal with the Communist challenge divided and in disarray."

Vice-President Nixon: "The time has now come to take the initiative in . . . establishment of the rule of law in the world to replace the rule of force."

Senator Kennedy: "With respect to the world outside, our purpose is not only to defend the integrity of this democratic society but also to help advance the cause of freedom and world law—the universal cause of a just and lasting peace."

And again Mr. Kennedy: "So far we have lacked the vision to present a comprehensive program for the development of a world community under law and we have lacked the courage to try small beginnings."

Nelson Rockefeller: "[The United States should seek] a political framework which someday may be comparable to the one we created for our own nation in the federation of states on a world-wide basis."

Chester Bowles: "The gradual growth of a framework of world

law will depend on the vitality and success of the multilateral agencies we now have, and we should be vigorously pursuing our objectives through these agencies wherever possible."

The phrase "the rule of law," I have noticed, means different things to different men. Mr. Nixon's amplification of the remark quoted above indicated that he found the rule of law in a strengthened World Court, which I think is to confuse international law with supranational law. I'm not sure I know what Mr. Kennedy means by the rule of law. President Eisenhower sometimes uses the phrase and leaves the interpretation up to the listener. Governor Stevenson goes as far as "a working cooperative Atlantic system" and "supranational cooperation." Governor Rockefeller comes right out with the federal principle and with a "political framework . . . comparable to the one we created for our own nation."

Well, politicians are busy men. Primarily they are not paid to indulge in the pastime of shaping the world in an ideal mold, out of pure theory and pure reason; they are paid to get us through the day as best they can. A public servant has a thousand pressing obligations as well as a strong distaste for theoretical ideas that are bound to irritate voters. But I believe that if a public man speaks of the rule of law at all, he should stay with the subject long enough to say what he has in mind: Who are the authors of this law? Who are the enforcers? From whom do they derive their authority? What are the geographical conditions? What is the framework within which it lives? The simple truth is, we in the West have not yet attempted a political inventiveness, we do not seek a political framework, the centrifugal forces causing friendly nations to fly apart are still operating, we are in disarray, and "the rule of law" is a cloudy phrase in a closing paragraph, not a clear gleam in somebody's eye.

Perhaps this is not the proper time to explore the foundations of unity of the West. Many people would say that although the vision of a federal union of free democratic capitalist states is a pleasing prospect for dreamers, actual work on it would be too upsetting, would shake us at a ticklish time. We might become so absorbed in establishing order on a higher level that we'd lose what little order we now enjoy, and thus play into the hands of our enemies. Others would say that if the political unity of free powers were to become an accomplished fact, it would merely increase the challenge and the fury of the East. Others would argue that most people find unity repugnant; it spoils the fun.

These are all good arguments against trying to bring greater order into Western society. As an American citizen, though, I would welcome the stirrings of political union with the United Kingdom, with Scandinavia, with the Western European nations —with any nation, in fact, that could show a long, successful record of government by the consent of the governed. For I would feel that although I was being placed temporarily in a more dangerous position, I was nevertheless occupying higher ground, where the view was better. I would know my destination at last. If from the shambles of the summit there were to emerge the first positive thrust of Western unity, then the summit would, in my book, go down as a smashing success, not a bleak failure.

The Communists have a shape they pursue; they propose an Eastern union that will eventually erode the West and occupy the globe. In a day when imperialism is despised and languishing, they brazenly construct an empire. To do this they engage us in a Cold War. I believe this war would be easier to fight if we, too, could find a shape to pursue, a proposal to make. Let us pursue the shape of English liberty—what Santayana once described as "this slow cooperation of free men, this liberty in democracy." English liberty in a federal hall—there's a shape to conjure with! "Far from being neutralized by American dash and bravura," wrote Santayana, "or lost in the opposite instincts of so many alien races, it seems to be adopted at once in the most mixed circles and in the most novel predicaments." A federation of free states, with its national units undisturbed and its people elevated to a new and greater sovereignty, is a long way off, by anybody's guess; but if we could once settle on it among ourselves, and embrace it unashamedly, then we would begin to advance in a clear direction and enjoy the pleasures and disciplines of a political destination. Liberty is never out of bounds or off limits; it spreads wherever it can capture the imagination of men.

In the long debate on disarmament, I encountered a statement that has proved memorable; it was in a piece in the *Times* magazine last October, by Salvador de Madariaga, who for a number of years watched disarmament from the vantage point of the League of Nations. Señor de Madariaga ended his article with an observation that should inform and enliven every free nation.

"The trouble today," he wrote, "is that the Communist world understands unity but not liberty, while the free world understands liberty but not unity. Eventual victory may be won by the first of the two sides to achieve the synthesis of both liberty and unity."

I have never seen the matter stated more succinctly, nor have I ever read a prediction I felt such confidence in. President Eisenhower often talks of "peace with justice," but fails to supply a sketch. Diplomacy, treaties, national aspirations, peace parley hot, peace parley cold, good-will tours, secrecy, spying, foreign aid, foreign trade, foreign relations—these seem to be the only building blocks we are trustful of. From them justice cannot be expected to arise, although occasionally some benefits do come from them, more by good luck than by good management. Our national strategy goes something like this: Keep your chin up, keep your powder dry, be willing to negotiate, keep your friends happy, be popular, be strong, get to outer space, stall for time, justice is bound to come eventually, and the rule of law.

I doubt whether justice, which is the forerunner of peace, will ever be pulled out of a hat, as some suppose. Justice will find a home where there is a synthesis of liberty and unity in a framework of government. And when justice appears on any scene,

on any level of society, men's problems enjoy a sort of automatic
solution, because they enjoy the means of solution. Unity is no
mirage. It is the distant shore. I believe we should at least head
for that good shore, though most of us will not reach it in this
life.

P.S. (July 1962).   To hold quixotic views about disarmament
is my lot, and it is not a happy one. What happens to arms in the
next few years may save all of us, or destroy all of us. In these circumstances a man feels uneasy at expressing any opinion at all,
since it might in some slight way affect adversely the course of
events.

Obviously my government does not regard disarmament as a
mirage; a special agency has been created to promote disarmament, and a detailed draft treaty will be before the Geneva Conference when it resumes later this month. I am reasonably sure
the Russian government regards disarmament as nonsense, but it
serves their purpose to believe one thing and say the opposite.
Most of the people I discuss the subject with feel that general
and complete disarmament (now known as G & C) is sensible and
desirable and that it is just a matter of finding a formula. John J.
McCloy, in a recent article in *This Week* magazine, said the
"weight of logic" is on the side of disarmament; but it appears
to me that logic is the one kind of weight it lacks—it certainly
doesn't lack the weight of public support and general wistfulness.
Almost everyone would like to beat a sword into a plowshare, and
I would, too, if I believed that plowshares made from old swords
were the principal arch of peace, order, and justice.

If there is a weakness or fallacy in the reasoning about disarmament, it is this: the belief that a supranational police force
can function effectively in advance of a supranational political
system. America's disarmament plan envisions a day when national

armaments will have been abolished and peace safeguarded by a United Nations Peace Force so powerful no nation would dare challenge it. Our goal, according to a State Department booklet called *Freedom from War*, is a free, secure, and peaceful world "of independent states," subjecting the use of force to the rule of law. This assumes that nations obey laws, and that nations can be punished for lawbreaking. It assumes that nations, collectively, can hold a preponderance of the world's arms and use them for everyone's protection and safety. This is an interesting assumption, but I've never seen any indication that it is a reasonable one. To turn the world's armed strength over to the United Nations (which is a treaty organization of about a hundred independent states) would be like turning New York City's police power over to a hundred civic organizations and societies—everything from the YMCA to Actors' Equity. The police themselves might be eager and willing to do their duty, but their duty, in specific episodes, would be far from clear. Order would be most unlikely. New York's cops are effective because they serve the city government and the people, rather than a group of societies. I think a world police force, if it is to be reliable, will have to serve a world government, not a group of states.

Another fallacy, as I see it, is that "keeping the peace" is the sole purpose of national arms. The chief purpose of arms is not to keep order but to protect and maintain political principles. American arms are directly associated with the American concept of liberty. I think we can't sensibly merge our arms in a general world force until such time as there is an agreement on principles. One of the clauses in the State Department booklet reads: "States shall agree to refrain from indirect aggression and subversion against any country." But at this point in history, indirect aggression and subversion are basic procedures in the Soviet system. This being the case, how can we seriously propose appointing the United Nations as a custodian of our arms?

Another fallacy is the assumption that a state that you go to bed with tonight is the same state that you will wake up to in the morning. States change overnight and what might seem like a responsible use of police power to, say, Cuba under Batista might seem different to Cuba under Castro, and still different to a democratic regime in Cuba.

Quite unintentionally, the *New York Times* recently jiggled whatever logic there may be in disarmament. A *Times* editorial noted with pride that the government had submitted a plan looking toward total disarmament "under a United Nations police force." But a little earlier in the editorial, the *Times* remarked that "Without our support, moral and financial, this world organization would collapse and chaos would be the result." It would appear, then, that the *Times* would be willing to disarm and turn police power over to an organization that is liable to collapse if so much as one nation out of a membership of more than a hundred were to withdraw its support. I find this hard to credit. Of course, our arms proposals are contingent on a greatly strengthened U.N., and perhaps the *Times* is justified in thinking that the new, improved U.N. will be less likely to go to pieces under stress. But I think you could strengthen the U.N. till the cows come home, and you would still have a treaty organization, whose members were unpredictable and whose people were unrepresented.

When this "Letter from the West" appeared in *The New Yorker*, the *Washington Post* picked it up and reprinted it with one typo. Then Senator Moss of Utah picked it up from the *Post* and, there being no objection, installed it in the *Congressional Record*, retaining the typo. The word "supranational," in one of the Stevenson quotes, became "supernatural" in the *Post* and remained "supernatural" in the *Record*. Thus Adlai Stevenson became the unwitting proponent of "supernatural cooperation," and that's the way it stands in the archives. I am not ready (and I'm sure Governor Stevenson isn't, either) to concede that Western unity will have to be the work of spooks. Many natural occurrences in recent weeks and months indicate that the tide of unity is running strong. You can hardly pick up a paper or a magazine or a book without seeing the lift of this tide on both shores of the Atlantic. The most notable evidence of it was President Kennedy's speech in Philadelphia on the Fourth of July, in which he issued our Declaration of Interdependence. This declaration is about fifty years late in coming, as such things usually are. Even at this late date, it took courage to make the speech. By making it, the President at last brought the theme out into the open, from behind the many curtains that so many people have tried to conceal it with.

I think Nelson Rockefeller made a valuable contribution, too, in his Harvard lectures, when he proposed the federal design as the correct *theoretical* solution to mankind's urgent problem. This is the first and hardest step. Until a design is welcomed *in theory* by persons high in public life, not much progress can be made among the people toward the political goal of liberty-in-unity.

THE SHAPE OF TELEVISION

Allen Cove, November 21, 1960

All kinds of new, interesting developments are taking place around me, and I feel always a little behind events. Our new post office, now nearing completion, has two picture windows in the front, and I think this is in preparation for the day when the mail arrives in town by rocket. The windows will give the postmaster an unobstructed view of the sky, so he will be able to see the mail coming. A rocket group over in Lincolnville have been making some test shots from their pad, and everything has been going pretty well. They have retrieved quite a lot of mail from Penobscot Bay, not much the worse for its trip, and I imagine their aim is improving all the time and one of these days a sack of mail will drop into the center of town or possibly go right through one of the picture windows. It will probably contain a letter for me from the National Geographic Society notifying me that I am now eligible for membership.

We have a brand-new mail-delivery system in Maine now, called the Metro system. Instead of letters being sorted in a nearby office, the way they used to be, they are now sorted in the county seat. This has greatly stepped up the distance a letter travels if it is just headed for somebody in the neighborhood. Many a letter that would formerly have gone a mile or two is now quite well travelled by the time it reaches its destination. If

I write a letter to a friend in the village a couple of miles away and drop the letter at the post office that is nearest my house, the letter gets taken all the way to Ellsworth, which is about twenty-five miles in the wrong direction. There it gets placed in either the right sack or the wrong sack, according to the way things are going in Ellsworth that day, and then it is rushed back across the county and goes down the road to the addressee. A better way, really, would be for me to take the letter in my hand and start out on foot with it, wearing a bright-orange cap so as to negotiate the deer crossings safely, and hand it to my friend. This would get me out into the air.

Before the Metro system went into effect, I could put a letter for New York in the mailbox in front of our house toward the end of the afternoon and get an answer back in four days. With the new, improved system, it takes five days. Postmaster General Summerfield is still not satisfied and is full of plans for a new kind of electronic "speed mail," by which a letter can be flashed across the country in a matter of seconds. He says that although the letter must submit to being reproduced, the sanctity of the mail will be preserved, because "no one but the machine" will have a chance to read it. I have thought this over and am still undecided about letting a machine see my private correspondence. The modern machine is rapidly acquiring man's characteristics, and nothing I have read lately has convinced me that machines are as closemouthed as we have always tended to think they are.

Some of the lobstermen along the coast are complaining about a new hazard in their business—skin divers. They say the frogmen swim down and steal lobsters from traps on bottom. The Sea and Shore Fisheries Department is taking the matter seriously and is thinking of hiring two skin divers as underwater enforcement agents. These, I guess, will be our first submarine policemen, and their work will be almost as complex as that of the United Nations troops in the Congo. I presume they will be armed with bows and arrows, and will shoot anyone found robbing a trap.

Over on Mount Desert Island, there has been a population explosion among white-tailed deer, and this poses a problem in game management. Hunting is illegal on the island, and the National Park Service people are faced with whittling down the deer population without actually killing any deer. The plan is to shoot about two hundred deer with tranquillizing pellets, capture them while they are tranquil, and remove them to the mainland, where they will be released in the woods, lose their tranquillity, regain their suspicion, and then be shot in the normal manner by licensed hunters with real bullets. You have to meet these modern problems head on. Of course, there are always a few deer that swim back and forth between Mount Desert Island, where hunting is illegal, and the mainland, where hunting is permitted. This constant movement back and forth keeps changing the population count in a very vexatious way, and it may become necessary to post extra skin divers beneath the surface along the principal water crossings. A deer will not be able to smell the frogmen, because of their being under water, and the men can take a census by looking up from below. It is believed that if the tranquillizing program proves ineffective the deer on the island will be shot by game wardens with live ammunition, and the meat distributed to schoolchildren and hospital patients. This would save one step in the process of getting a piece of venison from the woods to the table.

During the Presidential campaign, both candidates flirted around with America's farm problem; they discussed quotas, surpluses, the soil bank, price supports, and controls. To the best of my knowledge, though, neither candidate put his finger on the root of the farm problem; namely, that the farmer himself has disappeared. In his place stands a wholly new man, a fabulous fellow, part industrialist, part mechanic, part chemist. The farm as a source of individual needs and a supplier of personal wants has almost vanished from the scene. In its place is a sort of dirt-factory operation, and the land is not so much cultivated as it is mined for gold. Curiously enough, among the few farmers who are still doing things in an old-fashioned or backhanded way are fellows like me, not truly countrymen at all but merely dudes who have the time or the money, or both, for such bygone frivolities as raising some of the stuff they eat and drink.

Thirty years ago, almost every house along this road was hooked up to a family cow. In summer you would see her in the pasture or staked out in a field; in winter her presence would be known by the conical pile of manure against the barn, its apex under the window of the tieup. Most homeowners planted a garden, raised fruits and vegetables and berries, and put their harvest in jars against the long winter. Almost everyone had a few hens picking up the assorted proteins of yard and orchard. If you walked into a man's barn, you found a team of work horses shifting their weight from one foot to another. This pleasing rural picture has been retouched until it is hardly recognizable. The family cow has gone the way of the ivory-billed woodpecker. Householders no longer plant gardens if they can avoid it; instead, they work hard, earn money, and buy a TV set and a freezer. Then, acting on advice from the TV screen, they harvest the long, bright, weedless rows at the chain store, bringing home a carton of tomatoes with eye appeal and a package of instant potatoes. The family flock of hens has also disappeared. I still have a flock secreted in my barn, but it is not considered the thing any more if you are to enjoy a high standard of living. Hens, if kept at all, must be kept in multiples of a thousand. The largest building that has been erected in this vicinity in recent years is an egg factory—a handsome four-story ovulation arena housing about eight thousand birds. An elevator lifts boughten grain to a high bin, from which an endless chain carries it around the pens in troughs. The owner, one helper, and the Bangor Hydro-Electric Company can take care of the whole operation. The pens do not contain roosts and dropping boards, which are now old hat. The modern hen just sleeps around.

A farm paper that I subscribe to recently sent a poultry re-porter to the Maritime Provinces, and he came back with the news that the family flock is on the wane in New Brunswick, Newfoundland, and Nova Scotia, and that farming in those regions is on the move. He attributes some of the new ways to television. A lot of farm families who used to rise early are now late sleepers, and this has worked changes in their husbandry. Both Nixon and Kennedy have been guests of Jack Paar, but I don't recall that they found any connection between the lateness of the hour and America's farm problem. "In travelling," wrote the reporter, "we could hardly get a cup of coffee before 10 A.M. We thought it interesting to see how quickly customs of people change with a little higher economic level of living." As a man who tries to keep his level of living high, I find it necessary to walk steadily back downhill toward where we all used to be. I still live fairly high on the hog, but it takes an unfaltering spirit of retrogression to accomplish it. The minute I follow the crowd, my standard of living goes down.

I heard a TV comedian the other day make a crack about one of the early-morning educational programs on the air. "It's O.K.," he said. "Anybody who watches television at six in the morning is stupid and needs educating." But I tuned in at seven one morn-ing to watch a program listed as "Today on the Farm," hoping to find out what's the matter. The thing started off with a hillbilly singer plucking away at my early cobwebs and then swung into a study of modern pig farming. The picture showed a sow during farrowing. She was in a white-walled hospital room, under anesthesia. The farmer, dressed for surgery and sterile up to his elbows, was removing her uterus and its interesting load, in order that the pigs might come into the world without being exposed to disease germs. I watched for a while, but I had chores to do and had to turn it off before I found out what the man did with the uterus—whether he replaced it in the sow or used it for pack-aging potato chips. Anyway, it was a clear picture of Today on the

Farm, and it stayed in my mind while I was down in the barn cellar in a high state of unsterility, tending some females of a different order. There is still a pigpen in my barn, and it recalled to my mind certain delicious nights when I had sat up with a sow, receiving each tiny pig as it came slithering into the lantern gleam and placing it in a fairly sterile whiskey carton until such time as its mother was ready to receive it. I couldn't help comparing the scenes I remembered with the progressive scene I had just watched on television. And I couldn't help feeling pleased that among the females with whom I was at the moment engaged every uterus was in place.

The effects of television on our culture and on our tone are probably even greater than we suspect from the events of the last few years. TV's effect on political campaigning was great, and, as Richard Rovere recently pointed out, not entirely healthy. The debates were not conducive to reflection and sobriety; they encouraged quick, cagey answers delivered in headlong style to beat the clock. TV has kept the farmer up late at night, has lured the unwary candidate to offshore islands, and has drawn quiz contestants first into chicanery, then into perjury. It has given liver bile and perspiration a permanent place in the living room—the world's most honored secretions.

John Crosby, who watched television for a living until he felt himself getting loopy, wrote a very instructive column about the whole business several months back. Viewers, he reported, are less concerned about the falsity and fraud of commercials than about the annoyance of them. This is true, and it is unsettling. But you have to go beyond the mere characteristics of commercials to get at the real source of the annoyance. The physical form of TV is so familiar to all of us by this time that we seldom examine it with a fresh gaze. I believe that the basic shape of the audio-visual world is inferior to the shape of the world of journalism and the world of the stage and music hall. The trouble with TV is not that the programs are poor and the commercials sometimes repulsive but that the advertising matter is not in direct com-petition with the editorial matter, as it is in newspapers and magazines. I see no hope of improving television until this struc-tural fault is corrected.

Take the world of journalism, which is the one I am most familiar with. If you open a copy of the *Times* to a page that has in one column a Macy ad displaying a set of china and in an adjoining column a news story about China itself, your eye makes a choice; you read about Macy's china or about Mao's China, according to your whim. It's a free selection. But if you turn your TV set to a channel, only one image appears, and after you have watched for a few moments, an advertiser buttonholes you and says his piece in a loud voice while you listen or try not to listen, as the case may be. Thus, your attention is not just in-vited by the commercial, it is to a large extent pre-empted. Pre-emption of this sort does not occur in periodicals. It cannot occur. There, advertising matter competes with editorial matter for the reader's attention, and it is fair competition.

Open *The New Yorker*. You may start reading a Profile and, in mid-course, switch to a shoe ad, either because the author of the Profile has allowed your attention to wander or because your feet are killing you. Or you may start reading an automobile ad and switch to the Race Track column, horses suddenly seeming, by contrast with cars, more amusing or more profitable. What-ever happens to you as you dip and sway in those pages happens because of competition. The text and the ads are on an even footing. The choice is yours. I think the cause of my own ex-asperation with television is that I resent having my attention pre-empted by anyone at all, whether pitchman or prophet. And because television has access to both eye and ear it presents a far more complex problem than do newspapers and magazines, which command only the eye. The problem is stickier, and no easy solution suggests itself.

Another structural difference between television and publishing

THE POINTS OF MY COMPASS

is that in the case of magazines each article or poem or story is supported by the whole body of advertising, lumped, and not by an individual advertiser. In television it's the other way round; a TV show is usually identified with a sponsor and his product. The sponsor not only backs the show, he gets it up—with the help, of course, of his Madison Avenue outriders. Thus, Chevrolet has Dinah Shore for its girl, Kraft Cheese has Perry Como for its boy. Suppose this passionate arrangement obtained in the world of periodicals; you'd have Walter Kerr reviewing the theater for Hart, Schaffner & Marx, and you'd have Walter Lippmann cleaning up the political scene for Fab. Such an arrangement would be unnerving, to say the least. If Hart, Schaffner & Marx happened to own a piece of a show, Mr. Kerr would twitch in his seat so violently that he would wear out his critical judgment before the first-act curtain.

In newspapers and magazines (good old newspapers and magazines!), a great number of advertisers (the sum total of those represented) simply join forces in supporting the daring venture of putting out an issue; they buy space and hope to attract some unwary reader's glance, but they don't buy a writer or an artist, they don't create material, and their products are dissociated from the work and the personalities of the men and women who do create the editorial content. How different is TV, where the sponsor and his agency are in the saddle most of the time!

The TV industry should realize that being in possession of a customer's ear is a responsibility unlike that of being in possession of his eye. The eye can reject an image, but the ear cannot escape from sound. TV from the start has seized this advantage and exploited it to the hilt, and from the start the audience has resented it. The exploitation mounts, the resentment mounts, and I think the resentment will continue to grow until something gives way and busts.

I'm a firm believer in the system of having private enterprise support public utterance; advertising is the safest and best foundation for free speech. It is also diverting and instructive in itself, being the showcase for our national dream, and people like to study advertising, provided they do so of their own free will. Advertising becomes objectionable and irritating only when it gets the upper hand, and that is exactly what it has got in television. The basic design of the medium is somehow defective.

Ideally, if TV is not to pre-empt the attention of the viewer and is to permit him a free choice of material, such as he enjoys with newspapers and magazines, a TV set should have two screens, one right next to the other—a delightful, if chaotic, situation. One screen would be the showcase for advertising, the other the showcase for editorial matter. The revenue from Screen 1 would support the material on Screen 2—the debates, the panels, the drama, the weather, and the news. Stations and networks would be in the same boat with publications; the editors would put the whole show together, without one single assist from advertising genius. Ronald Reagan, instead of appearing for General Electric, would appear for Ronald Reagan. Advertising would be regularly scheduled and would have its separate listing in the guide. A master switch would be at the viewer's hand. If he desired utter confusion, he could watch both screens at once. If something occurring on one screen seemed more diverting than the thing occurring on the other, he could flip. The viewer would enter his living room and find both screens going full blast —bedlam. On the advertising screen Zsa Zsa Gabor would be giving the news of underarm security; on the editorial screen the Secretary of State would be giving the news of national security. The viewer could decide which presentation, which person, seemed the more attractive or instructive. No program would have a patron, every program would enjoy the support of the entire field of advertising, and Dinah Shore could see the U.S.A. in a moving van if she wanted to. I do not sketch the outlines of this dizzying structure to show the solution to the problem of TV, merely to show what the problem really is—or what I think it really is. The problem is how to support the editorial stuff with the advertising stuff without subjecting the viewer to a thousand indignities and without compelling singers and actors and reporters and philosophers to identify themselves with hair sprays, bug sprays, floor wax, and marshmallows. If television advertising were truly in competition with editorial matter, instead of being in command of it, the quality of TV advertising would immediately improve. It would have to, in order to stay alive.

The most troublesome result of television's format is that, slowly but surely, the industry has pushed almost every celebrated performer into the role of pitchman. There is hardly a person of any note in the TV world who does not lead a double life; right in the middle of whatever he is saying or doing there comes a pause, and the performer holds up a can of cleaning fluid and recites the lesson. Prior to this unseemly pause, the actor or the singer or the ballplayer was obviously a person whose opinions and ideas were spontaneous and his own; then it suddenly turns out that his good opinion of the sponsor's product has been prefabricated and is, in reality, the opinion of somebody else. (Next week the sponsorship may change and his good opinion will shift smoothly to the new product, for the same or more money.) This is a relatively new cloud in the American sky, this practice of commandeering people in the arts for advertising and promotion. Across the TV screen marches an endless procession of peddlers. There is no parallel to it in the publishing world. Some TV performers like it, some hate it, some, like Godfrey, are switch-hitters, as happy in one role as in the other; most (I think) simply accept it as an occupational hazard. No matter what a man thinks of it, he is not in a good position to hold out against it; the pressure is always on.

As a viewer, I feel demeaned. I hate all kinds of fuzziness. I believe that when a TV personality speaks disinterestedly one moment, interestedly the next, it does something to the performer and something to me. Even after so many years, I experience a slight internal twinge, as though I had taken a tiny bullet from a distant gun.

A year or so ago, payola was in the news and TV was in the doghouse. Americans were shocked at the way money was being passed around for sly promotional services. But payola strikes me as much less disquieting than pay. Payola has been around since the invention of money; it will always be around, because there will always be a new crop of alert characters willing to take money for undercover service. Payola is simply an evil associated with the human character, which is less than perfect. But the steady drift of people from the lively arts into the ranks of advertising is not an evil; it is a mist settling on our pond. The old clarity simply isn't there any more. In its place we have the new, big, two-headed man, one mouth speaking his own words, smiling his own smile, the other mouth speaking the words that have been planted, smiling the smile that has been paid for in advance. This is nationally demoralizing.

If anybody thinks I'm implying that TV artists have compromised themselves by giving the pitch, he fails to understand my complaint. I do not think anybody has compromised himself; I think everybody has fallen heir to a system that is disagreeable, disenchanting, interruptive, and unhealthy. Any creative person who, as a sideline, engages in promoting the sale of a product subjects his real line of work to certain strains, and fogs the picture of himself in the minds of all. It seems sad that the TV industry, on which ride the country's hopes for entertainment, education, and information, should have felt it necessary, as a first step, to equip its pundits, its clowns, its reporters, and even its children, with something to sell.

THE YEARS OF WONDER

By the Sea, March 13, 1961

Russia's foolish suggestion that a dam be thrown across Bering Strait brings back happy memories of that body of water and of certain youthful schemes and follies of my own. I passed through the Strait and on into the Arctic many years ago, searching for a longer route to where I didn't want to be. I was also in search of walrus. A dam, I am sure, would have been an annoyance.

I was rather young to be so far north, but there is a period near the beginning of every man's life when he has little to cling to except his unmanageable dream, little to support him except good health, and nowhere to go but all over the place. This period in my life lasted about eight years, and I spent the summer of one of those years in and around Alaska. It was the summer of 1923. In those days, I kept a diary, entering in it whatever was uppermost in my mind. I called it my journal; the word "journal," I felt, lent a literary and manly flavor to the thing. Diaries were what girls kept. A couple of years ago, when Alaska achieved statehood, I began digging into my journal for the year 1923, hoping to discover in its faded pages something instructive about the new state. This account, then, is a delayed account—some thirty-seven years late. I doubt that the reader will be able to put together a picture of Alaska from reading it, but he may catch a glimpse of the young diarist. And of the nineteen-twenties, that notorious decade that was almost a delirium.

My trip to Alaska, like practically everything else that happened to me in those busy years, was pure accident. I was living in Seattle; I was unemployed, my job on a newspaper having blown up in mid-June; and although I had no reason for going to Alaska, I had no reason for staying away, either. The entries in my journal covering the four-week period between the loss of my job and the start of my trip to the North reveal a young man living a life of exalted footlessness. I was a literary man in the highest sense of the term, a poet who met every train. No splendor appeared in the sky without my celebrating it, nothing mean or unjust took place but felt the harmless edge of my wildly swinging sword. I walked in the paths of righteousness, studying girls. In particular, I studied a waitress in a restaurant called the Chantecler. I subscribed to two New York dailies, the *World* and the *Evening Post*. I swam alone at night in the canal that connects Lake Union and Lake Washington. I seldom went to bed before two or three o'clock in the morning, on the theory that if anything of interest were to happen to a young man it would almost certainly happen late at night. Daytimes, I hung around my room in Mrs. Donohue's boarding house, reading the "Bowling Green" and the "Conning Tower," wondering what to do next, and writing.

My entry for June 15, 1923, begins, "A man must have something to cling to. Without that he is as a pea vine sprawling in search of a trellis." Obviously, I was all asprawl, clinging to Beauty, which is a very restless trellis. My prose style at this time was a stomach-twisting blend of the Bible, Carl Sandburg, H. L. Mencken, Jeffrey Farnol, Christopher Morley, Samuel Pepys, and Franklin Pierce Adams imitating Samuel Pepys. I was quite apt to throw in a "bless the mark" at any spot, and to begin a sentence with "Lord" comma.

On June 19th, I recorded my discharge from the *Times* and noted that the city editor said it was "no reflection on my ability." I didn't believe then, and do not believe now, that it was no reflection on my ability. As a newspaper reporter, I was almost useless, and it came as no surprise when one more trellis collapsed on me. When I left the *Times* office with my final pay check in my pocket, I "sauntered" down Pine Street. I can still recall experiencing an inner relief—the feeling of again being adrift on life's sea, an element I felt more at home in than in a city room. On June 25th, I clipped a sonnet sequence by Morley from the "Bowling Green" and pasted it in the journal. The second sonnet began, "So put your trust in poets." As though I needed to be told that!

On July 2nd, I entered in my journal a copy of a poem I had written and mailed anonymously to the Reverend Mark A. Matthews, pastor of the First Presbyterian Church, who had preached a sermon I found offensive. A résumé of the sermon had appeared in the Monday morning paper. Dr. Matthews had attacked nonchurchgoers, of whom I was one. On the following Sunday, I departed from my usual stance and became a church-goer, attending the morning service at the First Presbyterian to make a routine check on my man. "The smugness of his doctrine," I wrote in my journal, "made the air stifling." Probably what really made the air stifling for me was that in his sermon the minister made no mention of having received my stinging communication.

For one week I worked on Hearst's *Post-Intelligencer*, commonly called the *P.I.*, substituting for a reporter on vacation. My entry for July 18th (1:30 A.M.) begins, "A man scarce realizes what a terrible thing scorn is until he begins to despise himself." I doubt that I found myself despicable; I simply found life perplexing. I did not know where to go. On Friday, July 20th (3 A.M.), appears the abrupt entry, "I sail Monday on S.S. Buford for Skagway." No explanation or amplification follows, only an account of an evening spent with a girl who lived on Lake Union. (She fed me bread and apple jelly.)

I did, however, clip from the *P.I.* and paste into my journal the item that started me on my way to Alaska. The story was headed

S. F. CHAMBER
TO SEE ALASKA

and began:

"The resources and trade conditions of Alaska will be studied by a delegation from the San Francisco Chamber of Commerce, which will leave San Francisco today on the steamer Buford for an 8,300 mile trip to Alaska and Siberia, via Seattle. The group will also include citizens of other cities, among them ten Boston capitalists, and the trip will be in charge of B. S. Hubbard, vice president of the Schwabacher-Frey Stationery Company."

A number of things must have attracted me to this item in the news. First, the ship was to call at Seattle. I was a dockside regular at this period, and any ship at all was of interest to me. Second, Alaska was in the opposite direction from home, where I considered it unsuitable to be at my age. Third, a Chamber of Commerce was involved, and this opened up familiar vistas. As a reporter, I had spent many a lunch hour covering the noonday gatherings of fraternal and civic groups; Seattle was a hotbed of Elks, Eagles, Moose, Lions, Kiwanians, Rotarians, and members of the Young Men's Business Association. I had broken the hard roll countless times with Chamber of Commerce people, had laughed courteously at their jokes and listened patiently to their tales of industrial growth. I was under the influence of Mencken and Lewis, and felt proud disdain for business and for businessmen. It was important to me at that time to move among people toward whom I felt aloof and superior, even though I secretly envied their ability to earn a living.

Perhaps the clincher in the news story of the *Buford* was the list of the ports of call, names that were music to the ear of youth: Ketchikan, Taku Glacier, Juneau, Skagway, Sitka, Cordova, Seward, Kodiak, Cold Bay, Lighthouse Rocks, Dutch Harbor, Bogoslof Island, the Pribilof Islands, Cape Chaplin, Anadir. "From

Nome, they [the voyagers] will pass the ice pack, proceeding to
East Cape, Siberia, and then return to Nome. On the home trip
they will stop at St. Michael, Akutan and Seattle, the entire trip
requiring forty days."

Forty days! To me, forty days was a mere siesta in time's
long afternoon, and I could cling, for lack of anything else, to
the ship. The Pribilof Islands with ten Boston capitalists—sheer
enchantment! All I needed was a job on the ship, and this I
determined to get. The *Buford* arrived in due course and tied
up to Pier 7. Every day while she was there, I sneaked aboard and
hung about the corridors, waylaying ship's officers and offering
my services in any capacity. When, after three days, I found no
taker, I made inquiries and learned that for forty dollars I could
sail as a first-class passenger as far as Skagway, which is at the head
of the Inside Passage. This enabled me to shift my strategy; I *had*
forty dollars, and I decided to launch myself in the direction of
the Arctic by the sheer power of money. Once firmly entrenched
in the ship, I could from that vantage point pursue my job-hunting. The second steward gave me a bit of encouragement. "Anything can happen in a ship," he said. And he turned out to be
right.

To start for Alaska this way, alone and with no assurance of
work and a strong likelihood of being stranded in Skagway, was
a dippy thing to do, but I believed in giving Luck frequent
workouts. It was part of my philosophy at that time to keep
Luck toned up by putting her to the test; otherwise she might
get rusty. Besides, the nineteen-twenties, somehow or other,
provided the winy air that supported dippiness. The twenties
even supported the word "dippy."

You might suppose that the next few entries in my journal,
covering the days when I must have been winding up my affairs
and getting ready to sail on a long voyage of discovery, would
offer a few crumbs of solid information. Not at all. From Friday
morning, when I announced that I would soon be off, until the

departure of the *Buford*, several days later, my journal contains no helpful remarks, no hint of preparation, no facts about clothes, money, friends, family, anything. A few aphorisms; a long, serious poem to the girl on Lake Union ("Those countless, dim, immeasurable years," it begins); a Morley clipping from the "Bowling Green" about writing ("A child writes well, and a highly trained and long-suffering performer may sometimes write with intelligence. It is the middle stages that are appalling. . . ."); a short effort in vers libre written on Sunday morning and describing my boarding house slatting around in the doldrums of a summer Sabbath—that is all I find in these tantalizing pages. Mr. Morley was right; the middle stages are appalling. As a diarist, I was a master of suspense, leaving to the reader's imagination everything pertinent to the action of my play. I operated, generally, on too high a level for routine reporting, and had not at that time discovered the eloquence of facts. I can see why the *Times* fired me. A youth who persisted in rising above facts must have been a headache to a city editor.

Memory helps out on a couple of points. I recall that winding up my affairs was chiefly a matter of getting a Ford coupé repossessed by the finance company. My other affairs were portable and would go along—a Corona typewriter, a copy of *Lyric Forms from France*, and my wardrobe, which fitted cozily into one droopy suitcase. I owned an unabridged Webster's, but I am quite sure I did not take it—probably placed it in safekeeping with a friend. The luckiest thing that happened to me was that my wardrobe included a very old and shabby flannel shirt and a dirty pair of dungarees. Without these I would have been in some difficulty later on.

The *Buford* did not get away until almost ten on Tuesday evening, thirty-four hours behind schedule. As the lines were cast off, I stood at the starboard rail and watched the lights of the city—the Bon Marché sign, the tower of the Smith Building—and was shaken by the sudden loud blast of the whistle giving finality to my adventure. Then, it would appear, I sat right down and wrote what was for me a fairly lucid account of the departure. I listed some of the items that had come aboard: beeves, hams, nuts, machinery for Cold Bay, oranges, short ribs, and a barber's chair. I noted that when this last item was carried up the plank, the passengers lining the rail broke into applause. (Already they were starved for entertainment.)

At sundown the following evening, July 25th, we passed a tall gray ship that rode at anchor in a small cove near a fishing village. On board was President Harding, homeward bound from Alaska. A band on his ship played, and the President came to the rail and waved a handkerchief borrowed from his wife. The incident caused a stir among the passengers and crew of our ship; seeing the President of the United States in such an unlikely spot, on our way to the mysterious North, was reassuring. About a week later came the radiogram telling of his death.

The voyage of the *Buford* carrying the men of commerce to the Arctic wasteland was an excursion both innocent and peculiar. It inaugurated a new steamship line, the Alaskan-Siberian Navigation Company, and I think the company had been hard up for passengers and had persuaded the Chamber to conduct a trade tour and bring wives. The *Buford* herself, however, was in no way peculiar; she was a fine little ship. She had been a troop carrier in the war, and afterward had been reconverted to carry passengers and freight. She was deep, was not overburdened with superstructure, and had a wide, clear main deck. Painted in tall block letters on her topsides and extending half her length were the words "SAN FRANCISCO CHAMBER OF COMMERCE." This enormous label gave her a little the look of a lightship—all name and no boat—and in many a desolate northern port, where the only commerce was with Eskimos who swarmed aboard to peddle ivory paper cutters, the label acquired a bizarre and wistful meaning.

One of the things I know now, and did not know at the time, is that the *Buford* was being bought from the government on the installment plan. The owners never managed to complete their payments, and by 1925 she was being referred to in the San Francisco *Chronicle* as "the hard-luck ship Buford." Everything she touched turned to dross. The owners not only never completed their payments, they never fully completed the reconversion of the ship, either. I remember a room in the 'tween-decks that obviously dated from troop-carrying days. It was a spacious room furnished with a truly magnificent battery of urinals and toilets standing at attention and perfectly exposed—a palace of open convenience, seldom visited, except by me, who happened, at one juncture, to live close by. A lonely, impressive room. I have an idea that when the owners took possession of their ship, they must have taken one look at this panorama of plumbing and decided to let it stand. To have laid a wrench to it would have cost a fortune.

Our commander was Captain Louis L. Lane, a handsome, sociable man who delighted the ladies by his strong profile and reassured us all by his fine handling of the ship. He had been in the Arctic before, loved it, and was known and welcomed everywhere. I think he quite enjoyed the adventurous role he was cast in: shepherd of a crowd of landlubbers and dudes in wild, remote places where he had local knowledge and could display his special talents. No gunkhole was too small for Captain Lane to squeeze the *Buford* into. Before we were done with the voyage, though, I got the impression that our Captain operated under unusual difficulties. The strong tides and treacherous currents of the Inside Passage, the cold, enveloping fogs of the Bering Sea, the shifting floes of the ice pack in the lonely, silent, too bright Arctic—these were strain enough on a man, but they were slight compared to the cold white bank of boredom that gradually enveloped the passengers, several of whom, I believe, would gladly have paid any reasonable sum to have the ship turn about and head back for the Golden Gate. Captain Lane in mid-passage was the host at a party that was not going too well.

All pleasure cruises have moments of tedium, but usually the passengers can relax on sunny decks, swim in warm pools, go ashore every day or two where the ladies can plunder the shops and the men can stretch their legs and bend their elbows. The *Buford*, skirting the long coastline of Alaska in the early twenties, did not offer much relief of this sort. For some the *Buford* became a high-class floating jail—the food good, the scenery magnificent, but no escape. A hundred and seventy-odd passengers did a six-week stretch, and their spirits sagged as the scenery became increasingly familiar. In the fog, the scenic effect was dampening to many a spirit; for long periods the forecastlehead was barely visible from the door of the main cabin. The horn sounded daylong and nightlong.

Whoever planned this odd voyage for the expansion of trade had, of course, foreseen the need of entertainment and had done his best. Provision had been made for music, dancing, gaming, and drinking. Music was in charge of the Six Brown Brothers, a saxophone combo that had once performed in a show with Fred Stone. I have a fine, sharp photograph of the Brothers taken at the Akutan whaling station; they are standing in front of a dead whale, their saxophones at the ready. Adventure was in charge of H. A. Snow, a big-game hunter, who brought along his elephant gun, his movie camera, and his son Sydney. The ship was well stocked with private supplies of liquor. One of the owners of the ship, J. C. Ogden, came along for the ride, and this gave the thing the air of a real outing. But although there was an occasional diversion, the days were largely without incident and without cheer. Even such advertised treats as the stop at the Pribilofs to see the seal rookeries proved anticlimactic to many of the students of trade conditions; the place smelled bad and the seals looked like the ones you had seen in zoos and circuses. Some of the passengers, having gone to the great trouble and expense of reaching the Pribilof Islands, chose, when they got there, to remain on board and play bridge. As for me, I never had a dull moment. I lived on three successive levels socially, a gradual descent that to me seemed a climb: first the promenade deck, then the main deck, then below. I was busy, but not too busy to journalize, and I was young enough to absorb with gratitude and wonder the vast, splendid scene of Alaska in the time before the airplane brought it to our door and when it was still inaccessible and legendary.

When, in Seattle, I presented myself to the purser as a paying passenger, he assigned me to a small room with another man. This fellow turned out to be an oddball like me—not a member of the Chamber. He was a Laplander, a short, stocky man with a long mustache. His clothes were rough; he had no white shirts and almost no English. "I go Nomee," was all he could tell me at first. His name was Isak Nakkalo, and he was a reindeer butcher on his way to a job. Isak and I dwelt in peace and in silence day after day, until life changed abruptly for me and I began my descent. All up the Inside Passage, while the *Buford* skirted headlands and dodged rocks and reefs, Isak took no part in the social life aboard ship, but I did. I struck up a few acquaintances, danced to the sweet jazz of the Brown Brothers, nursed my clean shirts to get the maximum mileage out of them, and displayed affability (if not knowledge) in the matter of trade relations. I also lived a secret life. At every opportunity, I bearded stewards, engineers, and deck officers, and asked for work. My encounters with these people must have mystified them; at sea, a first-class passenger looking for work is irregular. I was probably worse than irregular; I was annoying.

Ketchikan was our first Alaskan port of call and the scene of the passengers' first disillusionment. In the minds of most of us aboard was an image of Alaska formed by Robert W. Service and Jack London—a land of deep snow, igloos, Eskimos, polar bears, rough men, fancy women, saloons, fighting sled dogs, intense cold, and gold everywhere. Ketchikan as we rounded the bend, delivered a shattering blow to this fine image; the village was a

warm, mosquitoey place, smelling of fish. Not an igloo was in
sight, and on the dock to greet us was a small, moth-eaten band
of Shriners in their caps. But, image or no image, this was our
frontier, and long before the ship was close enough for voices to
carry, the passengers began shouting questions to the group
ashore. One of our shipboard Shriners ached to know whether
there was going to be a ceremonial that night. The distant wel-
coming group cupped their ears. "I say is there going to be a
ceremonial tonight?" he bellowed. The words were lost in air.
Mr. Hubbard, our tour master, began bellowing, too. He wanted
to know whether a representative of the Ketchikan Commercial
Club was on hand.

I sat on a bollard in the warm sun, watching these antics in-
dulgently, I, a graduate of the University of Mencken and Lewis,
studying the spectacle of Babbittry northbound—men visiting a
strange land yet craving not strangeness but a renewal of what
was familiar. I can still recall the agitation of Mr. Hubbard on this
occasion—a pioneer in a sack suit glimpsing his frontier at last
and taut with emotion. As the ship was being warped alongside,
Mr. Hubbard saw the boatswain swing himself over the rail,
grasp a hawser, and slide down onto the dock. Eager to make
contact with the Commercial Club man, Mr. Hubbard stepped
over the rail and took hold of the hawser. But the dock was a
long way down, and there was still an ugly gully of water
between ship and dock. Twice Mr. Hubbard flexed his legs in a
test take-off, both times lost his nerve. His face wore a grim
look, and he soon had an audience, just as a suicide on a ledge
gets one. For a few tense moments, the launching of Mr. Hubbard
into Alaska held everyone spellbound, but it never came off. Pru-
dence conquered zeal, and our first brush with the frontier was
a defeat for the spirit of San Francisco.

Later, when I went ashore, via the plank, I "lounged down
the street" (I was always "lounging" or "sauntering" in my journal) and bought a copy of *Faint Perfume*, by Zona Gale. Because

the town smelled of fish, I considered this purchase clownish. Of such flimsy delights were my days made in those delectable years.

That evening, the Shriners had their ceremonial, the Commercial Club had its meeting, the ladies from the ship bought great numbers of Indian baskets, and one of the oilers from the *Buford*'s engine-room crew managed to get ashore and establish trade relations with a half-breed girl. "Big, like that," he told me afterward. (I was already cultivating the society of firemen and sailors, hoping to be admitted.) When everyone had satisfied his own peculiar needs and refreshed himself in the way he knew best, the *Buford* let go her lines and continued north through the tortuous straits of the Alexander Archipelago. I was an extremely callow and insecure young man, but as I examine my record of Ketchikan and translate it from the Chinese in which it is written, I can see that I was not alone in my insecurity; all of us were seeking reassurance of one sort or another—some with mystic rites and robes, some with the metaphysics of commerce, some with expensive Indian baskets and inexpensive Indian girls. I was enraptured with my surroundings—contemptuous of all, envious of all, proud, courageous, and scared to death.

On the morning of Sunday, July 29th, we sighted Taku Glacier, a scheduled point of interest. When we brought it abeam, Captain Lane stopped the ship and everyone rushed on deck. "The bridegroom," I noted in my journal, "dashed to get his polo coat and his yellow gloves. The bride put on her polo coat to match. Everybody put on something special. Walter Brunt, potentate of Islam Temple, put on his monkey cap in case he should get into a photograph with the glacier in the background."

The whale boat was lowered and Sydney Snow was rowed off to get pictures of the *Buford* against the glacier. But Captain Lane was not easily satisfied; he wanted his charges to see that a glacier is really a river of ice, discharging into the sea. Taku, in the manner of glaciers, was sulking in its tent and taking its

own sweet time about discharging into the sea; it needed prod-
ding. Accordingly, Mr. Snow was called on to stir things up. He
hurried to the bridge with his elephant gun and opened fire on
Taku, while Sydney, in the whaleboat, cranked away at his
camera. Nothing happened. For about an hour, there was desultory fire from the bridge while the passengers hung expectantly
at the rail. Then they wearied of the spectacle of a reluctant
glacier, and most of them drifted away toward the dining saloon.
A few minutes before noon, whether from rifle fire or from sheer
readiness, a piece of ice did fall into the sea. It made a fine splash.
Passengers who had deserted the deck rushed back but were,
of course, too late.

As I stood at the rail studying Taku Glacier, I was joined by
the *Buford*'s storekeeper, a solemn, thoughtful man. For a few
moments he stared quietly at the great wall of ice. "How do you
like it?" I asked, between volleys. He took my question seriously
and his answer was slow in coming. "I don't care for it," he replied, at last, and walked aft to resume his duties. As our voyage
progressed and we ventured farther and farther into nowhere,
with sea and sky and fog and ice and the white wings of gulls for
our backdrop, the storekeeper's measured words became more and
more expressive of the inner feelings of many of the tourists; they
did not care for it.

At Juneau, I watched one of the Brown Brothers fishing in
the rain, and wrote an unrhymed poem: "Grapefruit and oranges
in the green water off Juneau dock—grapefruit and oranges, part
of the ship's scum." Sandburg had me by the throat in those days.
Alaskan towns, I reported in my journal, "are just murmurings at
the foot of mountains."

One of the faintest of these murmurings was Skagway, where
my ticket ran out. The *Buford* tied up at the dock there on the
last day of July. My search for a job on board had been vain. I
put my Corona in its case, packed my bag, and went on deck to
sit awhile in sorrow and in fear, delaying until the last possible

moment my walk down the plank and into the forlorn street of
Skagway—a prospector twenty-five years late and not even primarily interested in gold.

While I was sitting there on deck (my journal says I was
"browsing" there), trying to sort out my troubles and wondering how I had managed to get myself into this incredible mess, I
received a summons to the bridge. A Miss Linderman, according
to my account, presented herself to me and delivered the message.
"The Captain wants to see you right away" was all she said. Oddly
enough, I did not associate this summons with my job-hunting; I
had no idea what was up, and felt like a schoolboy called to the
principal's office. The message seemed ominous, but less ominous
than the imminent trip down the gangplank into murmurous Skagway. I hustled to the bridge.

Captain Lane stared at me for a moment. Then he said, "We
can put you on as night saloonsman for the remainder of the
voyage—workaway passage. Is that satisfactory?"

"Yes, sir," I replied. I didn't know what a night saloonsman was,
or a workaway passage, but I was in no mood for quibbling, and
if Captain Lane had offered to tow me astern at the end of a long
rope I would have grabbed the chance. I thanked my Captain, reported to the second steward, and that night turned up in the
dining saloon wearing a white jacket and carrying a napkin
slung over my left forearm, in the manner of right-handed waiters
the world over. The crisis of Skagway was behind me, and
pretty soon Skagway was, too, as the *Buford* steamed west toward
the Aleutians at her steady pace of eleven knots.

I cannot recall Miss Linderman—she is a name on a page, that
is all—but among the handful of women who have distinguished
themselves in some great way in my life she occupies a high position. I never found out exactly what happened; I never even tried
to find out. This much is clear: the news that a job-hunter was
loose on board finally reached the Captain, just as the news would
have reached him that a harmless snake was loose in the hold,
and he reluctantly disposed of the matter in the easiest way,

as he settled many another small but pesky problem in the business
of running that crazy tour.

(Since beginning this account, I've been looking into the files
of the San Francisco *Chronicle* for 1923 for news of the *Buford*
and its company. One of the owners of the line, it appears, was a
Mr. John Linderman, and the passenger list shows the presence on
board of several Linderman girls—his daughters, I suppose. So I
guess I was baled out of Skagway by the daughter of an owner.
Inasmuch as Mr. Linderman and his partner Mr. Ogden were buying the ship on the installment plan, and had slim prospects of
making the thing pay, I think the management was foolhardy to
take on another mouth to feed. But I still value Miss Linderman
highly.)

Working in a ship is a far better life than sailing in one as a
passenger. Alaska, the sea, and the ship herself became real to me
as soon as I was employed; before that, all three had suffered
from a sort of insubstantiality. Passengers never really come to
know a ship; too much is hidden from their sight, too little is
demanded of them. They may love their ship, but without their
participating in her operation the identification is not established.
As saloonsman, I was a participant—at first a slightly sick participant. I worked from eight in the evening till six in the morning.
I set tables, prepared late supper for thirty, served it (sometimes
carrying a full tray in a beam sea), cleaned the tables, washed
the dishes, stropped the glasses, swept down the companionway
leading to the social hall, and shined brass. This was hard work,
dull work, and, until my stomach adjusted to the ripe smell of
the pantry, touchy work. But when, at around three o'clock, I
stepped out onto the forward deck for a smoke, with the sky
showing bright in the north and the mate pacing the bridge and
the throaty snores of the passengers issuing from the staterooms,
the ship would throb and tremble under me and she was *my*
ship, all mine and right on course, alive and purposeful and exciting. No longer was the *Buford* merely taking me from one
benighted port to another; now she was transporting me from

all my yesterdays to all my tomorrows. It was I who seemed to make her go, almost as though I were a quartermaster with my hand on the wheel.

My metamorphosis from passenger to saloonsman took the passengers by surprise and created a certain awkwardness at the late supper. A few of the first-class people knew me by name and most of them knew me by sight; naturally they felt uneasy when they found me at their service. There was the matter of tipping. Should a girl with whom I had danced between Seattle and Skagway leave a coin for me when I handed her a cold cut between Skagway and Cordova? A delicate question. One elderly female, flustered at seeing me in saloonsman's garb, cried, "Goodness! How long have *you* been a waitress?" I regarded my change in status as extremely comical, played it deadpan, and made quite a to-do about it in my journal, greatly exaggerating its comic value. Embarrassed at first, I soon felt an elevation of spirit and wore my white jacket like a plume. In my mouth was the taste of a fresh superiority over my fellow man; not only was I leading a secret literary life among the mercantile crowd but I was now a busy, employed man, gainfully occupied among wastrels and idlers. Always hungry myself and indulging in snacks at every opportunity, I nevertheless adopted a patronizing air toward those who appeared for the pre-bedtime meal, regarding their appetite at that hour as gross and contemptible. The hardest part of the job for me was remembering orders; I would stand attentively listening to a group of four telling me what they wanted, and by the time I reached the pantry the whole recital would be gone from my head. As a member of the Steward Department, I was permitted by the rules to go on deck to catch some air but was not permitted to sit down while on deck. I ceased mingling with the passengers and joined the much juicier fraternity of pantrymen and cooks, denizens of the glory hole in the stern of the ship next to the steering engine—a noisy, aromatic place, traditional seat of intrigue and corruption. I joined the glory-hole crowd, but I was not shifted to the glory hole itself; instead, I was assigned a bunk in a small, airless inside room, first class, with a young man named J. Wilbur Wolf. Wilbur was the other night saloonsman, and, like me, was burdened with a college education and an immaculate past. The second steward, a cagey man, chose not to inject Wilbur and me into the glory hole, where we properly belonged. The second may have feared that our morals would be corrupted, but I think he simply did not wish to disturb the gamy society of the hole by introducing two young dudes of almost unparalleled innocence. It would have made him uneasy.

At Cordova, we received by radio the news of Harding's death, and I copied into my journal the notice on the ship's bulletin board:

> San Francisco
> President Warren G. Harding died here tonight at 7:30 o'clock. He was stricken without any warning. Mrs. Harding was with him at the last. See the second steward about your laundry.

"Here," I wrote in pensive vein, "is a very fine illustration of how the world jogs on, come what may." Apparently the realization that people would continue to have their dirty clothes washed after the death of Warren Gamaliel Harding struck me forcibly.

At all events, the *Buford* jogged on, come what might. As she glided up the wide aisle of Resurrection Bay toward Seward, the Brown Brothers gathered in the social hall and rehearsed suitable numbers for an impromptu memorial service. Hearing the sad sounds of their muted horns drifting out and mingling with the crying of gulls, I was afflicted with melancholy at the loss of my President—I felt bereft. Mr. Harding is not greatly mourned these days, but we of the *Buford* blew him a heartfelt tribute from Seward that night, on six jolly saxophones hastily converted to solemnity.

In those northern waters in 1923, Captain Lane guided the *Buford* much in the manner of early aviators: he flew by the seat of his pants. Approaching Kodiak, we ran into thick weather. All afternoon the ship crept blindly through a cold, drizzly fog. We felt obliged to make Kodiak because we had a passenger to discharge, and for the newborn Alaskan-Siberian Navigation Company the discharge of even one passenger was an event of considerable moment, tending to add luster and credibility to the trip. The passenger in this case was an Airedale terrier, but that didn't diminish the matter. With visibility close to zero, the Skipper became unsure of his position, and his uncertainty was magically transmitted to the passengers. I heard a couple of ladies nervously ask an officer whether we shouldn't just drop anchor and wait for the weather to clear. (This would probably have been one of the longest sea waits on record.) After a while, a fishing boat appeared under our bow, its crew gave us our position by shouting and pointing, and away we went on an altered course. Captain Lane went ashore that night after a hard day at the chart table. He did not get back to the ship till late. I was called to his cabin at three in the morning to clear away glasses and bottles. I find the following entry, written an hour earlier:

Monday morning   4 bells.   Kodiak
The brass is shined. The dishes are put away. Wilbur sits across the aisle, dozing at another table. In the pantry the coffee urn simmers and from the ceiling the steam drops in little globules. The Skipper is not aboard yet, as far as we can tell. At any rate he hasn't appeared for his coffee: we have a place neatly set for him with cold meats, bread, and relishes.

This entry bears the telltale mark of a writer at work. The sixth sentence first read, "At any rate he hasn't appeared for his coffee yet," and I edited it, crossing out the word "yet," which was a sensible move, rhetorically, and shows that I was working away at a hard trade at a late hour. Wilbur, he who dozed, was also a diarist, although I didn't know it at the time. Two night saloonsmen, both of them diarists—a strange, unearthly ship in a strange, cold sea! A portion of Wilbur's diary is now in my possession. His widow recently sent it to me—a tiny notebook crammed with loathing for the menial life. "No more of this 'working your way' stuff—if I can't go first class I stay at home." Wilbur's urge to restore himself to a decent place in society was as compelling as my own urge to make my way farther down in the ship, sink to the depths, and try the rapture of human dereliction and drudgery.

My next entry is a poem called "Lament." It begins:

Millions of songs are knocking round, back and forth, inside my head: songs of praise and of wonder. But I can not give birth even to one song.

An odd statement. I was giving birth almost continuously, like a hamster. None of the songs had any merit, but there was no lack of parturition.

The passengers' disappointment with the Territory of Alaska was often quite apparent. Dutch Harbor, our next stop, did nothing to lift their spirits. A few deserted houses, a family of Indians, a sow and her three young ones—hardly a place made to order for San Francisco ladies bent on sight-seeing. I went ashore and followed a muddy path over a small hill and sat down in the grass where I could look across at Unalaska. This village, seen from that distance, was a picture-book place—a single row of white frame buildings, one of them a little Greek Orthodox church with two green onion spires. Behind the town, rising out of the sea in soft and billowing folds, were green treeless hills draped in swirls of drifting fog. They seemed incredibly lofty and massive, those hills—a backdrop for a dream sequence. I wanted desperately to visit Unalaska, but was not free to go, since I had duties on board.

While I sat there, staring, two ladies from the *Buford* came along and stopped in front of me.

"Is there anything over there worth seeing?" one of them asked, thinking I had been there. "From here, it looks to me as if it was pretty dead. If there's something special about that church, I want to go on, but otherwise, if there isn't anything special, I don't care about going. Do you, Kate?"

Kate shook her head. The two of them seemed ineffably sad and uprooted.

I told them I hadn't been to Unalaska but guessed there was nothing special. And on that report they turned listlessly back toward the ship.

Later on, I contrived to get over to the village; a boy in a small boat ferried me across. By some standards, the place could have been called dead, but, walking the length of Unalaska at the foot of the green, tumbled hills, alone and wonder-struck, I felt more alive than I had ever felt before in my life. I was about as far west as a man could conveniently get on this continent, I was a long, long way from home, songs of praise knocked in my head, and I felt a gush of exhilaration. Added to my cup of pleasure was the knowledge that when I returned to the ship I could go to bed instead of having to work all night; my job had changed abruptly. For the remainder of the voyage, I was to be messboy to the firemen.

At dawn that day, the second steward, my boss, had appeared in the pantry, where I was deep in dishes. "You can knock off," he said. "Tomorrow I'm putting you on as firemen's messboy— take care of eight men, firemen's mess, and you won't need the white coat. We'll sign you on the articles at fifty a month."

Although the second did not mention it, I had heard rumors of a fight below in the ship—someone had got knifed—and I was reasonably certain that my new job was connected with this affair. I figured I was the replacement for the knifee. This turned out to be correct. At any rate, I obeyed orders; I went to my room, fished my old flannel shirt and dirty trousers from my bag, and turned in, wondering why I was to receive fifty dollars for feeding eight people when I had been receiving nothing but my passage for feeding about thirty. I knew there was a catch in it somewhere, but I dropped off to sleep. At six the following

morning, I reported for work. This was the true beginning of the
voyage for me; I was below at last, where the ship's heartbeat
was audible and her body odor undispersed.

Why did I long to be below? I don't know. I just remember
that I did and that this descent seemed a difficult but necessary
step up life's ladder. The whole Alaskan experience was a sub-
conscious attempt to escape from the world, to put off whatever
was in store for me; the farther down inside a ship I went, the
better the hiding place. Moreover, I wanted to test myself—throw
myself into any flame that was handy, to see if I could stand the
heat.

The firemen's messroom proved to be a dandy crucible. No
young man could have asked for a more direct exposure to heat,
fumes, toil, and trouble. The room was small and rank-smelling,
with a porthole a few feet above the waterline. When I close my
eyes these days and think of Alaska, the picture always comes
to me in a round frame, for I viewed much of our future forty-
ninth state through the porthole of the firemen's mess, and the
picture has a special smell—a blend of cabbage, garbage, steam,
filth, fuel oil, engine oil, exhausted air, exhausted men. It is a
smell you get nowhere but in a ship.

At one end of the room was a warming table through which
live steam passed, a little of it always escaping in whispers and
causing the room to overheat. In the center stood the mess table,
flanked by two benches. On the side away from the porthole
were a sink, a garbage can, and our shrine—the coffee urn. This
urn was hooked up to the ship's steam lines. It had an intake valve,
an exhaust valve, and a glass gauge in which the coffee slowly
rose and fell with the motion of the ship. I soon learned to tell
the *Buford*'s angle of heel by glancing at my gauge. Filth set the
tone of the room, and the smell was steady and reliable. Filth
had accumulated in subtle ways: bits of tired soap stashed away
in tin cans, morsels of rotten meat tucked between the pipes
overhead, slices of raisin bread that had been deflowered and left
to die, cheese that had been placed in safekeeping behind the urn

—everywhere trinkets and keepsakes. The former messboy, like so many millions of people on land and on sea, had saved against a rainy day. It was easy to see why the firemen had taken matters into their own hands, finally, and brought his regime to a bloody close. But I think untidiness was only part of the story.

As I stood there on an empty stomach at six o'clock on that first morning and received my instructions from the second steward, I felt dizzy, sick, and scared. The instructions were sketchy, and the second acted as though he wanted to get away while I was still conscious and willing. He told me I was to carry the firemen's grub down from the main galley, serve it, clean up afterward, make the bunks in the forecastle, empty the garbage into a chute in the ship's side, keep the coffee always fresh and hot, keep the toilets clean, and do what the men said. "You take care of them—you do what they tell you," he said. "I'm still your boss, and if you get into any bad trouble, let me know. But they're the ones you have to satisfy." Then he introduced me curtly to my opposite number, a Puerto Rican youth named Luis, who was the sailors' messboy, and who would show me the ropes. The second then departed. I don't recall that he ever showed up again in the small world I now inhabited.

Luis was a twitchy youth swathed in a long, dirty sweater dangling to his knees. He had two eyes, but only one of them was on duty; the other peered straight ahead into another—and, I think, better—world.

"What job you come from?" he asked.

"Night saloon," I answered.

"Ahhh! Then you know how to steal. That is good." He seemed vastly relieved. My men, he explained, would expect delicacies obtainable only by the light-fingered.

Being shown the ropes by Luis turned out to be a dizzying experience—like being taught to fly a plane by a bright child. "Come ong, boy!" he said, and started out on the run, singing "Rock of Ages" in Spanish. Luis was evanescent, volatile, and loaded with interesting fancies and misconceptions, many of which did not pertain to the mess. He thought seals could fly, and he thought Harding had just been married, not buried. Steam valves mystified and excited him, and he couldn't keep his hands off them. As he scampered here and there, with me tagging along, he warned me about the low state to which I had fallen. The black gang, he said, were the lowest bunch in the ship, and I would be their servant, which made me low man. He described the firemen as having conceits and passions that were incredibly irregular and troublesome. And he warned me about the language in the messroom and forecastle. "Gee, boy," he said sorrowfully, "they use awfool language. Sonna mon beetsch, it is terrible the way they talk, those bastards."

I wasn't worried about any naughty words I might hear, but I had other worries. I knew I was a lamb set down among wolves, and I was greatly concerned lest the firemen, my masters, remember my face as belonging to first class and find out about my past, which was too dainty for a messroom. I was marred by gentility and stained with education. Worst of all, I had come aboard first class, and, thanks to the caprice of the second steward, I still occupied part of a first-class cabin. I knew well enough that these incriminating facts would have to be concealed if I were to survive. I felt like a man who has committed some monstrous crime in the past, one he will have to live down by good conduct. Stealing seemed my golden chance to redeem myself from my early infamy. I determined to be very brave and steal carefully and well. I decided to do my work, give good service, and keep my trap shut. My assets were that I was wearing a two-day beard and clothes that bore the clear imprint of toil.

The first breakfast was crucial and was served in a dense cloud of live steam. Luis had flipped the valves of my coffee urn in passing, the urn had erupted, and the room had become a Turkish bath. I could barely see the men's faces through the murk, blackened and stained as they were with engine-room oil and dirt. But they couldn't see mine, either, which was a break. They complained angrily about the steam bath, and when they found a new boy serving them, their curiosity was aroused, and I was required to answer questions and fill them in on my past. This I did in broad strokes, using place names and dismal events, always derogatory to management. Everywhere I had worked I had got fired, I said. The men were pleased with this familiar indignity, and they loved place names. (I was well fixed for names, as I had spent the previous summer crossing the continent, working at odd jobs.) In Cody, I said, I had sandpapered an open-air dance floor all day for a lousy three bucks. In Minneapolis, I had peddled roach powder, door to door. In Big Timber, I had worked as a hay hand. And everywhere I had got sacked. This was my simple card of admission. Sight unseen, the men hated all my past employers. I was now their boy. As I dodged about, dishing up oatmeal and trying to subdue the urn, my courage began to return. After the first loud outburst, the men settled into a dull guzzle and the question period came to an end. One or two of the faces looked positively amiable. Two of my fellows, I later found out, had been in jail, which I regarded as adventurous and laudable, and one of them was suffering from a venereal disease, which I found disquieting and worrisome. The memory of the famous Army film *Fit to Fight* was still fresh, and I assumed that I would soon contract the disease merely from using the same cutlery.

My name, I discovered, was Mess. "Get me an orange tonight, Mess!" one of the wipers said as he left the room after my debut. I knew from the sound of his voice that this was a direct order. I perceived, too, that the wiper was less interested in the sweetness of an orange than in the sweetness of having a personal servant to bedevil. Below decks, fresh fruit was not part of the diet; to get an orange, you had to either grow one or steal one. In the days that followed, I learned to pinch goodies at the source, or from staterooms with their doors left open. This was part of the

routine at sea. I became a floating Robin Hood, providing my men
with delicacies by robbing the rich. It was part of the stratagem
of survival, theirs and mine, and I laid my snares for a dill pickle
as artfully as a trapper for a mink. The men themselves were not
unreasonable. While I was carrying out my first assignment, I was
in a cold sweat, fearing that the sight of one orange in the messroom might lead to a demand for oranges right across the board.
This proved not to be the case. My firemen did not crowd their
luck. And except in rough weather, when their deranged stomachs
caused them to delve into the vast lore of seasick remedies and
dreams of miracle cures effected by combining the most rare
and unlikely substances, they asked of me only tasks I could
humanly perform. Thanks to my former job in the saloon, I had
valuable contacts in vital supply centers. In Wilbur Wolf I had
an actual confederate, who saved odds and ends from the night
buffet and turned them over to me as slyly as though we were
pushing dope. Never knowing when a fireman would strike, I
kept goodies always on hand in a hiding place by my bunk, as a
man in rattler country keeps a snake-bite kit at the ready.

    After breakfast the first morning, as the firemen drifted off to
their duties and the *Buford* steamed north into the Bering Sea, I
scrubbed the room, threw out the foul trophies, washed the cloth
bag in the coffee urn, and stole an orange. The first day passed
without mishap. I went on deck just long enough to see the
Buford dive into a wall of cold white fog. A lookout had been
placed on the forecastlehead, and Tony, the giant Negro watch-
man, was heaving the lead. Although I was busy getting squared
away in my new job, my journal for that date contains a long,
fancy description of the heaving of the lead. I was tired, but not
too tired for a burst of showy prose.

    The task of carrying the big stewpots of food down the almost
vertical ladder from the galley proved to be the most formidable
part of a messboy's job—far more ticklish than stealing. These
caldrons were as big as a bushel basket. They had two opposing
handles riveted to the rim. Even when empty they were heavy,

and when full of stew they were very, very heavy, as well as piping hot, and they required, of course, the use of both hands, leaving no hand for oneself. In a smooth sea, the trip down the ladder with one of these pots was, for a novice, sobering. In a rough sea, with the ship pitching and rolling, the descent appeared at first glance impossible. The ladder would lose its slant in mid-journey; slowly it would approach the perpendicular, then it would achieve the perpendicular. In a really heavy sea, it would go right past the perpendicular. Luis showed me how to get down. The trick was to wait at the top, stewpot gripped tightly, until the ladder presented a favorable angle for descent. Then you started down cautiously, gaining a round or two. As the ladder began straightening under you, you quickly poked one foot back between the rounds and hooked your toe around the side of the ladder, as an acrobat supports himself when hanging by his feet from a trapeze. As soon as the ladder's cycle was complete and it started back toward a favorable angle, you disengaged your foot and gained another couple of rounds, and so on down until the trip was completed. Those moments of being suspended between decks with a heavy pot full of hot stew and with the combined weight of body and stew supported by one leg and a terrible strain on the other leg seemed interminable. But I was young, and my ankles were as strong as my opinions. Fortunately, I mastered the ladder trick before the *Buford* ran into a whole gale in the North Pacific on her way home. By that time, I was an accomplished artist.

In the *Buford*, the sailors and the firemen were two distinct societies; they lived apart, ate apart, and thought apart. A ship is no melting pot; it hardens its class distinctions until the social bones are ankylosed. Fireman scorns sailor, sailor derides fireman, on general principles. This is, I guess, traditional, and helps keep everyone toned up. In dress and appearance, the *Buford*'s sailors were a cut above the firemen; they shaved oftener and kept their clothes clean, thus by personal daintiness further arousing the

scorn of the firemen. Each group took entire credit for making
the ship go and vehemently denied that the work of the other
group had any nautical significance whatever. This argument—
who makes the ship go?—was pursued endlessly, until logic reeled.
I heard it discussed by the hour in my mess as I stood dunking
dishes. My men were, in fact, nourished more on argument than
on stew meat; the most trivial subject awakened their forensic
powers and stirred their passions.

At St. Paul, in the Pribilof Islands, I went ashore during a lull
in the mess, trotted out to the rookery, and watched the seals.
Each big bull was surrounded by his harem. Many of the cows
had had their pups, and the place was like a gay, foul-smelling
nursery during a children's party, with fights breaking out among
the elders. I could have watched the fun for days but had to
hurry back to my urn. Luis was dispirited when I reported that
seals could not fly. He was filling a ketchup jar—a moment of
high drama complicated by this saddening piece of news.

At St. Lawrence Island, we anchored off the village of Gam-
bell and set a missionary and his wife ashore, a Mr. and Mrs.
Nickerson. It was the end of the voyage for them. Twenty
Eskimos came aboard, loaded with ivory goods and sealskin objects. They spoke no English except for a few key phrases like
"seventy-five cents," which they uttered clearly and firmly. They
could also say "napkin ring" and "paper knife" very nicely. The
ladies of San Francisco, starving for loot and long absent from
the bazaars, clutched wildly for the prizes and bid loudly against
each other. I watched from a vantage point while a pair of sealskin slippers was bid up from a dollar to six-fifty. The Eskimo
hesitated. At this moment, one of my firemen stuck his head
up from a companionway, caught the fellow's eye, and beckoned
to him. The Eskimo left the ladies and walked over to my man,
who thereupon produced from his shirt two dirty cakes of soap
and a roll of toilet paper. These items were accepted instantly
and the slippers changed hands—a severe setback for the trail

blazers of the San Francisco Chamber of Commerce. The ladies were furious. A few of the more alert and energetic ones rushed off to their staterooms and returned with soap and tissue, but trade between San Francisco, Alaska, and Siberia had taken an ugly turn, and the *Buford*'s high purpose seemed momentarily clouded. At noon, Luis and I served lunch to the Eskimos in the sailors' mess, Luis fairly transported by contact with savages in a strange land. Later, the six Brown Brothers unlimbered their horns, and the Eskimos danced, with surprising frenzy. None of them had ever heard a sax, and the sound made them drunk.

At St. Michael, we loaded fish. My poem for August 15th ran:

All day long barrels of fish went across the sky with a rattle,
Swung up from the lighter across the sky and down into the hold of the vessel.
The quartermaster had square shoulders and he drove the winches—all day long.
And at evening, when the sky got orange, and gray clouds mustered for a sunset, the fair-haired girl came and stood at the rail to watch the square-shouldered quartermaster.
She's his girl, I said. They'll get married, and the boys will grow up to be square-shouldered like the father.
A sea gull lifted itself from the water and glided peacefully into the orange west.

The quality of my verse plunged steadily down as the *Buford* plunged steadily north. One trouble the poet had was sheer fatigue; he was a mighty tired poet at the end of a day.

On Friday, August 17th, the *Buford* anchored off Nome; we had reached the gateway to the top of the world. The sea was rough, and for a while we were unable to unload cargo. All sorts of rumors were astir—that we were low on water, that we were low on oil, that we would not go to the ice pack, that we would be a week late getting back to the States. The tug *Genevieve* came alongside, and with some others I went down a ladder and got a ride ashore. *Genevieve* made hard work of it, and two ladies were stricken with nausea and were in bad shape when they set foot on the beach. On Saturday night, at about nine o'clock, I stood

outside the office of the Nome *Nugget,* across from the Nome
Tailoring Company, and watched the first copies of that weekly
paper come off the press. The *Nugget* office was full of men and
dogs. I bought a copy for twenty-five cents and read the streamer
head: "GREAT FUTURE ASSURED NOME; NOME–SAN FRANCISCO JOIN
HANDS NORTH OF 53." It was an eerie moment in mercantile history,
this joining of San Francisco and Nome. The ship was dressed
in flags, and the local population of the dreary little town was
delighted to see visitors come ashore, even if they vomited on arrival. I do not know how fruitful the occasion turned out to be
in the world of trade; the only fruit I saw with my own eyes
was in the window of Mrs. Wanger's shop, where a classy new
line of fall hats and dresses that had been hustled ashore from the
Buford was on display. I strolled about the ghostly town in the
bright night and took in the sights—the North Pole Bakery,
the Nome Sheet Metal Works, the Dream Theatre, Andrew Box's
Elite Baths & Hotel (Steam-Heated Rooms), and Mrs. Wanger's
red-hot finery.

The *Nugget* was celebrating the event with a special four-page
supplement dedicated to amity and trade. On the editorial page appeared an apology:

TO OUR PATRONS REGARDS THE DELAY OF THE PAPER

We wish to take this opportunity to say to the readers of the
Nugget that due to the fact that we have added another four pages
to today's edition we feel that an explanation is in order for our delay
in having the paper out on time. In order to add this amount to the
paper we worked all night Friday night not going to bed at all.

The "we" of this notice was George S. Maynard, owner and publisher of the *Nugget* and Mayor of Nome, a real night owl.

I've often wondered how San Francisco's business giants felt
when they glimpsed those tumbledown, almost deserted hamlets
of the North. Nome must have been a particularly heavy shock.
Nome's rickety houses were strung out in a long line fronting the
main street. Everybody in Nome lived out of tin cans, and the

disposal system was simple and direct; the empties got heaved out of rear windows, and landed on the beach. The beach was an enormous dump, with the accumulated pile of cans comparing favorably with the buildings themselves as an architectural mass. I'll say this for Nome, though: at a certain hour of the day, when the sun hit the place just right, the dump produced an extraordinary phenomenon. The top layer of cans would suddenly catch the sun's rays, and when this happened the crescent beach, viewed from the deck of a ship in the roadstead, would appear to burst into flames, and the down-at-heel gold town for a few breath-taking moments would wear a circlet of fire.

My strongest memory of Nome is of the close shave I had while there. I went to my garbage chute one morning and dumped a big load of slops overside, not knowing that a lighter had tied up to the ship during the night. The garbage took one of the lightermen fairly in the head. He was a big man, and he came aboard bellowing that he would kill whoever had done it. I rushed up to first class and hid, and he never found me. The episode gave me quite a turn, though. I can still see him, with all that stuff in his hair and blood in his eye, coming up the ladder to get me.

From Nome, the *Buford* steamed to Teller, where about a dozen white men remained from a gold-rush population of ten thousand, and then passed through Bering Strait and headed for the ice pack through quiet seas. We were the first passenger ship to invade this part of the world. Here in the Arctic, I began to feel the inadequacy of my wardrobe; I hadn't even brought along a pair of wool socks. Nights were cold and bright; the ship proceeded without running lights. One of our missions was to touch at Wrangell Island and take off two men stranded there. There had been a lot of talk about this, but the whole business fell through; at 70° North Latitude our path was blocked by ice, and we never reached Wrangell. Instead, we hunted walrus.

When the ice was sighted, Captain Lane went aloft in the shrouds and peered ahead through binoculars while the passengers

watched admiringly from the deck. Soon our Captain came down
and ordered the ship stopped. Then, to my great surprise, he left
us. With ice closing in all around us, he simply beat it—went off
for a hunt in a double kayak with three Eskimos we had taken
aboard at Nome. It gave everybody an uneasy feeling—the ship
nuzzled by ice, and no captain on board. The hunting party was
gone a long while. The passengers, alert and interested at first,
grew weary of watching and waiting, and when the hunters
finally returned, empty-handed, everyone felt let down. Next day,
the hunters had better luck; seven walruses were shot. They were
swung aboard by the boom tackle and dumped on the forward
deck, where they immediately began to ripen. These huge
corpses stayed with us for days; the heads and skins fetched up at
last in the Oakland Museum, whose curator, if the wind was
right, must have known long in advance that they were coming.
My whole account of the trip in the Arctic Ocean follows:

Wed. Aug. 22. The walrus hunt. Consensus of opinion among
ladies was that the icebergs were beautiful but the walruses were
disgusting. Mr. Snow, sitting on walrus and thinking of funny sayings.
Luis, the sailor's mess—"Surely this world it is a beautiful thing." The
bob-haired girl went on deck just long enough to find out what
walrus looked like, and then went back to the chief engineer's room
to play cards.

(There was always a card game in the chief's room—that is one
of the few things I remember about Alaska. I also remember seeing a polar bear in its natural habitat. Luis was right; surely this
world it is a beautiful thing.)

At about three o'clock in the afternoon of the twenty-third,
Luis darted into my messroom, flipped all valves, and made an
announcement: "Come ong, boy! Come quick, quick! Assia!"
He drew the name out lingeringly—"Ass-ee-a." He was all dolled
up in a clean shirt, ready to go ashore and send postcards. Together we rushed on deck, and there it was—Asia, a bleak head-
land called Cape Serdze, with patches of snow spotting the
ground. Whales were all around us as we closed with the land;

they blew and slapped their flukes. All over the deck lay the stinking walruses, the massive carcasses slashed and gouged by the knives of our hungry Eskimos, who gnawed at the raw trophies as you might work away at a cheese if you were in need of a snack. Blood leaked from the mutilated animals. It spread in rivulets across the deck and responded to the slight roll of the ship. The passengers, for their part, responded to the name Siberia; it was our Arctic *pièce de résistance*, justifying the trip and putting the authentic touch on the name Alaskan-Siberian Navigation Company. Mr. Snow went forward to the forecastle-head and cracked jokes about the Bolsheviki.

"No one knew what to expect," I wrote. "There was a good deal of speculation at first about whether the ship would be fired on. In a general way, the passengers felt that there was something hostile about Russia." Hostile or not, the San Francisco Chamber of Commerce was experiencing its most adventurous hour, and possibly its most footless, and I don't doubt that if we had been fired on, Mr. Snow would have returned the fire with what ammunition remained after our assaults on Taku and on the walruses. Mr. Hubbard, wandering gingerly among pools of blood, saw that Siberia was represented by a couple of dozen furry Eskimos and one squaw man; they came aboard from a skin boat as soon as the *Buford* dropped her hook. On shore we could see dogs curled up asleep among patches of tired snow. At this point, I shall quote from that other diarist of the *Buford*, J. Wilbur Wolf. Wilbur managed to get ashore. "Here," he wrote, "I witnessed the first real Eskimo huts. How shy the natives are, and how unsanitary."

Wilbur traded a few pieces of silver for a Siberian gun holster, Mr. Snow traded an old cap for a polar-bear skin, and we were off for East Cape, which proved to be a repetition of Serdze—headlands, a gray beach, a gray shack flying a small red flag, skin dwellings, vagrant fogs, snow in patches along the shore, and low hills hinting at the vast continent that lay beyond the fog and beyond the power of the imagination. (It may have been memories of the utter drabness of Siberia that caused the *Buford*'s co-owner Mr. Ogden to seek greener pastures for his boat; her next excursion was to Samoa and the Marquesas—a financial bust like the Siberian affair, but at least a languorous one.) Emotionally, the *Buford* and her passengers had had it; we were ready for home. Captain Lane guided his ship across the Strait, called again at Nome, just long enough to take on ten passengers, and then started the homeward journey, with parting salutes from the Coast Guard cutter *Bear*, the tug *Genevieve*, the Hudson's Bay Company's ship, and a whistle ashore. We steamed to False Pass, took aboard some workers from the cannery, and struck boldly out across the North Pacific in a direct line for Seattle. We had not been at sea long when the gale hit.

The new passengers at Nome had put a strain on the *Buford*'s accommodations, and Wilbur and I had been the first to feel the squeeze. We had been booted out of first class. There seemed to be no place to put us until some genius in the Steward Department remembered the ship's prison. This was a tiny steel cell, six feet by six feet, containing two hard, narrow bunks, one above the other—a cute little poky, well off the beaten track. It was located in the 'tween-decks, and Wilbur and I, after the surprise had worn off, were well pleased with it. For my part, I was glad to move into the brig because it relieved me of my fear of being discovered in first class by a fireman. Wilbur liked our new home because it was an outside room. "Somehow or other," he wrote in his diary, "a person can always adapt himself to new environment."

The gayest feature of our new environment was a large, noisy soil pipe running vertically through the room from a very popular toilet on the deck above. We arranged our clothes, wrapped in a sheet, behind this pipe. The door of our cell was heavy steel, and there was a steel sill about a foot high that you stepped over to get in or out. "We have fitted the cell out like a palace," wrote Wilbur in the first fine flush of nest-building. "Advantages: more secrecy [this was for hiding stolen food]; more light, outside room; better air, and more independence. The disadvantages will loom up later, I suppose."

They weren't long looming up. Our pint-sized palace felt the impact of the gale as soon as the *Buford* took her first big roll. The deadlight was leaky; it kept air out but let sea water in, in the mysterious manner of deadlights. Trapped by the high sill, the water in the room built up to a mean depth of about ten inches. Wilbur's stomach collapsed with the first roll of the ship, and he went to bed in the lower bunk, where he lay for three days *in extremis*, his groans blending with the mighty complaints of the soil pipe, his bunk awash like some bleak outer ledge, subject to the incessant rising and falling of our interior tides.

Most of the *Buford's* passengers, from long days and nights of wining and dining, fell horribly ill. More than half the crew were sick. My messroom was almost deserted, but as a matter of routine I had to set food on the table, regardless of the men's ability to retain it. I was also very busy mixing the extraordinary cocktails by which my men hoped to get relief from their agonies—pineapple ice cream laced with piccalilli, prune juice and tomato juice in equal parts with a sprinkle of mace, soft-boiled egg and marinated carrot, ginger snaps with ketchup.

On the second day of the storm, I had no sooner got the table set for lunch than the *Buford* rolled everything off onto the deck. The ship, which had been so quiet in the Arctic, set up a frightful banging. Down in the hold, the cargo shifted, and the sailors—those that could still stand—worked all one night getting it back in place. Barrels of fish, loose in the cold room, thrashed around and broke the refrigeration pipes, letting brine out all over the deck. On the main deck forward, some Husky dogs that were being brought back to the States by the more enterprising of our souvenir hunters took an awful beating from the storm. Two, I think, were washed overboard. Others got loose and wandered into the paint room, and soon were beyond recognition. Two of my firemen showed up in my messroom and engaged in a long, closely reasoned argument about whether one of them was sick and had vomited. During the storm, Luis lost his job—I never learned why.

For most of the passengers, the voyage ended on a note of nausea and gloom. For me, it ended on a note of triumph. The three gale-tossed days gave me a feeling of elation and well-being; it seemed exciting to be up and about, busily tending the sick and doing my duty. I felt victorious and hearty. My stomach held together and I was able to watch my first great storm at sea unimpaired. Even when a heavy mess bench fell on my foot and broke one toe, the accident and the pain failed to quiet my enthusiasm for the life of a messboy in a full gale. I was drunk with power, the Florence Nightingale of the mess and the brig, and this sensation of drunkenness was heightened by a trick I invented as an anti-sickness device; instead of bracing myself against the lurches of the ship, I let myself go and yielded to her every pitch and roll, on the theory that bodily resistance is—in part, at least—the true cause of nausea. There may have been nothing to this eccentric notion of mine, but for three days in the wild North Pacific I reeled crazily through the corridors, responding to the sea physically, as though the sea were a dancing partner whose lead I followed.

In a matter of hours, my long, evasive excursion to the Far North would be over. I was headed now toward the south and the east, toward unemployment and the insoluble problem of what to do with myself. My spice route to nowhere was behind me; I would soon be host again to the spectre that I commonly entertained—the shape of a desk in an office, the dreaded tick of the nine-to-five day, the joyless afternoons of a Sunday suburb, the endless and ineffectual escapes that unemployed young men practice (a trip to the zoo, a walk in the night, the opium pipe of a dark cinema). The shape was amorphous—I seldom attempted to fill in the outlines; it hung above me like a bird of death. But in the final hours of the *Buford* the gale granted me a reprieve. In the fury of the storm, thought was impossible; the future was expunged by wind and water; I lived at last in the present, and the present was magnificent—rich and beautiful and awesome. It gave me all the things I wanted from life, and it was as though I drank each towering wave as it came aboard, as though I would ever after be athirst. At last I had adjusted, temporarily, to a difficult world and had conquered it; others were sick, I bloomed with health. In the noise of battle, all the sad silences of my brooding and foreboding were lost. I had always feared and loved the sea, and this gale was my bride and we had a three-day honeymoon, a violent, tumultuous time of undreamed-of ecstasy and satisfaction. Youth is almost always in deep trouble—of the mind, the heart, the flesh. And as a youth I think I managed to heap myself with more than my share. It took an upheaval of the elements and a job at the lowest level to give me the relief I craved.

The honeymoon was soon over; the wind abated, the *Buford* recovered her poise. On September 4th, we docked at Seattle. I collected my pay and went ashore. My next entry is dated September 6th, from a room in the Frye Hotel—a poem called "Chantecler."

> How many orders of beef have you passed over the counter,
> Girl with white arms, since I've been gone?
> How many times have you said,
> "Gravy?"
>
> Your arms are still white,
> And you're still the thing in all the room
> That transcends foodstuffs.
>
> By standing there
> You make the restaurant part of September,
> And September, girl, is part of the world—
> A sad-voiced, beautiful part.
>
> How many orders of beef have you passed over the counter,
> Girl with white arms, since I've been gone?

Like so many other questions that stirred in me in those years of wonder and of wandering, this one was to go forever unanswered.